Politics in the United Nations

Politics in the United Nations

*A Study of United States Influence
in the General Assembly*

ROBERT E. RIGGS

ILLINOIS STUDIES IN THE SOCIAL SCIENCES: *Volume 41*

THE UNIVERSITY OF ILLINOIS PRESS
URBANA, 1958

Second Printing

Board of Editors: D. PHILIP LOCKLIN, D. W. GOTSHALK, AND FRANCIS G. WILSON

© 1958 BY THE BOARD OF TRUSTEES OF THE UNIVERSITY OF ILLINOIS. LIBRARY OF CONGRESS CATALOG CARD NO. 58-5601.

Contents

LIST OF TABLES

CHAPTER ONE

Introductory Observations

THE PRIMACY OF POLITICS

The General Assembly in its day-to-day operations bears witness to the primacy of politics in the United Nations. It would be commonplace to say that the Assembly is a forum where states and groups of states seek influence, prestige, political advantage, or whatever other values may be at stake. More than this, an extra-legal political structure has developed alongside the formal structure established by the Charter, which reflects the real power alignments and interests in the Assembly more accurately than the formal organization could. Delegates and groups of delegates meet casually outside the council chambers and committee rooms in lounges and eating places, often by prearrangement and in some cases with a fair degree of regularity, to discuss the important business at hand. Negotiations are initiated, compromises made, decisions taken, and the result is ratified in the debating chamber. This is not to say that the extra-legal structure is fully developed, easily identifiable in all its parts, tightly knit and smoothly running. No doubt the cooperative relationships existing between the Soviet Union and its reliable satellites approach a point of perfect coordination, but elsewhere power patterns and lines of common interest are not so clearly drawn, as it were, by a master draftsman. Nevertheless, on important issues the substance of the legislative process operates through structures and instrumentalities concerning which the Charter is totally silent.

Since the primacy of politics in national legislatures and parliaments is an undisputed fact of political life, no surprise is entailed at finding a similar state of affairs in an international parliamentary, or quasi-parliamentary, body. In fact it has much the same flavor and trappings. One finds the interplay of varied personalities, the importunings of special interests, cooperation in log rolling, fervent lip service to cherished values, and the oratorical play to the gallery. Of course the parallel is not perfect. There is no party system, although one might argue that groupings and blocs within the Assembly can be compared with rudimentary political parties. Moreover, a delegate to the General Assembly comes instructed by his government, and in the last resort he is responsible to it rather than to a party or constituency. His freedom of action is strictly and immediately limited by its policies:

1

another delegation which disapproves of his stand on an issue may, as a last resort, appeal to his government through regular diplomatic channels for a change in his instructions. The appeal need not await the next election.

A difference perhaps more profound in its effects upon the interplay of interests in the Assembly is the absence of a value system understood and accepted by all members of the organization. In most parliamentary bodies a common value system provides a frame of reference within which compromise and concession can prevail on matters of the most vital concern, leaving to partisan wrangles noisy questions not closely interconnected with the continued peaceful existence of the polity. Nevertheless, despite these differences one gets the distinct impression that in the General Assembly politics is prime and that its manifestations are not far different from what we have accepted in our national political life.[1]

The Problem: American Influence

For a study which purports to treat of politics, of "influence and the influential," no approach is more appropriate than an analysis of the policies of the United States—the most influential member of the organization. The Assembly,[2] until recently at least, has been characterized by an American-led majority running roughshod over a recalcitrant communist minority. The pattern has been altered somewhat by the growth of a tendency toward neutralism within the numerous new states of Africa and Asia which have representation in the Assembly, but American predominance is still more than a matter of past history. A glance at the voting record of any major United Nations organ reveals

[1] Raymond Dennett has commented concerning this phenomenon: "In the effort to utilize international machinery for the attainment of individual state aspirations, the politics being played differ in degree—but not in kind—from the politics used by special interest groups in domestic political organs. Politics is, after all, the interaction of diverse groups seeking different and often conflicting special treatment for varied interests in a particular institutional framework. The institutional framework may not be as satisfactory on the international as on the national level, but factors of power, of majorities and minorities, of basic differences in political values and methods operate within it in much the same fashion as they do in domestic governmental bodies." "Politics in the Security Council," *International Organization*, vol. 3 (Aug., 1949), p. 433.

[2] The choice of the General Assembly as an area for the study of political processes in the United Nations was dictated by its primacy among the major organs and its more universal membership. The overshadowing of the Security Council by the General Assembly has been commented upon so frequently as not to warrant exegesis here. See, e.g., Leland M. Goodrich, "Expanding Role of the General Assembly," *International Conciliation*, no. 471 (May, 1951); H. Field Haviland, Jr., *The Political Role of the General Assembly*, Carnegie Endowment, United Nations Studies No. 7 (1951); Hans J. Morgenthau, "The New United Nations and the Revision of the Charter," *Review of Politics*, vol. 16 (Jan., 1954), pp. 3-21.

that United States-sponsored measures receive a majority vote in nearly every instance. This tendency has not gone unobserved. In 1952 Leland M. Goodrich wrote, "No important action can be undertaken by the United Nations with any reasonable prospect of success in the face of United States opposition. Conversely, if the United States gives full support to a proposal, its chances of being adopted must be considered very good, unless of course the veto operates." [3] With particular reference to the General Assembly, Ernest A. Gross has offered impressive evidence of what he terms the "American leadership record." "The American leadership record in this forum is a proud one. In the years 1946 through 1953 the General Assembly adopted over 800 resolutions. The United States was defeated in less than 3 percent—and in no case where our important security interests were involved. In these eight years only two resolutions supported by us failed of adoption." [4] At the risk of undue repetition, another such observation may add emphasis: ". . . as the United Nations and the cold war have simultaneously developed, it is hardly too much to say that in many respects the United Nations has become a reflection or even an instrument of the policies of the western powers, almost always supported by a large majority of the other Members. If in one sense the United Nations continues to be a 'neutral' organization of which the U.S.S.R. is a member in good standing, it is also true in a perhaps even more significant sense that it is now committed to any number of positions flatly opposed to those taken by the Soviet bloc." [5] These statements and the facts which support them bear witness to an apparent predominance of American-held views.

Explanations of this phenomenon vary. From Soviet sources have come frequent charges of a "mechanical majority" manipulated at the will of the United States government. As early as 1946 this explanation of Soviet defeats in the United Nations was being propagated in the Soviet press. Imperialists, it was said, were attempting to turn the United Nations into a branch of the American State Department to implement their plans for "Anglo-Saxon domination." [6] With embellishments and refinements, this charge has since become the habitual response of the Communists to habitual defeat in the United Nations. The implication which it carries is that the United States secures its majorities by covert

[3] Leland M. Goodrich, "American National Interests and the Responsibilities of United Nations Membership," *International Organization*, vol. 6 (Aug., 1952), p. 376.

[4] Ernest A. Gross, "Why the U.S. Needs the UN," *Foreign Policy Bulletin*, vol. 34 (Sept. 15, 1954), p. 2.

[5] Rupert Emerson and Inis L. Claude, Jr., "The Soviet Union and the United Nations: An Essay in Interpretation," *International Organization*, vol. 6 (Feb., 1952). pp. 11-12.

[6] New York *Times*, Nov. 7, 1946, p. 35.

"pressures"—economic, financial, political—upon members of the United Nations. The United States government, by way of rebuttal, has vehemently denied the charge of mechanical voting with all its invidious implications. If the free world repeatedly rolls up huge majorities for its proposals, it is asserted, the reason lies in a fundamental community of interests in which differences are smoothed over through discussion, negotiation, and compromise—not in the dictation of any one member of the group. Characteristically, the charge of mechanical voting is flung back at the communist members, which almost invariably vote together.[7]

These conflicting interpretations raise two questions basic to an understanding of the functioning of the General Assembly: To what extent do American policies prevail in the Assembly? and How is this degree of influence achieved? The present study endeavors to answer these two questions through an analysis of the political issues which have come before the Assembly.

SUBJECT ORGANIZATION

The study is organized in two parts, one concentrating on the methods, the other on the extent, of American influence. Part One deals with the execution of policy—the methods by which the United States seeks Assembly approval of particular resolutions. This includes a survey of the American mission and Assembly delegation, a brief description of delegation groupings or blocs in the Assembly, and a comment on the political function of the Secretariat. The role of consultation and the nature and role of "pressure" are considered in their relationship to the whole Assembly political milieu. Against this background detailed accounts of Assembly action on two selected political questions provide an intimate glimpse of the Assembly political process, with the give and take of pressure and counter-pressure and the vigorous exertion of American influence.

The methods of influence, in part at least, are observable and identifiable. The extent of influence can be determined only with reference to arbitrarily defined categories or measuring rods. In this instance, influence is expressed in terms of positions fought for and won, positions compromised, positions abandoned, and a few fought for and lost. The evidence, as presented in Part Two, includes a discussion of each political question considered by the Assembly during its first nine sessions.

[7] This charge was thought important enough to be denied in the annual volume, *The United States and the United Nations*, report of President to Congress (1948), p. 5. For the rejoinder of a United States delegate under fire, see the comments of Senator Wiley as summarized in *Ad Hoc Political Committee*, 7th sess. (1952), p. 301.

Emphasis is placed primarily upon the position assumed by the United States with respect to each question. Any substantial modification of the American position on a given issue is noted, and an attempt is made to indicate the congruency of the final Assembly action with the American position. Since some questions are obviously more important than others, in terms of United States policy, an effort is made to elucidate the American position on this score. It can be said that the United States takes a position on every question before the Assembly, but in some instances it may be simply to favor any solution acceptable to the principal parties concerned.

The questions or issues are discussed individually within four more or less homogeneous groups. The first, admittedly, is something of a catch-all for questions not readily placed in the other three groups. It embraces exercises in the formulation of principles of international cooperation, various propaganda proposals, and a number of international disputes and "irritating situations." Treating such items in a single section affords a striking contrast of Assembly moods—the moments of harmony and unanimity with the notes of hypocrisy and discord. The second category includes questions of disarmament and collective security, the third the legacies of colonialism, and the fourth a group of questions relating to the internal operation and organization of the United Nations. Part Two is concluded with brief observations as to the extent of United States influence and a quantitative summary of voting patterns in the Assembly. A final chapter summarizes the findings of the study in the context of their relevance to American leadership.

DEFINITIONS AND PREMISES

Although an effort has been made to use words whose meanings are obvious, a few terms may not seem immediately clear in context. The concept of a "political question" is one which demands elucidation. For practical purposes the line of demarcation between "political" and "non-political," as the term is used in this study, is easy to draw: those questions are deemed political which are discussed by the Political and Security Committee of the General Assembly—the First Committee— or by the Ad Hoc Political Committee (in 1956 renamed Special Political Committee) which has been created each session since the second to handle the overflow of political questions. In a few instances items considered by the General Assembly in plenary session, without reference to a committee, have also been included, but they are for the most part identical in subject matter with questions normally considered by the two political committees. Any less pragmatic definition of a "political" question would have been hazardous. Substantively, as H. Field Haviland observes, the term "political" is "a rather slippery concept to deal with," although "it seems to be generally understood in connection with United Nations affairs to designate those questions that are so highly charged that they are a potential threat to international peace." [8] This definition is perhaps adequate to account for most agenda items referred to the two political committees. However, to those questions involving a potential threat to the peace must be added organizational matters—such as the admission of new members and the creation of the Interim Committee— which would effect some change in the formal pattern of power relationships within the United Nations organization. These also are regularly sent to the First Committee or the Special Political Committee and must enter into any substantive definition of a "political" question in the General Assembly.

Aside from the determination of what is political, there also arises the problem of deciding when an item is actually a separate "question" or "issue." Some items on the agenda of the committees have been subdivided into two or more parts and made the subject of more than one resolution. Other items have been inscribed on the committee agendas but never discussed as to substance. For instance, until recently the item entitled "Report of the Security Council" appeared regularly on the agenda of the First Committee or the Special Political Committee. Almost invariably the committee, without discussion, recommended that the Assembly take note of the report of the Security Council and pass on to the next order of business. In such matters the rule normally followed in this study has been to omit such items which are not discussed substantively, and to treat separately a subsection of a major issue, which is discussed and voted upon independently of the larger question.

A final definition concerns the use of the term "leadership." This expression is broad enough to cover a multitude of concepts, but in this study it is given a rather specialized meaning to distinguish it from the concept of influence. From one point of view leadership might be regarded as roughly equivalent to influence, or the possession of influence. In this sense leadership would be demonstrated when influence is exerted, and leadership would be successful when the exertion of influence achieves its objective. However, an effort has been made to use the word "influence" in all such instances. The term "leadership," for the purposes of this study, is used to connote something more than the exercise of influence. It is meant to imply also a relationship of mutual respect and confidence between the leader and those who are disposed to follow.

It might be well, as concluding observations, to set down explicitly

[8] Haviland, *op. cit.*, p. 12.

some of the author's general normative premises with respect to the United Nations, since they no doubt pervade the study implicitly at many points. The principal ones are these. International cooperation is desirable and the United Nations is a reasonably satisfactory agency for facilitating cooperation. As a center for airing problems and disputes, the desirable effects outweigh the less desirable ones. It is good to have an international parliament where the attention of the world can be called to existing problems and an attempt made to alleviate them, even though some may be exacerbated in the process. As a world security organization it cannot be expected to function effectively except in cases of localized conflict. As a defense system for one part of the world against another, it is inferior to old-fashioned formal alliances. Taken by and large, however, the United Nations deserves the continued support of the United States government and the American people. While its inherent limitations should be taken into account, the United Nations is about as good an all-purpose international organization as can be devised for the world of today. Any desirable goal that can presently be promoted through a general international organization can be promoted through the United Nations.

Part One

The Methods of Influence

CHAPTER TWO

Policy Execution: Instrumentalities and Protagonists

There is perhaps no better point of departure for a discussion of United States influence in the Assembly than the means or instrumentalities through which influence is exerted. A full recounting of the instrumentalities of influence would involve consideration of all the diplomatic agencies through which international intercourse is normally carried on, for United States policy in the General Assembly is not pressed forward in isolation or disregard of normal diplomatic processes. Quite the contrary: those who formulate and execute our foreign policies strive for a close coordination of means and objectives so that our efforts in the United Nations and through traditional diplomatic channels supplement each other. In order to carry a point in the Assembly, the United States may attempt to influence the Assembly delegations of other countries. But the State Department will often achieve more salutary results by contacting foreign governments through our diplomatic missions abroad, or through their missions in Washington. However, any detailed survey of the organization and operation of our diplomatic service as a whole is obviously beyond the scope of this study. At the same time, the manner in which the United States is represented at the seat of the United Nations is of particular concern.

THE MISSION

The United States is continuously represented at the headquarters of the United Nations by a Permanent Mission, which maintains contact with the Secretariat and the representatives of other member states having permanent missions in New York. For all practical purposes the mission is an embassy to the United Nations, with a "Permanent Representative to the United Nations" as Chief of Mission.[1] The functional components of the mission correspond to the major organs of the United Nations and subsidiary bodies in whose work the United States participates. Besides the Permanent Representative and his deputy,

---

[1] The mission finds its legal basis in the "United Nations Participation Act of 1945," as amended in 1949, and Presidential executive orders pursuant thereto. *U.S. Statutes at Large*, 79th Cong., 1st sess., vol. 59, p. 619, and 81st Cong., 1st sess., vol. 63, p. 734. The original executive order, 9844, was superseded by order 10108.

the mission consists of representatives to the General Assembly, the Security Council, the Economic and Social Council and its subsidiary bodies, the Trusteeship Council, the United Nations Military Staff Committee, the Disarmament Commission, and certain General Assembly functional committees and commissions.[2] The representatives to the organs of the United Nations are assisted by political, economic, and social advisers permanently attached to the mission. All representatives are subject to instructions from Washington and, on occasion, may be aided by State Department experts sent down to advise on a particular problem currently being considered.[3] The work of the mission is organized under the direction of a Counsellor of Mission who, so to speak, runs the mission for the Chief. His responsibility, partly political and partly administrative, is to plan and coordinate its daily activities.[4] Essential clerical and maintenance services are supervised by an Executive Director,[5] under whose direction some one hundred mission employees carry on the routine activities relating to personnel and security, finance, maintenance and supply, travel and accommodations, reporting and documentation, and a variety of necessary secretarial services.[6] Attached to the mission and directly responsible to the Chief is an Office of Public Affairs performing the multitudinous informational and publicity functions.[7]

[2] The Permanent Representative is also the United States representative in the Security Council and *ex-officio* representative in the Disarmament Commission and certain of the committees and commissions created by the Assembly.

[3] The representatives to the United Nations Military Staff Committee, while a part of the mission, receive instructions through the Joint Chiefs of Staff rather than through the Secretary of State, and the Chief of Mission is not responsible for the "internal administration of the personnel, budget, and obligation or expenditure of funds" connected with their activities. See Executive Order 10108.

[4] The title of Counsellor of Mission was not created until 1954. Before that time the duties of the position, as they had evolved through usage and practical necessity, were lodged with a senior adviser. When the title was created in 1954 it was largely formalization of the existing situation. The relative emphasis upon the administrative and political aspects of the Counsellor's responsibilities has varied with the personality and inclinations of the men holding the position.

[5] Until 1954 the chief of housekeeping services was called the Secretary-General instead of Executive Director, although his functions were largely the same.

[6] With the change to a Republican administration, the mission, like many other agencies of the federal government, was subjected to a "reduction in force." In January, 1953, the permanent personnel of the mission numbered 142. By January, 1955, the figure was 103. Although economy was the object, better coordination also resulted, according to the statement of one mission official.

[7] For organizational chart as of March, 1955, see Figure 1. Information relating to the organization and operation of the mission and delegation was obtained through personal interview with a number of mission officials, present and past. Printed materials on the general subject include Channing B. Richardson, "The United States Mission to the United Nations," *International Organization*, vol. 7 (Feb., 1953), pp. 22-34; George Barrett, "Our Global Embassy on Park Avenue," *New York Times*

The mission was established as the formal medium through which the United States government might maintain representation in the organs and activities of the United Nations. Like embassies to a foreign government, however, it carries on from day to day a wide range of two-way liaison and informational activities which extend throughout the Secretariat and the permanent missions established in New York by other nations. Views of the United States are disseminated and support for United States policies organized. Ideas, reactions, and suggestions from others are channeled through the mission to the State Department as grist for the decision-making process. Negotiations are undertaken and multilateral agreements reached. Close personal contacts with representatives of other nations, rooted often in friendship and mutual respect, are an invaluable asset both in the formulation and implementation of policy. This process of dealing with many nations simultaneously, on a continuing basis, in the attempted solution of international problems, has come to be called "multilateral diplomacy," and the mission is its focal point.

The Delegation

When the General Assembly is in session the processes of multilateral diplomacy are extended and intensified as the United States seeks to weld a two-thirds majority in favor of its positions and tailor policies to meet majority demands. Technically the delegation is a part of the mission, since Presidential executive orders designate all representatives to the various organs of the United Nations, together with their deputies, staffs, and offices, as "the United States Mission to the United Nations."[8] Budgetarily there is a distinction, however, and the representatives to the Assembly are instructed by the President as a delegation rather than as a part of the United States Mission. The Permanent Representative of the United States to the United Nations, presently former Senator Henry Cabot Lodge, Jr., thus wears two hats when the Assembly is in session. As Chief of Mission he receives instructions from Washington relating to the conduct of mission activities; in his capacity as a representative to the General Assembly he is instructed as a member of the delegation. The distinction may be illustrated further. One member of the delegation, according to the statute, is to be designated

---

Magazine, Nov. 27, 1949, pp. 14-15; Lincoln Palmer Bloomfield, "The Department of State and the United Nations," *Department of State Bulletin,* vol. 23 (Nov. 20, 1950), pp. 804-11; James M. Hyde, "United States Policy in the United Nations," *Annual Review of United Nations Affairs, 1951,* pp. 254-67; Hyde, "United States Participation in the United Nations," *International Organization,* vol. 10 (Feb., 1956), pp. 22-34.

[8] Executive Orders 9844 and 10108.

ORGANIZATION CHART

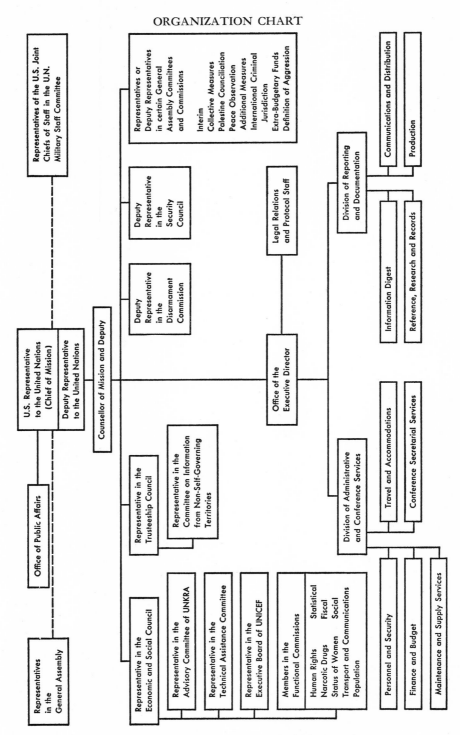

FIGURE 1. United States Mission to the United Nations

the "senior representative." Ordinarily the Permanent Representative is so designated. However, when the Secretary of State participates in the activities of the Assembly the Permanent Representative relinquishes the title of "senior representative" to him without any similar derogation from his status as Chief of Mission.[9]

REPRESENTATIVES AND ALTERNATES

At the top of the delegation pyramid stand the five representatives and five alternates, annual Presidential appointees and for the most part persons of prominence and demonstrated ability in public affairs. The twenty-nine men and women who have served as representatives during the first nine sessions include four Secretaries of State, two former Secretaries of State, fourteen members of Congress, eight high-level officials of the State Department and the United States Mission, one administrative assistant to the President, and two who held no governmental positions immediately prior to the time of their original appointments.[10]

Typically, the Secretary of State, the Permanent Representative, two Congressmen, and one or two prominent public figures or high-level diplomats comprise the front-line representation at the General Assembly. If the Secretary of State is present only for a short time, six different persons, although no more than five at one time, may be accredited as representatives to one session. Congress has not always been so heavily represented in the delegation as in recent sessions. Senator Arthur H. Vandenberg, Senator Tom Connally, and Representative Sol Bloom all served as representatives to the first session. From 1947 through 1949 only one member of Congress, Senator John Sherman Cooper, was so honored. Since 1950, however, the practice has been to include two members of Congress, one Democrat and one Republican, as full representatives to each session. Senators not running for re-election are appointed in election years and two members of the House in odd years. Alternates have included persons of somewhat lesser distinction in public affairs although not necessarily of lesser ability, and many of them have been persons without government portfolio. Turnover

[9] Administrative and clerical employees of the United States Mission, like the Chief, don a second hat during Assembly sessions. For the period of the Assembly they are assigned to the delegation as its secretariat.

[10] The two were Mrs. Franklin D. Roosevelt and Charles H. Mahoney. Mrs. Roosevelt was a representative to the first seven sessions while Mr. Mahoney was appointed only for the ninth. John Foster Dulles might be counted in this category also, since he served as a representative to several sessions before returning as Secretary of State and senior representative. James F. Byrnes, who as Secretary of State was senior representative to the first session, was also selected as a delegate to the eighth session. Edward R. Stettinius, Jr., Secretary of State when the Charter was framed, was a delegate to the first session.

among alternates has also been higher from session to session than among representatives. In nine sessions forty different persons have served as alternate, although ten of these at some time participated in the capacity of full representative as well. Only four were members of Congress, with the other thirty-six coming from the top levels of the State Department and the United States Mission or from private life.[11] For the past several years a studied attempt has been made to have the ten delegates and alternates be as representative of a cross section of the United States population as possible. Thus a prominent Negro, members of principal religious groups, and individuals from different sections of the country have been included.

DELEGATION ADVISERS

Standing next to the representatives and providing the expert knowledge and liaison contacts without which the efforts of the representatives would be ineffectual is the corps of delegation advisers. Together with the delegation secretariat they make the United States delegation the largest at the Assembly. Some of the advisers are selected for their knowledge of the peoples and problems of a particular geographic area: these are the political liaison men, officially titled area advisers who are sent out to inform and persuade other delegations and to report the attitudes, feelings, and comments of those delegations. Others are subject-matter specialists, or "subject" officers, chosen to supply technical counsel on Assembly questions within the area of their special competence. Some advisers, by virtue of their ability and experience, may serve in both capacities. The number of advisers varies from session to session but has averaged about fifty.[12] Sixty-one were used during the fourth session, while only forty and thirty-nine were found necessary during the eighth and ninth sessions respectively. At least half have been officials from State Department desks temporarily assigned to the delegation, and usually ten to twelve are permanent officials of the United States Mission. The others are for the most part men on rotating assignment from the foreign service, including perhaps two or three who have served in posts of ambassadorial or ministerial rank. Although some advisers serve for one session or part of one session only, the tendency is to use repeatedly the men who have gained experience with the General Assembly situation and who are familiar with the problems which arise perennially.

[11] See Appendix A for list of representatives and alternates by session.

[12] The members of each of the delegations to the General Assembly are listed annually in the prefatory pages of the *Official Records of Plenary Meetings*. The United Nations Secretariat also issues a special list of Assembly delegations under the document symbol ST/SG/Ser.A.

In recent years it has been found desirable to designate certain members of the delegation as "senior" and "special" advisers. During the first session a number of advisers whose preeminent status required special recognition were set off from the others by the title of Senior Adviser.[13] In subsequent sessions, however, the designation fell into disuse. All subject-matter experts and political liaison officers, whatever their experience or standing within the delegation, were listed together as "advisers" although they were not all separate and equal in function. In practice, coordinating functions which evolved with the organization were assigned to one or two of the more experienced advisers. Out of this situation a problem of protocol developed. Under the single designation of "adviser" a few men of ability, status, and long United Nations service were lumped together with a great number of newcomers and junior advisers. As a practical matter, representatives from other delegations who did not know the United States advisers personally needed a guide to designate which advisers were in fact the senior men. Because of these and other special considerations the title was revived in 1951. John C. Ross, already the coordinator of liaison activities, was formally designated as a senior adviser; Durward V. Sandifer, coordinator of the substantive work of the delegation, was given a similar title.[14] Once the process of differentiation was begun, pressures developed to carry it to great lengths. Only two officials, Ross and William Sanders, were named senior advisers at the seventh session, but four were so designated for the eighth, and an even more superlative category of "special" adviser was created for Robert Murphy, Assistant Secretary of State for United Nations Affairs. For the ninth session no less than twelve senior advisers and four special advisers were listed on the delegation roster.[15]

---

[13] They were Benjamin V. Cohen, James Clement Dunn, Green H. Hackworth, Leo Pasvolsky, and Adlai E. Stevenson.

[14] Special conditions in 1951 served as a catalyst for the change. Warren R. Austin, the chief delegate, was not well and quickly grew tired in the strenuous round of activities at the Paris session. To conserve Senator Austin's strength for the most important matters, Sandifer and Ross were placed as buffers between him and the outside world. Ross handled all liaison work and contact with other delegations. Sandifer lived in the delegation headquarters and coordinated the substantive work of the delegation. Every request and message for Austin came to him, and he decided whether and in what form the problem reached Austin for his decision.

[15] The special advisers were David M. Key, Assistant Secretary of State for International Organization Affairs (formerly United Nations Affairs); David W. Wainhouse, Deputy Assistant Secretary for International Organization Affairs; Ross, Deputy Security Council Representative; and Willard B. Cowles, State Department Deputy Legal Adviser.

Senior advisers were Brig. Gen. Stanton C. Babcock, James W. Barco, Philip Bonsal, John Dreier, William O. Hall, Preston Hotchkis, Jack McFall, Leonard C. Meeker, Mason Sears, Paul B. Taylor, Henry Villard, and Francis O. Wilcox.

DELEGATION FUNCTIONING

Coordination of the varied activities of the delegation in order to accomplish American objectives in the Assembly is an almost impossibly demanding task. As noted above, coordination at the political level—both as to problems of policy and liaison activities—is attempted by the senior advisers. At the administrative level the work of the delegation is organized by the Delegation Executive Officer. The central point of overall coordination is the delegation meeting, held almost daily throughout the session. Here the Delegation Executive Officer announces the agenda for the day. Members of the delegation hear and discuss State Department instructions, seek through mutual discussion a common understanding of objectives, and outline the broad strategy applicable to current agenda items. Ideally the meeting should ensure that the delegation functions as a team.

Detailed consideration of particular questions, both as to substance and tactics, is reserved to much smaller working groups within the delegation.[16] At the beginning of each session about twelve to fifteen working groups are assigned to deal with one or more related items on the Assembly agenda. The central figure of the group is the representative or alternate assigned as spokesman for the item or items in the Assembly and its committees. Working closely with him are one or two subject officers who may have been sent from Washington to work on a single problem. In addition to the substantive experts the working group will have an area adviser for each of the four principal geographic areas—Latin America, Europe, the Near East and Africa, and the Far East.[17] A Committee Executive Officer, who handles the strategy for all questions considered by one of the principal Assembly committees, serves as chairman or senior adviser for the working group.

[16] An excellent description of delegation functioning at the operational level, particularly with respect to the liaison officers, written by a former senior adviser to the delegation, is William Sanders, "Assignment to the United Nations," *Foreign Service Journal*, vol. 30 (Nov., 1953), pp. 24-27.

[17] The pattern of liaison assignments has in the past been relatively flexible. The relative merits of the functional adviser and the area adviser as liaison officers have not been definitely assessed, and both are used for the purpose. Nor has any rule been fixed for specific liaison assignments. As Sanders indicates, assignments in the political committees tend to be by committee and by region. In such cases the liaison officer participates in any working groups dealing with problems which come before the committee to which he is assigned, and contacts, primarily, only those delegations from the countries in his geographical region. However, the liaison officer may be assigned to a committee with the responsibility of contacting all delegations on the relevant agenda items; or he may even be assigned by subject and not by committee. The assignment to contact delegations regardless of area has greater applicability where the emphasis is upon purely informational activities rather than negotiation, persuasion, or discussion of tactics, and has been used very little for the two political committees.

When the delegation spokesman appears before the Assembly or one of its committees he has the assurance that tactically and substantively the ground has been as well prepared as circumstances will admit. Every possible aspect of the problem has been thoroughly explored, the views of other delegations ascertained, and all practicable efforts made to ensure that United States views will mesh with those of an Assembly majority. Sitting just behind the representative in the council chamber is his principal aide and briefing officer, the Committee Executive Officer. This man has kept close watch on all activities of interest to the committee—substantive, procedural, and liaison—and is ready with advice against almost any contingency that may arise. Immediately behind the Committee Executive Officer are functional advisers concerned with the problem. Standing farther back near the door of the committee room, trying to appear inconspicuous, are a number of area advisers prepared at the flick of a finger to make contact with any of the other delegations as the occasion requires.[18] With such backing the delegation spokesman can have reasonable assurance of representing his country well in the Assembly.

THE POLICY DISCRETION OF DELEGATIONS

Each of the members of the General Assembly, while sharing an area of common interest with others, has its own policies, interests, and aspirations. Each represents a sovereign government and operates on the basis of instructions from its foreign offices. The degree to which delegation policies are detailed in advance of the session varies from country to country. Clearly, the most carefully prepared plans must remain flexible enough to adjust to the sinuosities of debate and the inevitable compromises of off-stage negotiations. With leeway for necessary maneuvering, United States policies are in most cases carefully detailed beforehand by officers in the State Department. The proximity of the State Department to the site of the United Nations, with constant contact between the mission and the Department by mail, telegraph, and telephone, further limits the discretion of the American representatives on the spot. To the extent that discretionary latitude exists in the instructions, the delegation may exercise its own initiative in dealing with problems which arise. If the delegation disagrees with its instructions it may either request a certain amount of discretion or a specific change in the instructions. On one or

---

[18] To use a hypothetical situation by way of illustration, the United States representative may think that the Costa Rican delegate should talk to the representative from Ecuador in order to remove an erroneous impression which the latter has indicated in a committee address. He confers with the Committee Executive Officer, who concurs; the functional advisers are consulted and concur. One motions to the area adviser for Latin America in the group near the door, who gets his assignment and proceeds to the Costa Rican representative with his problem.

two occasions the delegation has exercised an important influence upon major questions of policy. Notably, in the spring of 1949 the United States delegation protested the decision of the State Department to support a Latin-American resolution lifting the diplomatic embargo on Spain. The Department subsequently authorized abstention, but even in this case, where the delegation was strongly at variance with its instructions, it took no independent course of action other than to request reconsideration. Nor was this a case in which the delegation was accorded discretion by virtue of a lacuna in the instructions. When the Secretary of State is present as a representative to the Assembly, the discretion of the delegation is of course substantially widened.

The Soviet Union and the United Kingdom, and, to a lesser extent, France, give similar attention to detailed pre-Assembly policy preparation. In contrast, smaller powers allow their delegations a higher degree of discretion.[19] The Canadian delegation, for instance, receives a policy outline of two or three hundred pages at the beginning of each session as a general guide for each agenda item, but many details remain to be filled in as Assembly developments warrant. Of course the extent of financial commitments is spelled out clearly, and no amount of pressure from all the other delegations could conceivably induce Canada to contribute more. This would be true of other members as well. But in most matters the initiative is left to the Great Powers and instructions are correspondingly broad. The Norwegian delegation, as perhaps typical in this regard of the smaller nations of Western Europe, has general instructions which allow considerable leeway for the exercise of discretion. In some instances the government may have a deep enough interest in a question to spell out its position in great detail. On occasion the delegates themselves may wire home for instructions with regard to an unforeseen contingency.[20] Frequently, however, the delegation is merely required to apply a general policy to a particular situation, and often the Norwegian representatives, being personally acquainted with the ministers in the government, know what the instructions would be if they were sent. Delegations from Latin America, the smaller countries of South Asia, the Near East, and Africa, with variations from state to state, have an even higher degree of discretion. The limited facilities of their foreign offices and their modest international commitments almost dictate such a situation. These delegations, too, receive general instructions and, on important questions, more de-

---

[19] Much of the information in this section was obtained through personal interview with members of foreign missions to the United Nations.

[20] For instance, the Norwegian delegation refused to take the responsibility for deciding on the bitterly contested question of India's participation in the political conference on Korea, debated in August, 1953, and asked the home office for instructions.

tailed orders, but many matters are left to the decision of the delegates, with a resulting increase in their on-the-spot personal bargaining capacity.

DELEGATION GROUPINGS

Just as each delegation has its own policies and interests which it seeks to promote, identifiable groups of delegations have common interests which they seek to promote through arrangements for more or less frequent consultation. These groups, often referred to as "blocs," range in unity and common purpose from the tightly knit communist bloc, whose members almost invariably vote alike, to the Western European states meeting occasionally for a mutual exchange of views.[21] The groups which clearly consult with a view to some degree of voting cohesiveness include the Soviet bloc, the Arab League, the so-called "Afro-Asian" bloc, the twenty Latin-American republics, and the British Commonwealth. India, Burma, and Indonesia, apart from their consultative relationships with other Asian and African states, maintain extremely close liaison with one another and constitute a cohesive, if diminutive, Southeast Asian bloc of votes. Irregularly the states of Western Europe also meet for the interchange of views. Within this rather inchoate group are two sub-groupings, the Benelux nations and Scandinavia, whose special consultative relationships stem directly from the cooperation of their governments at other levels. Occasionally, for particular issues, the Western European consultative group may be expanded by the addition of the United States, Canada, Greece, and Turkey to become a "NATO bloc." One other group which deserves mention is "The Sixteen," composed of all United Nations members which sent combat troops to Korea. These states have maintained close contact with each other when discussing the Korean question in the Assembly.

Indisputably the Soviet bloc is the most cohesive of Assembly coalitions.[22] Its members meet frequently and achieve a high degree of coordi-

---

[21] For detailed analysis of bloc voting in early Assembly sessions, see M. Margaret Ball, "Bloc Voting in the General Assembly," *International Organization*, vol. 5 (Feb., 1951), pp. 3-31. Useful observations also are found in Benjamin H. Brown and Joseph E. Johnson, "The U.S. and the UN," *Foreign Policy Association Headline Series*, no. 107 (Sept.-Oct., 1954), pp. 41-43; David Blickenstaff, "The General Assembly," *Annual Review of United Nations Affairs, 1952*, p. 36; Andrew W. Cordier, "The General Assembly," *Annual Review of United Nations Affairs, 1953*, pp. 61-74; Gwendolen M. Carter, "The Commonwealth in the United Nations," *International Organization*, vol. 4 (May, 1950), p. 259; Haviland, *op. cit.*, pp. 39-42; John A. Houston, *Latin America in the United Nations*, Carnegie Endowment, United Nations Studies No. 8 (1956), esp. pp. 297-314; Ernest A. Gross, "The New United Nations," *Foreign Policy Association Headline Series*, no. 125 (Sept.-Oct., 1957), pp. 22-29.

[22] From 1946 to 1949 the Soviet bloc was made up of six countries: Byelorussia, Czechoslovakia, Poland, the Ukrainian Soviet Socialist Republic, the U.S.S.R., and Yugoslavia. With the defection of Yugoslavia in 1949 the number was reduced to five. In December, 1955, Albania, Bulgaria, Hungary, and Rumania were admitted

nation in speaking and voting in the Assembly. Consultation among them is made easier by the physical proximity of their delegation headquarters in midtown Manhattan. They constitute the one solid voting bloc in the General Assembly, almost invariably voting together.

The members of the Arab League meet almost daily while the Assembly is in session to discuss questions of tactics and coordination of policy.[23] Customarily the chairman at such meetings is the representative of the Arab League sent to the United Nations as an observer. On questions of immediate interest to the Arab world, and in Assembly elections, the group attempts to present a solid front. On other questions more room is allowed for the expression of individual differences. By tacit agreement the Arab choice for one Assembly vice-presidency is invariably elected. The Arab states also stand together in support of candidates from their own region for other Assembly offices and for positions in other organs of the United Nations subject to approval by the Assembly. Since representation in most United Nations organs is distributed roughly on a geographical basis, the group selection is frequently governing. The Arab states have also met often to discuss a wide range of questions with other Asian and African delegations.[24] Such meetings are irregular and, as with most group meetings, no records are kept, although each group renders a report to its home government on any significant transactions. The chairmanship is rotated monthly in alphabetical order. The Afro-Asian group, which assumed its present configuration as a result of the Korean crisis, has tended to become somewhat more cohesive with the passage of time. The permanent representatives to the United Nations of the Afro-Asian states carry on consultations throughout the year.[25]

Numerically one of the most powerful blocs in the General Assembly is the group of twenty Latin-American states. From the very first Assem-

---

to the United Nations, increasing the number of the Soviet-controlled vote to nine. These four new members had no part in the activities of the Assembly during the period covered by this study.

[23] The Arab states in the Assembly are Egypt, Jordan, Iraq, Lebanon, Libya, Saudi Arabia, Sudan, Syria, and Yemen. Jordan and Libya, which were not admitted to the United Nations until December, 1955, and Sudan, admitted November, 1956, had no part in Assembly decisions during the period covered by this study.

[24] Besides the members of the Arab League the group has included eight Asian states—Afghanistan, Burma, India, Indonesia, Iran, Pakistan, the Philippines, and Thailand—and two African states—Ethiopia and Liberia. Cambodia, Laos, Ceylon and Nepal, admitted to the United Nations in 1955; Tunisia, Morocco and Japan, admitted in 1956; and Ghana and the Malayan Federation, admitted in 1957, are now associated with this group.

[25] Information concerning Arab and Afro-Asian organization was obtained through personal interview with an official of the Saudi Arabian delegation. A useful published commentary is Harry N. Howard, "The Arab-Asian States in the United Nations," *The Middle East Journal*, vol. 7 (Summer, 1953), pp. 279-92.

bly their representatives have met to decide upon Latin-American candidates for Assembly elections and to discuss other matters of common interest. It has become an established precedent for the Latin-American delegate who holds an Assembly vice-presidency to be chairman of the caucus for the year. As with the Afro-Asian states, their permanent representatives also meet during the year when the Assembly is not in session. In the early years the Latin-American caucus met principally to select candidates for elective offices allotted to the Latin-American region, although important questions of substance were discussed from time to time. Recently meetings have become more frequent, and in the ninth session the caucus chairman instituted the practice of holding regular fortnightly meetings for the conscious purpose of increasing Latin-American influence in the General Assembly through prior agreement on important questions. No binding decisions are taken by the group, but "understandings" as to policy and tactics are frequently attained among a substantial majority. Increasingly, too, the caucus has become a forum where advocates, upon their own initiative or at the invitation of the caucus, explain and seek support for a measure in advance of its presentation to the Assembly.[26]

The delegations from British Commonwealth countries meet weekly while the Assembly is in session, on a fairly regular but informal basis.[27] There is no weekly agenda as such, but one delegation may circulate to the others a list of suggested topics or propose that a particular question be emphasized at the next meeting. Polices are discussed and efforts made to harmonize them to the extent that divergent interests will permit. Where positions are irreconcilable, one side may be persuaded to abstain in order to avoid opposition among members of the Commonwealth. Of course even this sort of unity cannot always be obtained. Subjects which cause tension between Commonwealth countries or on which Commonwealth countries are known to be totally at variance, such as the question

---

[26] For instance, at the request of Henry Cabot Lodge, Jr., the American atoms-for-peace plan was outlined to the Latin-American caucus for comments and criticism before being presented to the ninth Assembly. At the same session Secretary of State Dulles accepted an invitation to explain United States policies in the Far East to the caucus.

In some instances the activities of the organization have extended beyond matters of immediate concern either to the Assembly or to the United Nations as a whole. In two cases cited by Ambassador José Vicente Trujillo, Permanent Representative of Ecuador to the United Nations, the group intervened to stay executions pending in Guatemala and Egypt. Such action, particularly in the field of human rights, could conceivably increase in the future.

The principal source of information concerning the organization and activities of the Latin-American delegations was a personal interview with Ambassador Trujillo, chairman of the caucus during 1954-55, on March 8, 1955.

[27] Australia, Canada, India, New Zealand, Pakistan, the Union of South Africa, and the United Kingdom, and, since December, 1955, Ceylon. Ceylon is not included in any of the tabulations relating to Commonwealth voting in the Assembly.

of Indians in South Africa, are never discussed at such meetings. But Commonwealth ties are at least one consideration in the evolution of policies and tactics, and meetings of the Commonwealth delegations furnish an instrumentality through which common action can be evolved.[28]

The Soviet bloc, the Arabs and Afro-Asians, the Latin Americans, and the Commonwealth nations are readily identifiable as delegation groupings organized, with varying degrees of formality, to facilitate consultation and joint action on a wide range of topics. Contrasted to such groupings, which retain the same membership and meet with relative frequency and regularity, are groups of states thrown together *ad hoc* in support of a particular resolution. Somewhere between these extremes is the group of Western European states which meets from time to time for the exchange of views without any degree of regularity or formality of organization and with little intention of acting as a West European "bloc."[29] The initiative for getting together may come from any state in the group feeling the need for it, and a representative from the delegation calling the meeting will in all likelihood serve as chairman or discussion leader in an informal way. A similar ascertainment of views might be obtained by an interchange of cables between foreign offices, but it is easier and quicker for the delegates who are all in New York to meet and brief each other on their respective positions.[30] "The Sixteen," as a delegation grouping, functions in close coordination under American leadership when Korea is an issue, but it is too limited in scope to deserve the appellation of "bloc" in the same sense as the communist states or the Latin-American delegations. Likewise, the NATO countries usually operate in the General Assembly on the basis of affiliations and interests other than their Atlantic alliance.

The existence of organized blocs of states in the Assembly is a generally recognized political phenomenon. The extent and significance of bloc voting, however, is more controversial. Some indication of relative bloc cohesiveness may be gleaned from Tables 1, 2, and 3, in which the various delegation groupings are ranked according to the extent of voting agreement within each group. The tables are based upon eighty-six selected roll-call votes on political questions, which are sub-classified into cate-

---

[28] These comments are based principally on an interview with an official of the Canadian Mission, March 4, 1955. Gwendolen M. Carter, surveying the record of the Commonwealth nations in 1950, concluded that the individual states were acting independently in the United Nations, despite their group consultations and the increased cooperation in Commonwealth relations outside the United Nations. *Op. cit.,* pp. 247-60.

[29] Somewhere in between also is a bloc of so-called "underdeveloped" states, including most of Latin America, Africa, and Asia. Although they lack regular institutional arrangements for consulting they do work together and vote together with a fair degree of cohesiveness on many questions.

[30] Interview with an official of the Norwegian Permanent Mission, March 8, 1955.

gories of "colonial" and "non-colonial" questions.[31] The primary ranking is based on the number of times 15 per cent or fewer of the members of each bloc voted differently from the majority of the bloc. This is not quite the same as 85 per cent agreement, since on a given question one or more members of the group may not have voted at all. Bloc voting agreement expressed as a percentage was chosen as the primary criterion of relative cohesiveness in order to put the groups with many members on a comparable basis with those having only a few. However, the tabulations of unanimity and disagreement frequencies may shed additional light on the question of cohesiveness.

TABLE 1. BLOC VOTING AGREEMENTS FOR 86 ROLL-CALL VOTES ON POLITICAL QUESTIONS

Bloc	Times 15% or fewer members voted differently from majority of bloc	Times voted unanimous	Times actual disagreement
Soviet bloc	86	86	0
Arab League	72	62	0
Latin America	59	30	22
Western Europe	52	40	19
Afro-Asia	41	26	21
Commonwealth	36	16	35
Burma-India-Indonesia	—	72	1
Benelux	—	71	2
Scandinavia	—	60	6
All members but Soviet bloc	32	1	45

TABLE 2. BLOC VOTING AGREEMENTS FOR 56 ROLL-CALL VOTES ON POLITICAL QUESTIONS CLASSIFIED AS "NON-COLONIAL"

Bloc	Times 15% or fewer members voted differently from majority of bloc	Times voted unanimous	Times actual disagreement
Soviet bloc	56	56	0
Latin America	49	26	7
Arab League	42	33	0
Western Europe	41	35	7
Commonwealth	32	15	11
Afro-Asia	18	9	12
Benelux	—	49	1
Burma-India-Indonesia	—	44	0
Scandinavia	—	41	4
All members but Soviet bloc	26	1	18

[31] See Chapter Seven for a detailed discussion of political questions dealing with legacies of colonialism. For an explanation of the basis on which the eighty-six roll-call votes used in the tables were selected, see Chapter Ten, pp. 167-70.

TABLE 3. BLOC VOTING AGREEMENTS FOR 30 ROLL-CALL VOTES ON POLITICAL QUESTIONS
CLASSIFIED AS "COLONIAL"

Bloc	Times 15% or fewer members voted differently from majority of bloc	Times voted unanimous	Times actual disagreement
Soviet bloc	30	30	0
Arab League	30	29	0
Afro-Asia	23	17	9
Western Europe	11	5	12
Latin America	10	4	15
Commonwealth	4	1	24
Burma-India-Indonesia	—	28	1
Benelux	—	22	1
Scandinavia	—	19	2
All members but Soviet bloc	6	0	27

The Soviet bloc stands without peer as the most highly coordinated voting bloc, with unanimity on all eighty-six questions. The states of the Arab League run a surprisingly close second, achieving unanimity on sixty-two votes and on ten others one vote less than unanimity. On colonial questions the Arabs voted together twenty-nine times out of a possible thirty, a feat exceeded only by the Soviet bloc. The record on non-colonial questions indicates a fair amount of non-agreement, although the degree of mutual concurrence is still impressive. In all eighty-six votes, not one occasion arose in which a member of the League cast a vote contrary to the others. All deviations from the majority vote took the form of abstentions. Latin America and Western Europe, despite the formal caucus organization of one and the extremely casual consultative arrangements of the other, score much the same on all three tables. As an overall score the Latin-American group has fifty-nine agreements at the 15 per cent deviation level to fifty-two for Western Europe; but Western Europe achieved ten more unanimous votes and had three fewer disagreements. Both rank relatively high on non-colonial questions and quite low on colonial matters. The Afro-Asian bloc clearly functions effectively only in the area designated as colonial. It has fewer agreements and more disagreements on non-colonial questions than any of the other groups and, in the 15 per cent deviation column, scores well below the fifty-five non-communist members taken as a whole.[32] The Commonwealth, with its high rate of disagreement and otherwise unimpressive agreement scores, scarcely qualifies as a voting bloc at all. It should be noted, how-

[32] For the purpose of this tabulation Yugoslavia is counted as communist through the third session and non-communist thereafter. The twenty-two new members, admitted since 1955, of course do not figure in any of the tabulations.

ever, that the five non-Asiatic members of the Commonwealth do concur frequently. Exclusive of India and Pakistan the Commonwealth nations were unanimous forty-four times on non-colonial questions and ten times on colonial questions, and voted in opposition to one another on only nine occasions. The Benelux nations, Scandinavia and Iceland, and the South Asian triad of Burma, India and Indonesia, while hardly large enough to be termed blocs, all have a very high degree of voting agreement within their own small groups, as the tables attest. The extent of bloc voting, in absolute terms, becomes more apparent when bloc agreement scores are compared with the agreement scores calculated for the Assembly as a whole, excluding the Soviet bloc.

The extent of bloc voting in the Assembly can be precisely calculated for questions on which a roll-call vote is taken. But even if individual voting records were available for all questions, this would give no infallible key to the influence of the group upon the voting of its members. When an overwhelming majority of Latin-American states vote in favor of a particular resolution, are they acting on the basis of a group determination? Are they simply all following the lead of the United States? Or is it a matter in which there was no group consultation, no vigorous exertion of American influence, and each state independently reached the same decision on the merits of the case? Such questions can be answered only by reference to particular situations, and, with the limitations of available data, much must still be left to conjecture. A few summary statements appear to be warranted, however. It is evident that, except for the Soviet bloc and, to a lesser extent, the Arab League, the various groups achieve a high degree of voting cohesiveness only on particular questions which fit neatly within the area of common interest. On other issues members of the groups tend to vote together but with much less regularity. Sometimes the members of a so-called bloc may be split almost evenly on a controversial measure. The interests of individual states are too compelling and varied to be subordinated in important matters to a nebulous group interest. There is a certain group loyalty springing from personal relationships and a sort of "united we stand, divided we fall" psychology. But since the group, with whatever formal structure it may have, is basically a creature of convenience and the coincidence of interests, a member will scarcely hesitate to break its bounds on an important question when convenience and interest so dictate. It can be said without exaggeration that the completely *ad hoc* meetings, fluid in composition and varying in number from two or three to twenty or more, as the case may be, result in decisions more significant for the Assembly legislative process than the more stable group associations. The permanent blocs are based upon an area of common interest within which a given Assembly question may or may not fall, but the *ad hoc* meetings spring from a particular interest in a particular issue. The immediacy of the interest is greater. And the decisions reached in such meetings, being based on particular, immediate interest, will be supported in the Assembly and its committees.[33]

THE SECRETARIAT AS A PROTAGONIST

In contrast to the national delegations, the Secretariat is not ordinarily characterized as a protagonist in the Assembly melee. The Secretary-General, as chief of the Secretariat, is assigned functions which are primarily administrative. By Charter prescription the Secretary-General is "chief administrative officer" of the organization, subject at all times to the directives of the other major organs of the United Nations.[34] However, the framers of the Charter authorized the Secretary-General to exercise something more than administrative discretion when they enjoined him to "make an annual report to the General Assembly on the work of the Organization," [35] and his Charter right to "bring to the attention of the Security Council any matter which in his opinion may threaten the maintenance of international peace and security" involves a wholly political function.[36] Moreover, the Assembly, the Security Council, the Economic and Social Council, and the Trusteeship Council have recognized the political role of the Secretary-General by granting him, in their rules of procedure, rights with respect to the preparation of provisional agendas, the proposal of agenda items, and participation in their debates. In the Assembly and Security Council the Secretary-General may present his views, orally or in writing, on any subject without a prior invitation.[37] The constitutional and legal rights of the Secretary-General to exercise political initiative have been confirmed, although not fully delimited, by

---

[33] Bloc voting has been both praised and blamed, depending on the viewpoint of the commentator. See, for instance, Herbert V. Evatt's deprecatory comments in his lectures published under the title of *The United Nations* (1948), pp. 82-83. Carter, *op. cit.*, p. 259, and Haviland, *op. cit.*, pp. 39-42, present an opposite point of view.

[34] *United Nations Charter*, Article 98. See also Articles 97-101. For detailed treatment of the political role of the Secretary-General, as the office had developed to 1951, see Stephen M. Schwebel, *The Secretary-General of the United Nations: His Political Powers and Practice* (1952), and esp. the chapter entitled "Relations with the General Assembly," pp. 63-83. An excellent brief commentary on the Secretariat and its functions is Leland M. Goodrich and Edvard Hambro, *Charter of the United Nations: Commentary and Documents,* 2nd and rev. ed. (1949), pp. 497-98. A somewhat more detailed general study of the Secretariat is *The United Nations Secretariat,* Carnegie Endowment, United Nations Studies No. 4 (1950). More recent observations are to be found in Schwebel, "Secretary-General and Secretariat," Commission to Study the Organization of Peace, *Charter Review Conference* (Aug., 1955), pp. 198-211, and Gross, "The New United Nations," pp. 30-34.

[35] *United Nations Charter*, Article 98.

[36] *Ibid.*, Article 99.

[37] See, e.g., *Rules of Procedure of the General Assembly*, document A/520/Rev.3, 12 and 72.

precedent. Trygve Lie, as the first to hold the office, staunchly defended what he regarded as the political prerogatives of the Secretary-General. His policy recommendations on controversial questions more than once ran counter to previously announced positions of one or more of the Great Powers.[38] The principal reason for his resignation in 1953 was inability, in the face of the Soviet boycott, to exercise the political functions of the Secretary-General as he believed the Charter had intended.[39] The present incumbent, Dag Hammarskjöld, while not given to tilting at windmills, has on occasion vigorously asserted the Secretary-General's political prerogative.[40]

The Secretariat may thus play an important part in decisions of the Assembly. While maintaining impartiality as to country and ideology, the Secretariat can and does examine issues in their relation to the Charter. The concept which emerges is that of an impartial but not necessarily neutral Secretariat. If the Secretary-General believes that the objectives of the Charter can be promoted by his intervention, he will unquestionably do so. On other questions he will remain neutral as well as impartial. There are no clearly defined categories of questions concerning which the Secretary-General feels obliged to intervene or not to intervene. However, certain general principles are relevant to his decision on a particular question.[41] For obvious reasons complete aloofness from "propaganda" resolutions is maintained. Likewise, active participation is avoided when opposing views are so clearly irreconcilable as to make intervention pointless. On the other hand the Secretary-General is virtually certain to express his views with regard to issues affecting the organization and operation of the Secretariat. The attitude of the Secretariat under these circumstances is almost categorically predictable. In other situations, however, the intervention of the Secretariat is conditional. The Secretary-General may intervene with the object of harmonizing differences if this

---

[38] E.g., the questions of Iran, Greece, Palestine, Korea, and Chinese representation.

[39] See Trygve Lie, *In the Cause of Peace* (1954), pp. 39-54, 74-88, 409-11.

[40] During the early months of Hammarskjöld's incumbency there appeared to be a tendency to characterize Trygve Lie as having unduly emphasized the political role of the Secretary-Generalship, in contrast to Hammarskjöld's concentration upon the purely administrative aspects of the position. Lie, for instance, crossed swords with the United States government when it backed away from partition of Palestine in the spring of 1948. Later he won the undying enmity of the Soviet Union by his advocacy of vigorous United Nations action in Korea. However, the distinction between the two men on this basis is scarcely valid. Hammarskjöld may perhaps be a better administrator than his predecessor, and he has certainly been more discreet both in the positions he has chosen to advocate and in the manner of pressing his views. But at the same time he has utilized and increased the political potential of his office, as his action with respect to the imprisoned American airmen, the atoms-for-peace program, and the Suez crisis will attest.

[41] The author is indebted to Andrew W. Cordier, Executive Assistant to the Secretary-General of the United Nations, for these general criteria of judgment given in personal interview, March 8, 1955.

appears feasible.[42] If the Secretary-General is to be charged with some new function or responsibility he may suggest drafting changes in the projected resolution, or even changes of substance, to ensure that the resolution is workable.[43] As a catch-all principle, he will act to influence the determination of policy whenever, in his judgment, the purposes and principles of the Charter may be furthered thereby. This, of course, is broad enough to justify a multitude of interventions, and, in the last analysis, its application depends upon the Secretary-General himself.[44] While the Secretariat under some circumstances becomes a protagonist in the Assembly, it is never strictly comparable in this respect to one of the national delegations. The principle of impartiality, in a sense, sets it above the strife of battle. The Secretariat may be consulted by national representatives from time to time, but respect for the Secretariat's impartiality, as absolutely essential to the continued functioning of the United Nations as a world organization, prevents outright importuning of the Secretary-General.

There are many other levels, mostly informal, at which the Secretariat enters into the Assembly policy process. Members of the Secretariat are consulted continuously on a wide variety of questions, both as experts and as friends. The secretaries of each of the Assembly Main Committees are important points of contact between the Secretariat and national representatives. As a member of the Secretariat responsible for the administrative and procedural details of committee operation, the secretary has duties which include arranging the time of meetings, keeping records, preparing the speakers' list, and advising the committee chairman on matters of procedure. As an individual he tries to keep well informed on committee developments in order to supply the numerous requests for information made of him. Recognizing this, members of delegations will often give him advance notice of prospective departures in policy and tactics, and otherwise cultivate his friendship. Then, in the course of debate, the secretary's timely advice to the chairman on procedure may extricate a friend from a difficult parliamentary situation. Or advance notice of a rearrangement in the speakers' list may enable a delegation to be prepared for an eventuality that might otherwise have come as a surprise in the committee. Such activities by members of the Secretariat are hard to evaluate but are not without significance in the Assembly political process.

[42] E.g., the Secretariat was active in promoting agreement on the atomic energy resolution, adopted unanimously by the ninth Assembly.

[43] This happened with the resolution requesting the Secretary-General to act in the case of the American airmen imprisoned in Communist China.

[44] This broad Charter mandate presumably was the justification for Trygve Lie's Twenty-Year Program for Peace, discussed in Chapter Six, and for the initiative of Hammarskjöld in undertaking studies relating to the development of atomic energy for peaceful uses.

CHAPTER THREE

Policy Execution: The Melee

THE ROLE OF CONSULTATION

CONSULTATION IN POSITION PREPARATION

When the Assembly is in session, the United States, through its delegation, works in varying degrees of cooperation and competition with other states to obtain a series of voting majorities for resolutions which it approves. In the context of the present study this is policy execution. It is accomplished by two closely interrelated processes—the preparation of a resolution acceptable to the necessary majority, and marshalling the necessary majority behind the resolution at the right time and place. In these processes the role of consultation is crucial.[1]

If the policy is right the United States delegation will encounter little difficulty in securing its adoption by the Assembly. What constitutes "right" varies from issue to issue, and sometimes from year to year on a similar issue. The position makers in the State Department are set the task

---

[1] A description of the policy formation process is beyond the immediate scope of this study except as it impinges on policy execution. Useful commentaries on this subject are Lincoln Palmer Bloomfield, "How the U.S. Government Is Organized to Participate in the U.N. System," *Department of State Bulletin,* vol. 35 (Sept. 17, 1956), pp. 442-44; H. Field Haviland, Jr., *The Political Role of the General Assembly,* Carnegie Endowment, United Nations Studies No. 7 (1951), pp. 49-50; James N. Hyde, "United States Policy in the United Nations," *Annual Review of United Nations Affairs, 1951,* pp. 254-67; Channing B. Richardson, "The United States Mission to the United Nations," *International Organization,* vol. 7 (Feb., 1953), pp. 22-34; Benjamin H. Brown and Joseph E. Johnson, "The U.S. and the UN," *Foreign Policy Association Headline Series,* no. 107 (Sept.-Oct., 1954), pp. 41-43. Of these Bloomfield is the best and most detailed concerning the technical aspects of policy formation with regard to the United Nations. Two articles which attempt to assess the impact of the United Nations upon American government and foreign policy are Daniel S. Cheever, "The Role of the United Nations in the Conduct of United States Foreign Policy," *World Politics,* vol. 2 (Apr., 1950), pp. 390-404, and Haviland, "The United Nations: Effects on American Government," *Current History,* vol. 22 (Jan., 1952), pp. 13-18. In a broader context Dean Acheson, in his article "The Responsibility for Decision in Foreign Policy," *Yale Review,* vol. 44 (Sept., 1954), pp. 1-12, presents an authoritative if brief analysis of the problems inherent in foreign policy decision making and stresses the personal responsibility of the President for major decisions. Useful also is Dorothy Fosdick, *Common Sense and World Affairs* (1955), a provocative and extremely readable analysis of some of the more general considerations involved in the making of foreign policy. For the present study, these commentaries were supplemented by personal interviews with members of the State Department and the United States Mission.

of determining in advance what will be regarded as "right" by a substantial Assembly majority, and then incorporating the essential ingredients into the United States position without compromising national interests.[2] As Haviland remarks, "When advance consultation is tardy and spotty, the task of gaining broad support during the Assembly session becomes that much more difficult."[3] The problem of execution is thus intimately connected with the process of policy formulation and adaptation.[4]

The striving for accommodation and intermeshing of American policies with the views of other nations goes on continuously through consultation and exchange of information with the Secretariat and the permanent missions in New York. Other exchanges take place with foreign diplomatic representatives in Washington and, through United States diplomatic missions abroad, with the foreign offices of other countries. This "diplomatic preparation" reaches a peak of intensity in the months immediately preceding the annual Assembly sessions. Before the Assembly convenes every United States embassy is sent a circular statement of American objectives in the forthcoming session and an outline of positions to be taken on each question. At this early stage positions will not always have been clearly formulated but their general direction can be indicated. The diplomatic representatives of the United States are thus in a position to answer questions and explain, at least in broad outline, what the United States hopes to accomplish. On many questions special consultation will be undertaken with friendly delegations and governments. These begin ordinarily with the United Kingdom, followed by talks with France, and from there spread out to include other countries as the importance and nature of the question warrant.[5] On such questions

[2] Primary responsibility for the preparation of Assembly position papers is lodged with the Bureau of International Organization Affairs, formerly designated the Bureau of United Nations Affairs.

[3] Haviland, *Political Role*, p. 49.

[4] The completed position paper sent to the delegation, if properly done, will reflect the positions of other states and take into account anticipated opposition. See Hyde, *op. cit.*, pp. 262-63.

Speaking to the American Association for the United Nations and the National Citizens' Committee for United Nations Day, New York, October 21, 1951, John D. Hickerson, then Assistant Secretary of State for United Nations Affairs, stated: "Our program has been worked out carefully within the United States Government to provide responsible and realistic policies for our delegation at Paris. We are continuously exchanging views with other free governments on important questions so that our policies will take into account the opinions and needs of other free peoples and represent a common and more effective approach." Reprinted in *Department of State Bulletin*, vol. 25 (Nov. 5, 1951), p. 733.

[5] Prior to the opening of the seventh Assembly, for instance, United States representatives had conferences on the Korean situation with nearly every member of the United Nations except the five in the Soviet bloc. New York *Times*, Oct. 1, 1952, p. 1.

as disarmament the United States quite naturally works more closely with members of the Security Council than with other states. The nature of the question determines who shall be consulted: on a question pertaining particularly to the interests and activities of the Western Hemisphere, the Latin-American states might be consulted first and Britain not at all, or only cursorily. However, the United States will try scrupulously to avoid stating a position on a question of any magnitude without first reaching an understanding with the United Kingdom. Cooperation with Britain in the Assembly is as essential as in other areas of international relations. Complete agreement is not always possible but efforts are made to achieve some sort of accommodation, and joint policies are frequently evolved.[6]

CONSULTATION IN THE ASSEMBLY

Despite the scope and extent of consultations in the policy preparation process, the working group in the Bureau of International Organization Affairs obviously cannot prepare position papers on all questions which definitively reconcile the views of all, or even most, of the members of the Assembly. Practical limitations of time and staff facilities prevent bringing every member government into the round of consultations. Some countries may, for all practical purposes, have no readily ascertainable views on numerous questions; others, such as the communist states, may have positions which are patently irreconcilable. No state can anticipate and provide against every eventuality that may arise during the course of the session. Given these conditions the American policy planners could not possibly eliminate all dissent in advance even if this were the sole objective. Beyond considerations of the need for obtaining a consensus, there comes a point in the formulation of detailed positions when, for the sake of coherency and consistency as well as the preservation of United States objectives, the suggestions of other governments must be passed over. Characteristically, too, the position papers are framed as negotiating documents with an acceptable minimum set somewhere below the initial demands. Extensive as the pre-position consultations may be, the United States delegation is still confronted with a considerable task of education, persuasion, and negotiation.

Consequently, the process of consultation and accommodation does not stop with the initial preparation of the position paper but continues throughout the course of the Assembly.[7] Increasingly co-sponsors are

[6] Private talks among leaders of the two great Western powers on some aspect of Assembly policy are frequently reported in the press. See, e.g., *ibid.*, Nov. 14, 1949, pp. 1, 5; Nov. 5, 1951, p. 1; Nov. 23, 1952, p. 1.

[7] Delegations sometimes complain that the United States has acted without consulting them in advance. Occasionally, giving advance notice of intentions is thought undesirable, and at other times, unnecessary. But usually the omission arises from the limitations of time and available personnel.

solicited for American resolutions in order to present them as group programs. This necessarily involves hammering out agreement among the
sponsors beforehand through tacit "understandings" of various passages
in the proposed resolution or outright textual revision. The practices of
negotiation, compromise, log rolling, and accommodation, so familiar in
domestic legislatures and for that matter in the annals of old-fashioned
bilateral diplomacy, are not scorned by the United States delegation in
the Assembly.[8] The United States is, in fact, highly sensitive to criticism
in the Assembly, particularly from non-communist nations, and will go
to considerable lengths to satisfy a legitimate complaint.[9] The United
States may indeed be moved to make substantial concessions to sentiment that is strong and widespread enough.[10] Consultation and cooperative action is further encouraged by the absence of a detailed American
position on some questions. The United States policy may be, simply, to
find a workable and generally acceptable solution to the problem before
the Assembly, and the delegation will actively solicit suggestions from
others.[11] As a result of this predisposition to accommodate others, many
policies advocated by the United States are, to a significant degree, what

---

[8] There are, of course, limits to compromise. Sometimes an offer of co-sponsorship,
made contingent upon the incorporation of some textual revision, must be politely
declined because the proposed amendment is unacceptable.

[9] As A. M. Rosenthal noted, "The job of finding out what effect American speeches
and ideas have on our friends is one that United States delegates take seriously."
New York *Times,* Dec. 9, 1951, sec. IV, p. 5. Rosenthal reported that the unfavorable
reaction of many European delegates to Secretary Acheson's "tough" opening speech
in the sixth Assembly led to an order the following morning "that American delegation speeches on all topics were to avoid adjectives and epithets."

[10] Such a case was the abandonment of its stand, in the third session, against reviving
discussions of the full Atomic Energy Commission. Commenting on this reversal,
Ambassador Austin declared to the First Committee: "No, believe me, the United
States respects the opinion of its colleagues on this committee and when it sees a
movement of opinion like that around this table, it gives attention to it. And, notwithstanding the fact that we still believe firmly that the only place where we can
unravel this tangle—the tangled threads—is on a higher level, nevertheless, we are
going to acquiesce in the obvious feelings of this Committee. We are going with
you. Don't let anybody assert that the United States tries to coerce or force its
opinion. I can give you evidence now, this minute, to the contrary. We are going
to vote for this although we still adhere to the opinion expressed in that report of
the Atomic Energy Commission and supported by our endeavors here with all the
strength we have." *Department of State Bulletin,* vol. 19 (Oct. 31, 1948), p. 540.

[11] Secretary of State Dulles, in his opening address to the eighth Assembly,
expressed a willingness to learn from others: "We shall state as clearly as possible
what we deem to be the just and the right solutions to the problems which we here
encounter, for we do not think that the United States ought to be ambiguous about
the problems of our time. But we also adhere to the basic United States belief,
expressed in our Declaration of Independence, that we owe 'a decent respect to the
opinions of mankind.' We are ready to learn from others and we also recognize that
our views may not always prevail." *Plenary Meetings,* 8th sess. (1953), p. 17.

the State Department represents them to be—the common policies of a majority of the members of the United Nations.[12]

THE ROLE OF PRESSURE

TACTICS

There sometimes comes a point in the task of fashioning a two-thirds majority when consultation is not enough. The United States must then apply to reluctant or indifferent states methods of persuasion which are commonly termed "pressure." Phrased in its simplest terms, the application of pressure is the attempt to persuade a delegate or his government to support the United States position by methods which extend beyond a factual exposition of the merits of the case. Admittedly it is not always easy to determine where a presentation of the facts shades into the application of pressure, but there are certain observable activities of the United States delegation, the Department of State, and, on occasion, other agencies of government which constitute pressure within the present definition. While official spokesmen resent the implication of coercion which the expression "pressure" frequently conveys, members of the State Department and Assembly delegation readily admit that other nations are importuned on bases other than the facts immediately relevant to a given question.

In the task of gaining a consensus, the eyes, ears, and mouth of the delegation are its liaison officers, sometimes less respectfully referred to as "arm twisters." [13] When pressure is applied at the delegation level the liaison officer is the most common instrument.[14] Primarily his duties are informational—to inform other delegations of the United States position and report their views, reactions, and suggestions to his own delegation.

---

[12] Communist charges of an American "mechanical majority" in the Assembly, to which the State Department and the United States delegation are very sensitive, are usually met with the assertion that the majorities spring from cooperation, not dictation. The following passage taken from *The U.S. and the U.N.*, report of President to Congress (1948), p. 5, is illustrative. "The [third] Assembly did not automatically adopt the proposals made by any one Member, as often alleged by Soviet spokesmen. On the contrary, national proposals were, in practically all instances, modified through the process of discussion. They expressed the views of a large majority, and they emerged with the support of practically the entire Assembly except the Soviet bloc."

[13] See, e.g., New York *Times*, May 11, 1949, p. 25, and Dec. 9, 1951, sec. IV, p. 5.

[14] Almost uniformly officials of other delegations who were queried on the matter of United States "pressure" denied that it was ever applied to them. They did readily admit being consulted by American officials and urged to support particular resolutions. Most seemed to feel that the Latin-American states were perhaps subjected to pressure, if any members were. A Peruvian official interviewed denied personal experience of American pressure but stated that if pressure were applied it would be upon the home governments rather than at the delegation level.

Keeping other delegations informed of United States attitudes is an important factor in winning support. Other delegations appreciate advance notice of American intentions, which, on many not greatly publicized issues, are not always clearly apparent. Commonly, however, the presentation of an American position is accompanied by supporting arguments calculated to persuade as well as to inform. The "pressure" which the liaison officer applies is a function of his insistence and the degree of emphasis which he gives his arguments. If a friendly delegation upon first consideration of the American position agrees with the views expressed, there is no occasion to speak of pressure or arm twisting. If, however, the liaison officer repeats his importunings after delegation representatives have indicated reluctance to support the United States position, his activities may be said to constitute pressure. The appeal of facts, having proved unconvincing, is then being supplemented by personal insistence and, it may be assumed, emphasis upon the importance of the question to the United States government. The amount of pressure which may be applied in a given situation depends upon the importance of the question and the officer's estimate of how effective such tactics will be.[15] Some delegations can be favorably influenced by repeated solicitations, at least on certain questions; others are merely incensed. The objective is to apply pressure only where it will do some good, and the subtler the better. In extreme cases this may involve none too subtle remonstrations with a delegate in lounges, at luncheons, in corridors and halls, in his apartment, or wherever he may be found, until the desired assent is given. It may also involve contacting his government for a change in instructions to support the American position. The liaison officer, in what he can actually say, is largely limited to arguing the merits of the United States position. The pressure springs more from his insistence than from the content of his message. Of course in presenting arguments he may dramatize the extreme importance of the issue to his government. He may speak in terms of the possible consequences of alternative courses of action including, perhaps, the unfavorable reaction of Congress or the American people if the resolution should fail to pass. But if his arguments and his persistence are not persuasive, the liaison officer has no further recourse. He has no authority to impose sanctions or even to threaten. Some liaison

---

[15] William Sanders emphasizes the need for discrimination on the part of the liaison officer. "The central objective of the liaison work," he states, "is to exchange views and to obtain information. It is not the indiscriminate corralling of votes. Varying degrees of emphasis are called for in the presentation of the views and attitudes of the United States, depending on the importance of the subject. The 'crisis psychology' . . . must be guarded against to avoid dissipating good will on matters of relative unimportance. Good judgment in determining the matters that must receive special attention is indispensable. Although such decisions are not his alone to make the area adviser has a special responsibility in carrying them out." *Op. cit.*, p. 62.

men may become overzealous and persist to the point of annoying another delegation, but their capacity to apply pressure extends no further.[16]

Presumably, officials in the State Department, when they cable an American mission abroad to make special representations to a foreign government, are in a better position than the liaison officers to suggest specific rewards or reprisals. In practice, however, this is not done.[17] On important questions special circulars are sent out to American diplomatic missions for the information of the governments to which they are accredited, and a very high degree of emphasis may be indicated.[18] Particular governments may also be singled out for special attention. However, in its representations the United States government tries carefully to avoid the appearance of exercising coercion. The support and confidence of other states over the long haul cannot be built by highhanded coercion in special cases. Just as a liaison officer may use poor judgment in his approach to other Assembly delegations, an official of a United States embassy abroad may, through an excess of zeal and impatience with the slow process of international negotiations, assume a somewhat dictatorial attitude. If knowledge of this conduct reaches the State Department the officer will invariably be told to stay within his instructions.

UNDERLYING FACTORS

The effectiveness of pressure tactics is almost wholly dependent upon the more fundamental ingredients of American national power. Like consultations the use of pressure tactics makes a significant contribution to American influence only in the context of other conditions. The representatives of Yemen might consult, importune, or even threaten until they collapsed from exhaustion, but Yemen would still not be recognized as wielding great influence in the Assembly. Fundamentally the United States has influence in the Assembly because of the wealth and power which make it influential in every other area of international affairs.

---

[16] A former adviser to the United States delegation colorfully described this process of "turning on the heat": "You sit down with the delegate, tell him the United States position, and ask for his support. You present your arguments and tell him that such and such consequences may flow from one action or the other. You catch him in the lounge or take him out to lunch, and keep after him until you make his life miserable. Then he may say, 'I'm cabling my government for instructions.' You think he's lying so you cable his government; then you go to him with the cable. You keep after him until he gives in. No actual threats are made—it's just a process of hounding him to death." Interview, March 7, 1955.

[17] State Department officials interviewed were all emphatic on this point.

[18] Cables are frequently sent out as a means of soliciting support, but often the purpose is a dual one. Besides letting the foreign government know the American position, the cable also puts the State Department on record as actively championing the measure. This is for its own protection in case, for instance, a Congressman complains that nothing was done to secure adoption of a particular resolution.

Almost any program of action which the Assembly might initiate must rely heavily upon the cooperation and the resources of the United States. Most members of the Assembly recognize, at least in principle, that a policy to be rationally formulated must take into account the views of those states which bear chief responsibility for its implementation. Representatives from smaller states speak out freely on matters which are of particular concern or interest to them but otherwise are inclined to follow the lead of the Great Powers, among which the United States stands foremost. Certainly this rule has many exceptions. Not infrequently representatives of small states will call for strong action by the Assembly which, in actual practice, will have to be carried out by others. In many instances the temptation to bellicosity without responsibility proves irresistible. But on the whole small powers tend to leave the initiative in important questions to the larger states. Unquestionably American views have weight in the Assembly simply because the United States is a Great Power.

Another element which lends cogency to American appeals for support is the economic dependence of many non-communist nations upon the United States government. This factor is so obvious that its significance can be overestimated. Probably the situations are few in which a foreign government supports an American resolution in the General Assembly solely, or even principally, because of the economic assistance it receives and hopes to continue receiving from the United States. The question of economic aid is just not made an issue. No one is threatened with a cut in aid if he fails to go along, or bribed with an offer of more if he does. No enduring framework of cooperation among sovereign and independent states can be erected upon a foundation of crass coercion. There is wisdom if not rhetorical euphony in the observation of Henry Cabot Lodge, Jr., United States Permanent Representative to the United Nations: "If we say they had better do what we tell them because we have got all the money, then that would irritate them. The worst thing we could do would be to do that."[19] Nevertheless, the relationship is there and cannot be ignored. Although the American minister, when making a special request for support of a foreign government, may meticulously guard against any reference to underlying economic relationships, such fundamental realities as technical assistance, mutual security aid, and trade and tariff concessions may lurk within the consciousness of the foreign official and influence his decision in some degree. United States officials, likewise, are aware of the connection between aid programs and United Nations activities, as the following colloquy between United States

---

[19] U.S. House, subcommittee of Committee on Foreign Affairs, *Hearings on International Organizations and Movements*, March 27-July 29, 1953, 83rd Cong., 1st sess., p. 103.

Representative Jacob K. Javits and Henry Cabot Lodge, Jr., bears witness:

Mr. Javits. What about the mutual security bill with reference to our whole United Nations position? Where does it fit?

Ambassador Lodge. . . . I think among the nations other than the Communist nations in the United Nations, they naturally watch very carefully the extent to which we want to cooperate with them. In that total contemplation the foreign aid legislation plays a major part. There is no doubt about that.

Mr. Javits. Do you feel, therefore, that there would be a serious change in cooperative activities through the United Nations if we should reverse our policy on the mutual security program which is being so widely discussed?

Ambassador Lodge. If you reverse the policy then you have to expect them to reverse their policy. This whole thing is going to hang together. . . .[20]

The effects of economic aid are subtle and exceedingly difficult to evaluate in relation to General Assembly voting, but they are undeniably part of the pattern of American influence in the Assembly.

The words of American representatives have weight in the Assembly because the United States is a Great Power which must bear a lion's share of responsibility for implementing Assembly policies. Their weight is greater still because of the manner in which the United States government has chosen to distribute economic aid throughout the non-communist world. Yet a third factor, perhaps of more direct and immediate significance for Assembly voting, is the role of the United States as the leader of a world coalition against communism. As the only nation with economic and military resources sufficient to raise a bulwark against the spread of Soviet communism and imperialism, the United States commands in varying degrees the allegiance of all countries which feel the need for protection against communist encroachments.[21] The voting pattern on many political questions in the General Assembly is clearly determined by cold war alignments. On question after question the vote characteristically has found communist states standing in isolated

---

[20] *Ibid.*, p. 108. For a brief analysis of foreign aid as an instrument of American policy, see George F. Kennan, "Foreign Aid in the Framework of National Policy," *Proceedings of the Academy of Political Science*, vol. 23 (Jan., 1950), pp. 448-56. Kennan recognizes the virtual necessity of rendering economic aid to others but cautions against regarding it as "a sort of an unlimited letter of credit, to be held by us, upon the future policies of other governments in any and all matters, whether related or otherwise to the immediate purpose of our aid." A useful reference volume on the same general subject is Raymond F. Mikesell, *United States Economic Policy and International Relations* (1952). See esp. pp. 264-73.

[21] Thomas J. Hamilton, reviewing the record of the sixth session, commented, "Fundamentally, United States leadership in the United Nations remains secure if only because the United States is the only country with military and financial strength to keep the flag of freedom flying." New York *Times*, Dec. 16, 1951, sec. IV, p. 4.

opposition to a large majority of non-communist members, with a handful of neutrals refusing to commit themselves to either camp. It is safe to say that but for the cold war the United States would win fewer and smaller majorities in the Assembly than it now does. On issues not involving a large measure of East-West conflict, such as those relating to dependent peoples, the United States often finds itself in the minority or a part of a very tenuous majority. In a very real sense, therefore, the Soviet Union is itself responsible for the consistently large majorities which the United States is able to muster on political questions.

For the most part this "non-communist bloc" forms without pressure from the United States. It springs from mutual interest in maintaining a united front against Soviet expansionism.[22] Individual members of the non-communist coalition will remonstrate with the United States to secure modifications in the American position, and to a great extent the United States is willing to accommodate them. But when unity of action can be preserved only through sacrifice of the preference of the smaller states, considerations of unity are likely to predominate unless the principle is very strongly held. There is a feeling that United States leadership must be upheld if it is to function effectively as a rallying point for the non-communist world.[23] Opposition to Soviet imperialism provides the amalgam which binds the non-communist nations together. On more than one occasion when differences have arisen, a poorly timed Soviet broadside of abuse and derision has driven them to resolve their differences and once more present a united front. This was spectacularly the case with the prisoner-of-war repatriation issue in the seventh Assembly. At a time when the United States was at loggerheads with many of its allies with respect to amending the Indian draft resolution, Andrei Vishinsky made the differences purely academic by roundly denouncing the Indian proposal. Shaken by Vishinsky's "meat grinder touch," the non-communist members immediately closed ranks, found an acceptable for-

---

[22] The New York *Times* commented editorially with regard to this phenomenon: "Any meeting of the United Nations General Assembly reveals the existence of blocs of nations, some of them permanent, some of them for temporary purposes. There is, of course, the Communist bloc. There sometimes seems to be a Western European bloc, a Latin-American bloc, a Far Eastern bloc, an Arab bloc. But there is one sort of bloc that develops whenever the Communists apply enough pressure. This is the non-Communist bloc. . . . We believe that this solidarity of the non-Communist nations will always appear when Russia pushes any issue to its basic point of contention." Nov. 30, 1952, sec. IV, p. 8.

[23] Just after the committee vote on Indian participation in the proposed political conference on Korea, in August, 1953, one "prominent Latin-American delegate" was cited by the New York *Times* as stating that some of his colleagues who voted with the United States would have preferred to see India invited, but they felt that the dominant consideration was not to let the United States go down to defeat on a major political issue. Aug. 28, 1953, p. 3.

mula, and adopted the resolution with the greatest demonstration of solidarity since the beginning of the Korean war.[24]

EVALUATION

Pressure tactics in this context may be regarded as the means for asserting American influence in the Assembly—influence based on economic, military, and, one might add, moral strength. Without the essential power base the tactics of persuasion would be of little avail. But without the application of pressure, American leadership potential would remain dormant. Majorities must be mobilized outside the council chambers and the tactics and strategy of the campaign worked out in advance. Even though a substantial majority of members may be assumed to have a wide area of common interest with respect to a given question, support for a particular resolution must be organized if victory is to be assured. Otherwise minor differences in approach, the reluctance of some delegations to take a firm stand, the uncertainty of others, and, perhaps, the indifference of a few may result in the loss of needed votes. In such situations the application of pressure by the United States can mean the difference between a feeble majority, or none at all, and an overwhelming endorsement of the policy at issue.

There are, of course, limitations to the effectiveness of arm twisting. Certainly no pressure that the United States is willing or able to apply would force Egypt and Israel to reach a mutually acceptable settlement of their outstanding differences. India cannot be persuaded to vote against Chinese Communist representation in the United Nations, nor can Greece, with all its economic and military dependence upon the United States, be induced to relinquish its claim to Cyprus. Persuasion is possible only where differences are reconcilable within an area of common interest. Attempts by the United States to exercise pressure beyond this

[24] The vote was 54-5-1. *Plenary Meetings*, 7th sess. (1952), p. 301. For the Vishinsky speeches see *First Committee*, 7th sess. (1952), pp. 149-51, 177-79. See also comments of New York *Times*, Nov. 30, 1952, sec. IV, p. 1, and Dec. 3, 1952, p. 3.

Another such occasion was Vishinsky's attack upon United Nations aims and objectives in Korea, during the August meeting of the seventh Assembly, at a time when other delegates, with eulogies for the Korean war dead, were paying tribute to the United Nations armed forces in Korea. This episode came hard upon the heels of the bitter squabble over India's participation in the proposed political conference.

Henry Cabot Lodge, Jr., has testified to the solidifying influence of Soviet speeches upon the non-communist states: "Just when the free nations begin to drift apart, which they have a natural tendency to do, being free, a Soviet speaker will say something that is so monstrous and so senseless that you can see the free world getting together right in front of your very eyes." U.S. Senate, Subcommittee of Committee on Foreign Relations, *Hearings on Proposals to Amend United Nations Charter*, pt. 1, Jan. 18 and Mar. 3, 1954, 83rd Cong., 2nd sess., p. 48. Pertinent also are comments of Thomas J. Hamilton, New York *Times*, Sept. 27, 1953, sec. IV, p. 5.

rather ill-defined area are bound to encounter resentment and engender hard feelings. Nations, though acutely conscious of their dependence upon American leadership in international affairs, are all the more jealous of their right to differ. Pressure, consequently, is useful and effective but only within proper bounds.[25]

THE ASSEMBLY MILIEU

The activities of the United States delegation to the Assembly appear in clearer perspective when considered in their proper setting. When the Assembly is in session the United States is but one, though an extremely important one, of the nations seeking to influence the policies of the organization. If the United States solicits votes, makes deals, and engineers compromises, so do Britain and the Soviet Union and, as the occasion arises, Yemen, Guatemala, Indonesia, or any of the other members. And the United States is by no means immune to pressures. As the Assistant Secretary of State for United Nations Affairs remarked to a Senate investigating committee, "foreign governments usually are not particularly modest in letting us know about things of major interest to them. . . . They do not stand on ceremony. They usually find ways and means of bringing to our attention things that they want us to do in their behalf."[26] When the State Department receives a letter or a cable from a friendly power saying a particular resolution will cause the government to fall, or seriously affect its standing, the pressure on the United States is real and severe. According to one State Department official, at least once a year the United States government receives a communication of this type, forcing reconsideration of a position already fully prepared.[27]

Other countries certainly are well versed in the tactics of persuasion. When in 1954 the Indonesian delegation secured a greater than two-thirds majority in the First Committee for a resolution on West Irian, the Netherlands government immediately went to work through its embassies in Latin America. The result was a shift of Latin-American votes in plenary meeting sufficient to defeat the resolution.[28] The defeat of the

[25] A State Department official interviewed confided that on one occasion the Department received a query from some agency in the Turkish government, "Do we have to vote with you every time?" A terse reply of "No!" was immediately dispatched. When this incident was repeated to a prominent Turkish official at the United Nations, the man bristled with indignation. "No real Turk would ask such a question," he said. "We make good allies but poor satellites!"

[26] John D. Hickerson before a subcommittee of the Senate Committee on Foreign Relations, *Hearings on Resolutions Relative to Revision of the United Nations Charter, etc.*, Feb. 2-20, 1950, 81st Cong., 2nd sess., p. 425.

[27] Interview with an official of the State Department, March 1, 1955.

[28] *First Committee*, 9th sess. (1954), pp. 457-58, and *Plenary Meetings,* 9th sess. (1954), pp. 120-21. An official of the Peruvian Permanent Mission, in personal interview, March 8, 1955, confirmed the fact of Dutch diplomatic activity during the interval.

Arab-Asian resolution on Tunisia in the seventh session was due at least in part to French lobbying in the Assembly and pressure exercised through diplomatic missions abroad.[29] In 1947 the Arab states used every possible tactic, even though unsuccessfully, to prevent the partition of Palestine.[30] Latin-American delegations lobbied intensively and openly in the third and fourth sessions to obtain for Italy the right to administer a part of her former African colonies.[31] These are only illustrative of the diplomatic give-and-take which characterizes an Assembly session. Significant also, with regard to some questions, is pressure from non-governmental organizations. Representatives of the Spanish Republican government-in-exile labored diligently in lounges and corridors to obtain United Nations support for their cause, particularly in the first session when hope of a restoration was still alive.[32] On more than one occasion when the protection of Jerusalem and its Holy Places was at issue, the Roman Catholic Church, through messages and pronouncements, intervened in support of an international trusteeship.[33] Perhaps the most notorious case of pressure from private and non-governmental interests was the highly effective Zionist campaign for partition of Palestine in 1947.[34]

When old-fashioned interest-group politics combine with the new multilateral diplomacy, the lot of the delegation official becomes harrowing indeed. The demands of the Assembly situation are arduous and exacting. Keeping abreast of some seventy or eighty agenda items taxes the capacity of even the larger delegations. In the words of a former senior adviser to the United States delegation,

Space and time is compressed in the need for instantaneous and simultaneous contact with the great number of delegations; there are deadlines of

---

[29] See comments of New York *Times,* Dec. 13, 1952, p. 3.

[30] See, e.g., *ibid.,* Sept. 23, 1947, p. 1, and Sept. 25, 1947, pp. 1, 6.

[31] *Ibid.,* Apr. 20, 1949, p. 10; Apr. 27, 1949, p. 18; Nov. 23, 1949, p. 3. This was a particularly notorious case of bargaining and pressure between contending interests. For fuller details of the third session fiasco see Benjamin Rivlin, "The Italian Colonies and the General Assembly," *International Organization,* vol. 3 (Aug., 1949), pp. 459-70.

[32] See New York *Times,* Nov. 19, 1946, p. 12, and "Assembly: Maneuverings Behind the Scenes," *Newsweek,* vol. 28 (Nov. 18, 1946), p. 48.

[33] New York *Times,* Nov. 12, 1949, sec. IV, p. 1; Dec. 8, 1949, p. 22; Dec. 11, 1949, sec. IV, p. 1; Dec. 19, 1952, p. 11. A State Department official interviewed March 1, 1955, considered the influence of the Church an extremely important factor in the decision of the Assembly on the Jerusalem issue.

[34] The press carried numerous accounts of the pressure being exerted both for and against partition. A very revealing if biased report of Zionist activities by a participant in the campaign is David Horowitz, *State in the Making* (1953). See esp. pp. 150-304. Alfred M. Lilienthal, *What Price Israel?* (1953), gives a detailed, anti-Zionist account of the matter. This question is discussed in some detail in Chapter Four.

speeches, votes and decisions to be met, and a watchful eye must be kept on sudden surprise moves. When sixty countries are concerned simultaneously with the same problems, when at least seven such problems are under active consideration in that many committees, and many other such problems are being prepared for the next round of debate, inter-action and adjustment of views becomes a highly complex and far-flung operation.[35]

Observers have been impressed with the "rush hour" atmosphere that grips the Assembly when committee work begins—the milling delegation officials, crowds gathered about bulletin boards, packed lounges, intense corridor conversations, and everywhere groups of delegates meeting in caucuses.[36] This is the setting in which United Nations diplomats carry on the continuous, day-to-day process of multilateral diplomacy, with the object always of building the coveted two-thirds majority.[37] It is an arena in which delegations operate simultaneously on two levels—one formal, legal, and moralistic; the other informal, extra-legal, and political. The pattern is not unfamiliar to domestic legislative assemblies. In the melee the United States stands foremost, but no one carries off all the honors.

[35] Sanders, *op. cit.*, p. 26.

[36] See, e.g., New York *Times*, Sept. 28, 1947, sec. IV, p. 2.

[37] The busy round of daily activities, rigorous enough to daunt the most hardy of diplomats, has been sketched by two former participants in the melange: "The new multilateral diplomat goes on almost around the clock. On an average busy day during a General Assembly it carries a UN delegate through his morning delegation meeting, private consultations, a public morning meeting at UN headquarters, an official luncheon, more private consultation before an afternoon public meeting, a regional caucus, a formal reception, an official dinner, and frequently a late evening caucus in a Manhattan delegation office.

"These are not occasions of relaxed social intercourse. They are all part of the day's work. The discussion of policy, strategy and tactics goes on with few interruptions." Brown and Johnson, *op. cit.*, p. 13.

CHAPTER FOUR

Partitioning Palestine

In some respects the question of partitioning Palestine is unique rather than typical. The debates on few, if any, other actions of the Assembly have been the object of such sustained interest, such persistent pressures on the part of many governments, and such lasting effects upon relationships within the Assembly.[1] It is unique, too, in that the United States and the Soviet Union reached agreement on a major question of substance. Nevertheless, as a case study in the execution of policy it throws into bold relief many of the pressures and influences to which members of the Assembly are subjected when dealing with a controversial question.[2]

PARTITION WITHOUT IMPLEMENTATION

The United States approached the question of Palestine warily notwithstanding President Truman's repeated statements in favor of more

---

[1] The New York *Times* reported: "Never before had the United Nations action on a major issue remained so long in doubt. Never before had the delegates themselves displayed such sustained interest on any major problem. Never before had a United Nations decision been awaited with such anxiety." Nov. 30, 1947, sec. IV, p. 1.

[2] The methods of policy execution and their immediate setting in the second Assembly are stressed in this study, to the exclusion of many substantive aspects of the Palestine question which are relevant to an understanding of the problem as a whole. For the reader who wishes to pursue the question in somewhat greater detail, L. Larry Leonard, "The United Nations and Palestine," *International Conciliation*, no. 454 (Oct., 1949), pp. 607-786, is a valuable digest, providing essential background facts and a resumé of events to the summer of 1949. Of full-length monographs, perhaps the best survey of Arab and Jewish politics in Palestine, 1936-48, is Jacob C. Hurewitz, *The Struggle for Palestine* (1950). This is a balanced, factual, and scholarly study. Jorge García-Granados, *The Birth of Israel* (1949), an account by a member of the Special Committee of events during 1947 and 1948, should be approached with caution since even his Zionist friend and well-wisher David Horowitz described García-Granados as one who "at times built up whole systems of thought which had little foundation in reality." Passionately pro-Zionist, the book provides an intimate if distorted glimpse of the processes through which partition came about. An anti-Zionist polemic, Alfred M. Lilienthal, *What Price Israel?* (1953), presents the Arab case with some brilliance. Sumner Welles, *We Need Not Fail* (1948), is an appeal for collective security and American support of Israel's independence and territorial integrity. A revealing account of the highly successful Zionist campaign for independence, 1945-48, is David Horowitz. *State in the Making* (1953), the memoir of an active participant.

Jewish immigration to Palestine. At the first special session, called to deal with the problem in the spring of 1947, the United States evinced no preference whatever as to the ultimate disposal of the British mandate. The American delegation was inclined rather to establish the United Nations Special Committee on Palestine, dubbed UNSCOP, and to wait for its conclusions. When the Special Committee made public the substance of its report on August 31, 1947, Zionist spokesmen were quick to announce acceptance of the principle of partition as recommended by the majority of the committee, and Arabs as quickly denounced both the majority plan and the minority proposal for a single federal state.[3] But the United States, hesistant to offend either Arab or Jew, maintained a discreet silence. Secretary of State George C. Marshall, in his opening address to the Assembly on September 17, indicated that the United States would give "great weight" to the UNSCOP majority recommendations for partition, but otherwise made no commitment. A week later press reports indicated that the American position was still not decided upon.[4] Not until October 13, after more than two weeks of committee debate, did the United States finally announce its determination to support partition.

American vacillation and hesitation stemmed from divided opinion within the United States government as to the best course of action. The Jewish vote and campaign contributions bulked large with the President and his advisers. High officials in the Defense and State Departments, somewhat more removed from domestic political pressures, were preoccupied with strategic interests and oil concessions in the Near East which might be jeopardized by support of a Palestine solution unacceptable to the Arabs.[5] Both points of view were reinforced from day to day by pressures from pro-Arabs and pro-Zionists. As the opening of committee discussions drew near, one public figure after another announced support of the majority partition proposals. Among others, Governor Thomas E. Dewey of New York, House Speaker Joseph W. Martin, and Senate Republican Leader Robert A. Taft made public declarations in favor of an independent Jewish state in Palestine. Twenty-three state

[3] New York *Times*, Sept. 2, 1947, pp. 1, 3, and Sept. 3, 1947, p. 7. Jews asked the Assembly to accept and improve the majority report, while Arabs threatened forcible resistance to attempts to implement either recommended solution.

[4] *Plenary Meetings*, 2nd sess. (1947), p. 21; New York *Times*, Sept. 24, 1947, p. 1; Sept. 25, 1947, p. 1.

[5] See *ibid.*, Sept. 24, 1947, p. 1; Sept. 25, 1947, p. 1; Dec. 14, 1947, sec. IV, p. 5; Benjamin V. Cohen, "The Impact of the United Nations on United States Foreign Policy," *International Organization*, vol. 5 (May, 1951), p. 277; Sidney B. Fay, "Arabs, Zionists, and Oil," *Current History*, vol. 14 (May, 1948), pp. 270-76; Walter Millis (ed.), *The Forrestal Diaries* (1951), pp. 309, 323, 344-45, 358-60, 508; Lillie Shultz, "The Palestine Fight—An Inside Story," *Nation*, vol. 165 (Dec. 20, 1947), pp. 675-76; Welles, *op. cit.*, pp. 74-80.

governors sent a telegram to President Truman endorsing partition, and twelve others called on the President to take firm action, without expressly recommending any particular settlement.[6] Arab spokesmen, for their part, poured out an almost continuous stream of threats and protests. The Arab Higher Committee, representing the Arab population of Palestine, expressed its readiness to "fight to the last man" to defend Palestine "as an Arab country," while responsible officials of Arab countries warned that partition would sooner or later lead to war in the Middle East. Arab League representatives talked of a "complete economic and cultural break with Europe and the United States," including cancellation of oil concessions.[7] Small wonder that the United States government had difficulty in formulating a position.

The Ad Hoc Committee on the Palestinian Question, created by the Assembly for the purpose of considering this one explosive issue, began its deliberations on September 25. The report of the United Nations Special Committee on Palestine, with its majority and minority recommendations for partition and federalism, respectively, formed the basis of discussion.[8] The partition plan, recommended by seven members of the Special Committee,[9] provided for the division of Palestine into separate Jewish and Arab states, each, as a result of demographic considerations, composed of isolated districts joined by narrow corridors. The two nascent states were to achieve full political independence with economic union after a transitional period of two years, during which time the mandatory power was to carry on the administration of Palestine under United Nations auspices. Jewish immigration for the two-year transition period was set at 150,000. An international trusteeship administered by the United Nations was prescribed for Jerusalem and its environs.

Three members of UNSCOP—Iran, India, and Yugoslavia—offered a plan for an Arab and a Jewish state federated in a single national state, to achieve independence after a transitional period of three years. Constitutional organization of the federal state was laid down in some detail, including a federal executive, a judiciary, and a bicameral national legislature with proportional representation of the whole population in one chamber and equal repesentation of Arab and Jewish citizens in the other. Jewish immigration during the transitional period was "not to exceed the absorptive capacity of the Jewish state," and the city of Jerusalem, with appropriate guarantees of all interests concerned, was to be the

---

[6] New York *Times*, Sept. 12, 1947, p. 12, and Sept. 22, 1947, p. 5.

[7] See *ibid.*, Sept. 1, 1947, pp. 1, 3; Sept. 2, 1947, p. 1; Sept. 7, 1947, sec. IV, p. 4; Sept. 9, 1947, pp. 1, 3; Sept. 10, 1947, p. 3; Sept. 16, 1947, p. 10; Sept. 23, 1947, p. 1.

[8] Document A/364.

[9] Canada, Czechoslovakia, Guatemala, the Netherlands, Peru, Sweden, and Uruguay.

capital of the federal state. The minority report recommended the creation of a permanent international body to supervise and protect "Holy Places, buildings and sites." No specific suggestion was made as to who should be the administering authority during the period of transition.

Although UNSCOP was thus divided, with Australia refusing to endorse either plan, all members of the committee were in accord on certain general principles which should govern the Palestine solution. All agreed on the desirability of an early end to the mandate, independence for Palestine, United Nations responsibility during the transitional period, special consideration for the Holy Places and religious interests, the need for alleviating the plight of displaced European Jews, the protection of minorities, a peaceful settlement, the economic unity of Palestine, and renunciation of any existing capitulations pertaining to Palestine.

The report of UNSCOP which the Ad Hoc Committee was now meeting to consider consisted thus of a majority plan for partition, a minority recommendation for a single federal state, and certain general principles on which all members of UNSCOP had agreed. At its initial meeting the Ad Hoc Committee on the Palestinian Question selected Herbert V. Evatt of Australia as chairman and agreed to invite representatives of the Arab Higher Committee and the Jewish Agency for Palestine, the authorized spokesmen for the respective Arab and Jewish inhabitants of Palestine, to participate in committee deliberations.[10]

Before long it was evident that the United States was not the only member reluctant to state its position.[11] Of all the Great Powers only the United Kingdom was willing to make an early statement to the committee, and Arthur Creech-Jones, the British Colonial Secretary, carefully avoided the advocacy of any specific solution. The United Kingdom would accept—that is, not impede—any solution recommended by the General Assembly, but it would not impose a policy in Palestine by force of arms nor implement any policy not acceptable to both Arabs and Jews. Furthermore, Mr. Creech-Jones was instructed to announce "with all solemnity" that in the absence of a settlement the United Kingdom had a plan for early withdrawal of British forces and adminstration from Palestine.[12]

With this announcement the problem took on added urgency, since the Assembly had to act or face the possibility of chaos in the Holy Land. But the other Great Powers maintained their silence. In response to press

---

[10] *Ad Hoc Committee on the Palestinian Question,* 2nd sess. (1947), pp. 1-2.

[11] García-Granados claimed that the Latin-American states meeting in their caucus were unwilling to take a vice-chairmanship of the Palestinian committee because of the touchiness of the subject. Most European and Asiatic delegates whom he consulted reportedly were unwilling to assume any responsibility and regretted having to vote for or against the Special Committee's report. *Op. cit.,* p. 247.

[12] *Ad Hoc Committee on the Palestinian Question,* 2nd sess. (1947), pp. 2-5.

queries, State Department spokesmen explained that the United States intended to wait until the British, the Arabs, and the Zionists had all spoken before taking a final stand.[13] In the Palestinian committee the British statement was followed within the week by arguments from representatives of the Arab Higher Committee and the Jewish Agency for Palestine. A second week passed in which the committee heard from Czechoslovakia, Lebanon, Panama, Iraq, Uruguay, Pakistan, Poland, Egypt, Colombia, El Salvador, Syria, and Sweden, but not a word from the United States, the Soviet Union, China, or France. In the hope of forcing action the chairman suggested an October 13 deadline for the submission of proposals on the question, and the Pakistani delegate, Sir Mohammed Zafrullah Khan, proposed immediate closure of debate in view of the reluctance of "certain delegations" to take part in it. The chairman set the October 13 date for proposals and ruled that no more names should be added to the speakers' list after October 11.[14]

At last, on October 11, the silence of the Great Powers was broken. Herschel V. Johnson, the United States representative in the Palestinian committee, read out his government's carefully prepared statement.[15] It noted first the urgency of the problem and briefly sketched a history of American policy toward Palestine since the first world war. Then came the anxiously awaited commitment:

The United States Delegation supports the basic principles of the unanimous recommendations and the majority plan which provides for partition and immigration. It is of the opinion, however, that certain amendments and modifications would have to be made in the majority plan in order more accurately to give effect to the principles on which that plan is based. . . .

The General Assembly did not, by admitting this item to its agenda, undertake to assume reponsibility for the administration of Palestine during the process of transition to independence. Responsibility for the government of Palestine now rests with the Mandatory power. The General Assembly, however, would not fully discharge its obligation if it did not take carefully into account the problem of implementation. . . .

The United States is willing to participate in a United Nations program to assist the parties involved in the establishment of a workable political settlement in Palestine. We refer to assistance through the United Nations in

---

[13] New York *Times*, Sept. 26, 1947, p. 10.

[14] *Ad Hoc Committee on the Palestinian Question*, 2nd sess. (1947), pp. 5-52.

[15] Text of the October 11, 1947, statement is found in *United States Mission Press Release*, no. 260, Oct. 10, 1947. Official committee records contain only a summary of remarks. Concerning the preparation of the statement the New York *Times* wrote: "A special 'Palestine team' composed of a few members of the American U.N. delegation had done spadework for it. It had been written in Washington, edited in New York, re-edited in Washington. It had received a thorough going-over from the full American delegation. Finally it had been sent to the President of the United States for his comments and approval. On Friday morning at the delegation's offices at 2 Park Avenue in New York, press officers had put in the final capitals and commas." Oct. 12, sec. IV, p. 1.

meeting economic and financial problems and the problem of internal law and order during the transition period. The latter problem might require the establishment of a special constabulary or police force recruited on a volunteer basis by the United Nations. We do not refer to the possibility of violations by any member of its obligations to refrain in its international relations from the threat or use of force. We assume that there will be Charter observance.

The speech was painstakingly phrased to convey an assurance of American support for partition without a commitment to implement partition by the use of American regular troops, a contingency which the United States Joint Chiefs of Staff had considered and advised against.[16] The United States government favored partition as a solution most likely to succeed under the circumstances. Economically and financially it was ready to contribute a fair share to the implementation of an Assembly decision. But responsibility for the administration of essential services and preservation of order during Palestine's transition to independence rested, in the United States view, primarily with the mandatory. The United Nations might properly render assistance through the establishment of an international constabulary force. The United States, however, would make no promise to use its own troops in the enforcement of partition.

The United States thus stood for partition, without accepting any major share of responsibility for enforcing it. Two days later the Soviet representative declared the decision of his government to support the principle of partition and stressed the need to make definite arrangements for implementation. During the general debate on the question, which lasted another full week, delegates returned time and time again to the matter of implementation. Mr. Creech-Jones found himself forced to clarify the British stand. The United Kingdom, he averred, would agree to adminster Palestine during its transition to independence only in the event of a settlement between Arabs and Jews. In the absence of a settlement it would consider an invitation to take enforcement measures in partnership with others. But in no case would the British government bear responsibility for enforcement either alone or in a major role.[17] The success of partition, or any other decision the Assembly might make, clearly hinged on the crucial problem of implementation.

---

[16] *Ibid.*, Oct. 13, 1947, p. 1. The Joint Chiefs regarded the use of American troops in Palestine as unwise. Senator Arthur H. Vandenberg publicly questioned the President's authority to send troops without the express authorization of Congress, whether or not it were thought advisable. In view of these and other considerations, the New York *Times* reports, "Mr. Truman urged caution on the United States delegates to the United Nations last week and expressly instructed them not to make any commitment that could obligate this country to use Government troops to carry out any settlement of the Palestine problem." *Ibid.*, pp. 1, 10.

[17] For debate on the question see *Ad Hoc Committee on the Palestinian Question,* 2nd sess. (1947), esp. pp. 69-106.

SUBCOMMITTEE DELIBERATIONS

By the conclusion of general debate the alternatives had been narrowed to two antagonistic proposals—partition or an independent Arab state in Palestine. The next step was the creation of a subcommittee to prepare a detailed recommendation on which the committee might make a decision. The United States and the Soviet Union pressed for an immediate decision in favor of the general principles of the majority plan, after which the subcommittee could be appointed to fill in the details. In the absence of detailed proposals, however, most members of the committee were unwilling to make a decision on the substance of the question. A Soviet motion, supported by the United States, to make the substantive decision prior to the creation of a subcommittee was rejected by a vote of 26-14.[18] The committee then voted for a Swedish-American draft to establish a subcommittee to formulate a plan for partition, and created another to make concrete proposals for a single Arab state. With expressed reluctance the United States incorporated into its own draft Canadian amendments which specifically suggested some form of trusteeship for the period of transition to independence and called special attention to the need for implementation.[19] The committee approved without objection a proposal for a conciliation subcommittee to attempt privately and informally a reconciliation of Jewish and Arab views.[20] After rejecting a Soviet proposal that subcommittee 1 on partition be composed of the eleven members of the Security Council, plus Czechoslovakia, Sweden, Uruguay, and Venezuela, the committee decided that each of the two principal subcommittees should have nine members appointed by the chairman. The chairman, vice-chairman, and rapporteur were to constitute the conciliation committee.[21]

[18] *Ibid.*, p. 136. Remarks of American representatives are found pp. 132-33, 135. For text of American proposals for a subcommittee see document A/AC.14/17.

[19] The Swedish-American proposal, as amended, was approved 35-0-8, and creation of the second subcommittee was authorized 30-10 with 6 abstentions, the United States voting in the opposition. There were no roll-call votes on these proposals but the position of the United States was clear. For voting see *Ad Hoc Committee on the Palestinian Question*, 2nd sess. (1947), p. 137. Text of U.S.-Swedish draft is document A/AC.14/17, and Canadian amendments, document A/AC.14/23.

[20] *Ad Hoc Committee on the Palestinian Question*, 2nd sess. (1947), p. 136.

[21] *Ibid.*, pp. 138-39. Vote on the Soviet motion was 6-32-10, and on the proposal to let the chairman determine the membership, 40-6-4. The chairman appointed as members of subcommittee 1 on partition, Canada, Czechoslovakia, Guatemala, Poland, South Africa, the U.S.S.R., the United States, Uruguay, and Venezuela, all strongly pro-partition. Members of subcommittee 2 on a single state were Afghanistan, Colombia, Egypt, Iraq, Lebanon, Pakistan, Saudi Arabia, Syria, and Yemen, all Moslem countries except Colombia, which subsequently withdrew when Chairman Evatt refused to comply with the subcommittee's request to replace two of the Arab members with neutral states. See documents A/AC.14/32 and Add.1, and A/AC.14/34, Corr.1 and Add.1.

Subcommittee 1 on partition parcelled out the task of preparing detailed proposals among seven working groups, each dealing with a specialized aspect of the problem.[22] The working groups accepted in principle most of the Special Committee majority recommendations but made numerous modifications in detail, particularly with respect to boundaries and the plan of economic union. Implementation, which required a decision on the length of the transition period and the nature and powers of the transitional administering authority, proved the thorniest problem. On October 31 the United States representative in the subcommittee proposed to solve the problem by having the United Kingdom progressively turn over the government and administration of Palestine to the new states as the British withdrew, with partition to be in complete effect by July 1, 1948. A three-member United Nations commission, acting under the direction of the Assembly, would advise and assist Arab and Jewish leaders in the formation of functioning governments. With the transitional period between British withdrawal and assumption of authority by the local governments thus eliminated, no international constabulary as earlier suggested by the United States would be needed. The United States assumed that the British government would help in every way possible and that the two new states would through self-interest maintain public order in their respective areas.[23]

The immediate reaction of the British representative sitting with the subcommittee was to read the September 26 statement of Arthur Creech-Jones, to the effect that the United Kingdom would under no circumstances implement a solution not acceptable to both Arab and Jew.[24] Inasmuch as the new American proposal left the British with full responsibility for implementation, it appeared to many delegates to be based as much on wishful thinking as on the facts. In reality the United States was taking a purely pragmatic approach to implementation, as indicated by remarks of Herschel Johnson to the press. When questioned as to the feasibility of the new proposal, he replied that something else would have to be tried if the mandatory refused to cooperate.[25]

Four days later the Soviet Union submitted a rival plan for implementation, under which the United Kingdom mandate would end January

[22] The seven groups dealt, respectively, with the Holy Places, citizenship, international conventions and financial obligations, economic union, boundaries, implementation, and the city of Jerusalem. See document A/AC.14/34 and Corr.1 and Add.1, for report of subcommittee activities.

[23] New York *Times*, Nov. 1, 1947, pp. 1, 4, and *U.S. Mission Press Release*, no. 297, Oct. 31, 1947.

[24] New York *Times*, Nov. 1, 1947, pp. 1, 4. Unofficial British comment led to the same impression: they would accept if the United States could get the Jews and the Arabs to accept the plan.

[25] *U.S. Mission Press Release*, no. 299, Oct. 31, 1947.

1, 1948, and all British troops would be withdrawn by April 30. During a transitional period, to end no later than January 1, 1949, Jewish and Arab armed militia would keep order under the supervision of a United Nations commission responsible to the Security Council.[26]

With a determination on both sides to reach agreement, and the intermediary assistance of the Canadian representative, Lester Pearson, the United States and the Soviet Union found a basis for compromise. The termination of the mandate was set for May 1, 1948, with Jewish and Arab states to become independent not later than July 1. A United Nations commission to implement the resolution, composed of five members not representing any of the Great Powers, would follow directives laid down by the General Assembly but act under the supervision of the Security Council.[27]

The agreement evoked a fresh statement from the United Kingdom representative. Notwithstanding the schedule envisaged by the subcommittee, the British government would not complete withdrawal until August 1, 1948. And while British troops remained in any area of Palestine they would retain responsibility for law and order in those areas, although civil administration would not necessarily be maintained throughout the intervening period until the completion of evacuation. This statement forced the working group on implementation to revise their recommendations. The dates for troop withdrawal and independence were changed from May and July to August and October, respectively, and the commission was entrusted with responsibility for the civil administration of Palestine during the transitional period, in cooperation with the United Kingdom. It was specified that prior to the termination of the mandate the United Kingdom would maintain order and direct the main public services to the extent that these functions were not transferred to the commission or to agencies of the provisional Palestine governments. With minor modifications the recommendations of the working group were approved by the subcommittee for submission to the Ad Hoc Committee on the Palestinian Question. The subcommittee recommended that the five members of the commission be Guatemala, Iceland, Norway, Poland, and Uruguay.

In the meantime subcommittee 2 proceeded with its assignment to draft a plan for a unitary Arab state. On November 19 both subcommittees presented their reports to the full Palestinian committee.[28] The British,

---

[26] New York *Times,* Nov. 5, 1947, pp. 1, 14.

[27] *Ibid.,* Nov. 7, 1947, p. 9; Nov. 11, 1947, p. 1; *U.S. Mission Press Release,* no. 317, Nov. 10, 1947; document A/AC.14/34, Corr.1 and Add.1.

[28] The reports are contained in document A/AC.14/34, Corr. 1 and Add. 1, and document A/AC.14/32 and Add.1. Chairman Evatt, reporting for the conciliation subcommittee, said that everything possible had been done to bring the parties to agreement but without success. *Ad Hoc Committee on the Palestinian Question,* 2nd sess. (1947), p. 146.

however, were not yet satisfied. Although unwilling to make constructive suggestions, they were forthright in saying what they would not accept. In this case the United Kingdom representative stated that the transfer of administrative authority to the commission during the transitional period, while the United Kingdom was still the mandatory, would only create confusion. As long as the United Kingdom held the mandate it would insist upon undivided control of Palestine. Furthermore, the British government would not transfer authority to provisional councils or any other agencies of local government, since this would amount to participation in the implementation of the partition scheme. British administration would terminate at a date to be announced in due course, after which the United Nations must assume responsibility for implementing any decision it might make.[29] Faced with these objections, subcommittee 1 produced a further revision of its recommendations to provide for progressive transfer of authority from the mandatory to the commission and in turn from the commission to the provisional governments. The United Kingdom was not required to deal with agencies of local government and was recognized as retaining full control and responsibility for administration in all areas from which its troops were not withdrawn.[30]

A TIME FOR DECISION

On Saturday, November 22, subcommittee 1 presented its final amended report.[31] The Ad Hoc Committee on the Palestinian Question, with two detailed alternative proposals before it, had now to make a decision. Up to this point the United States had tried for the most part to confine its activities in behalf of partition to arguing the merits of the case in the Palestinian committee and the partition subcommittee. On other important questions before the Assembly the United States had not hesitated to press its views upon delegates and their home governments.[32] In this case, however, the United States government hoped that a two-thirds majority would materialize without the use of pressure by the American delegation. The United States did not wish to antagonize the Arabs further, and

[29] *Ibid.*, pp. 153-55.

[30] Document A/AC.14/34/Add.2.

[31] The United Kingdom representative subsequently made plain that, whatever the wording of the revised subcommittee recommendation might imply, the British government would remain in full control of all Palestine until the termination of the mandate, and only then would there be a progressive transfer of authority to the commission in areas from which troops were withdrawn. *Ad Hoc Committee on the Palestinian Question*, 2nd sess. (1947), pp. 168-70.

[32] This was particularly true of the Greek question and the creation of the Interim Committee. See New York *Times*, Oct. 20, 1947, p. 1; Oct. 26, 1947, sec. IV, p. 2; Nov. 28, 1947, p. 10.

it was feared that strong advocacy might turn partition into an American decision which others would expect the United States to enforce. If the Assembly could reach the decision without prodding, the moral responsibility for implementation of partition would rest with the Assembly as a whole rather than predominantly with one member.[33]

The weekend of November 22 was marked by a change in the United States attitude toward the passage of the partition resolution. Convinced that partition would otherwise fail, the United States began actively to solicit votes from other delegations.[34] A decision, it was felt, had to be made. With all its imperfections, the plan for partition with economic union appeared to offer the least unsatisfactory solution. On November 22, Herschel V. Johnson read out the strongest American statement yet prepared on the question:

> . . . My delegation will support and vote for the partition plan recommended to this Committee by Subcommittee 1. If this Committee and the Assembly in its turn approve the recommendation of the Subcommittee, the Assembly, in the view of my delegation, will have properly discharged the function of making recommendations "concerning the future Government of Palestine." . . . It is too much to hope that there will be unanimity or anything approaching unanimity in the final decision of the General Assembly. But my delegation fervently hopes that the General Assembly will approve this plan by as large a majority as possible and that all members will cooperate loyally in giving it full effect and implementation. . . . We hope that those who have doubts will not be deterred from taking a stand because the Assembly Committee have not been able to attain an impossible perfection.[35]

Later the same day he offered another plea for the Assembly to act decisively and firmly:

> This is a situation, it seems to me, where we should grasp the nettle and go ahead. This is not something to be afraid of. If we drop it and let it go it will be worse next year than it is now. The time now is for decision and work out

---

[33] Contemporary accounts bear out the unwillingness of the United States to use pressure in all but the last stages of debate. See *ibid.*, Oct. 26, 1947, sec. IV, p. 2; Nov. 26, 1947, p. 4; Nov. 27, 1947, p. 14; Thomas J. Hamilton, "Partition of Palestine," *Foreign Policy Reports*, vol. 23 (Feb. 15, 1948), p. 290. Two journalistic commentators claimed personal knowledge of the fact that officers of the United States delegation had, prior to November 22, told other delegations to vote "according to their conscience," that it was a matter of indifference to the United States. Shultz, *op. cit.*, p. 677, and R. H. S. Crossman, "Politics at Lake Success," *New Statesman and Nation*, vol. 34 (Oct. 25, 1947), p. 324.

[34] Members of the State Department and the Assembly delegation who were questioned on this matter all had a similar recollection: that the United States did turn the "heat" on other delegations but only tardily and reluctantly, in the conviction that otherwise no decision would be made by the Assembly. See accounts of New York *Times*, Nov. 26, 1947, p. 4; Nov. 27, 1947, p. 10; Nov. 28, 1947, p. 10; Nov. 30, 1947, sec. IV, p. 2; García-Granados, *op. cit.*, p. 269; Hamilton, *op. cit.*, p. 290; Horowitz, *op. cit.*, p. 301; Shultz, *op. cit.*, p. 677.

[35] Verbatim text of address in *U.S. Mission Press Release*, no. 339, Nov. 22, 1947.

the inequities later on. The United Nations machinery is quite sufficient for that purpose if we can just make up our minds to move now.[36]

Debate on the reports of the two subcommittees was concluded on Monday afternoon, November 24, and that evening the recommendations contained in the report of subcommittee 2 were put to the vote.[37] Besides the plan for a single unitary state, subcommittee 2 had submitted two additional draft resolutions, one to request of the International Court an opinion on the legal aspects of partition and the other dealing with the problem of Jewish refugees in Europe as distinct from the Palestinian question. These recommendations were voted upon first. The question of seeking an advisory opinion was rejected in two parts by extremely close votes of 18-25-11 and 20-21-13. The United States voted with the majority on both parts. Eleven separate divisions were taken on the resolution relating to the repatriation and resettlement of Jewish refugees. Several paragraphs received committee approval when voted upon individually, but the draft as a whole failed to pass when sixteen members voted in the affirmative, sixteen in the negative, and twenty-three abstained. On every recorded vote the United States voted in the negative. The plan of subcommittee 2 for a unitary Arab state was voted upon only once as a whole and rejected 12-29-14, the United States again opposing the measure.[38]

These measures were but preliminary. The real battle was yet to be fought. No one expected the Arab plan for Palestine to be adopted nor was there a reasonable possibility that the committee would vote to postpone the decision for a year by waiting for an advisory opinion of the International Court of Justice. The future government of Palestine was regarded by most members as a political matter to be settled according to the realities of international politics as best they could be ascertained, not by fiat of a panel of jurists who would be limited to a consideration of the legal aspects of the problem. The fate of Jewish refugees, while a

---

[36] *Ibid.*, no. 340, Nov. 22, 1947. The decision on the part of the United States government to take a firm stand does not mean that all differences of opinion were resolved. Many officials in the State Department still held to their belief that a course of action so certain to arouse Arab wrath was unwise. The delegation, too, was split deeply on the question. But the final word came from the White House. When President Truman gave the instructions to push the partition resolution the Department and the delegation cooperated loyally. For comments on the role of the White House, see Shultz, *op. cit.*, pp. 675-78; Horowitz, *op. cit.*, pp. 269-70, 301; Welles, *op. cit.*, p. 63; Millis, *op. cit.*, p. 323; Chaim Weizmann, *Trial and Error: The Autobiography of Chaim Weizmann* (1949), vol. 2, pp. 458-59.

[37] *Ad Hoc Committee on the Palestinian Question*, 2nd sess. (1947), pp. 189-210. For reports of subcommittees 1 and 2 see document A/AC.14/34 and Corr.1 and Add.1, and document A/AC.14/32 and Add.1, respectively. The reports contain a brief record of deliberations and the text of recommendations.

[38] For record of voting see *Ad Hoc Committee on the Palestinian Question*, 2nd sess. (1947), pp. 203-6.

pressing and emotionally charged problem, and one intimately connected in debate with the problem of a Palestine settlement, was in fact peripheral to the central issue of the future government of Palestine. The Arabs, without anticipating Assembly approval, had placed their position on record and forced the Assembly to declare itself. But the real question was whether or not the recommendation for partition with economic union would command a two-thirds majority.

Before a decision could be made, the draft recommendation of sub-committee 1 was subjected to the inevitable process of amendment and discussion. Most of the amendments were of a technical nature relating to such matters as boundaries and economic provisions, and the majority of these were adopted without objection. Two amendments, however, were particularly significant. The subcommittee had agreed upon Guatemala, Iceland, Norway, Poland, and Uruguay, all clearly in favor of partition, as members of the United Nations commission to assist in the implementation of partition. Pakistan and Norway now proposed that members of the commission be elected on a broad basis, "geographical and otherwise." Representatives of Norway, Uruguay, Guatemala, and Iceland all made graceful statements in support of the proposal. Although some delegations desired to eliminate the phrase "and otherwise" as implying that states not in favor of partition might be elected to the commission, the amendment was approved by the committee without objection.[39] This move seemed designed in part at least to placate the anti-partition forces, particularly in view of the fact that Moslem Pakistan, whose representative Sir Mohammed Zafrullah Khan had taken a leading part in the debate, was co-sponsor of the amendment. Although the United States did not speak in committee on this particular amendment, Jorge García-Granados, the Guatemalan representative, subsequently claimed it was the subject of extensive American lobbying. According to García-Granados the United States had actively supported the amendment because of its belief that putting two such vehement pro-partitionists as himself and E. R. Fabregat of Uruguay on the commission would unnecessarily antagonize the Arabs. García-Granados was obviously highly incensed at being squeezed out of the commission, whatever the actual circumstances may have been, and offered his support for the amendment only to avoid the embarrassment to himself and his country that a losing fight on the issue would have entailed.[40]

---

[39] Document A/AC.14/46 and *Ad Hoc Committee on the Palestinian Question*, 2nd sess. (1947), pp. 206-9.

[40] García Granados, *op. cit.*, pp. 258-60. Regarding United States lobbying, he says, "the various United States liaison men were very busy in the delegates' lounge. They held long and vehement conversations with one delegate after another. By a curious coincidence, after speaking with the Americans, one of my friends after another would tell me that perhaps the Commission as now constituted was badly balanced

The second amendment of great importance dealt with the matter of implementation. Denmark proposed that the Security Council be requested to "take the necessary measures as provided for in the plan for its implementation," to "take measures to empower a United Nations commission . . . to exercise in Palestine the functions which are assigned to it by this resolution," and to "determine as a threat to the peace, breach of peace or act of aggression . . . any attempt to alter by force the settlement brought into effect by this resolution." In short, the Danish amendment would request of the Security Council an advance commitment to meet force with force in Palestine. The amendment lay on the table for a day while interested parties carried on private negotiations. The next day Denmark submitted a revised amendment requesting the Security Council to consider, if circumstances should warrant, whether the situation in Palestine during the transitional period were a threat to the peace and, if so, to take such measures as were necessary to enable the commission to carry out its functions. This version required no commitment from the Security Council to act otherwise than it would ordinarily act in the case of a threat to the peace. Remarks of Herschel V. Johnson to the committee indicated that the United States had taken part in the backstage negotiations with Denmark and that, despite its recently found determination to round up votes for partition, it was still determined to avoid all advance commitments to the use of American military forces in Palestine.[41] The revised Danish amendment was approved 19-14, with the United States voting affirmatively.[42]

With the adoption of the Danish amendment the time had come for the final committee vote. By November 22, when the United States began in earnest its campaign for the partition plan, representatives of thirty-seven states had expressed their views on the question. Of these, eighteen had

---

and that perhaps countries less committed to partition should be substituted." *Ibid.*, p. 259. See also García-Granados' article "Behind the Palestine Reversal," *Colliers*, May 22, 1948, pp. 26, 76-77. Freda Kirchwey also gives credibility to the claim that the United States was in fact responsible for the elimination of Guatemala and Uruguay from the commission. "United Nations Victory," *Nation*, vol. 165 (Dec. 6, 1947), pp. 610-11.

[41] Mr. Johnson stated: "My delegation, I must say quite frankly, would not have been able to support the original amendment put up by the Delegation of Denmark. We are prepared, however, to accept this revised version. The revised version does not ask the Security Council to act on a hypothetical situation, but requests them to act in the event that a situation which constitutes a threat to international peace and security should arise. This at best can only be an admonition to the Security Council. The Security Council by its own constitution has the duty to exercise surveillance over such situations and to determine when a threat to international peace and security exists." *U.S. Mission Press Release*, no. 346, Dec. 9, 1947.

[42] For text of Danish amendment see documents A/AC.14/43 and A/AC.14/43/Rev.1. Voting is recorded in *Ad Hoc Committee on the Palestinian Question*, 2nd sess. (1947), pp. 221-22.

endorsed partition, twelve opposed it, and seven remained uncommitted or announced their intention to abstain. Those who had opted for partition, with varying degrees of enthusiasm, were three Great Powers—the United States, the Soviet Union, and China; two Soviet allies—Poland and Czechoslovakia; two Scandinavian countries—Norway and Sweden; two Commonwealth states—Canada and South Africa; and nine Latin-American republics. The hard core of opposition rested with the six Arab states, Cuba, Yugoslavia, and four South Asian countries—Afghanistan, India, Iran, and Pakistan. The opposition of Yugoslavia and the Soviet Union to one another was perhaps a forerunner of things to come. On the final committee vote, three days later, the configuration was changed to twenty-five in favor, thirteen against, seventeen abstaining, and two, Paraguay and the Philippines, absent.[43] The pro-partition vote was bolstered by the addition of the Ukraine and Byelorussia, Australia, Denmark, Iceland, and four Latin-American states—Brazil, Costa Rica, Ecuador, and Nicaragua. China, which had given only halfhearted support to partition, moved into the abstention column, as did also Haiti, a move which was a complete surprise to most of the Assembly delegations. The opposition gained Thailand and Turkey but lost Yugoslavia to the abstentions.

The question thus came to the plenary meeting one vote short of a two-thirds majority in favor of partition.[44] As the ground had been thoroughly covered in committee debate, a decision was expected to be reached on Wednesday, November 26. Herschel Johnson took the floor in the morning meeting to sum up the situation as viewed by the United States, perhaps in the hope of encouraging a few of the waverers. While admitting again the imperfections of the plan, Johnson spoke for partition as holding out the best hope of a peaceful settlement in Palestine. In remarks clearly aimed at Britain and others who had chosen to abstain rather than offend either party, he trenchantly observed that there was no delegation present which did not know "that no plan has ever been presented, either to this Assembly or to the mandatory Government during its long years of tenure, or in any other place, which would meet with the acceptance of both the Arabs and the Jews." [45] The Johnson statement, incisive and pointed as it was, did not create the sensation that had earlier greeted the remarks of the Philippine and Greek representatives. The Philippines, which had not voted in committee, and Greece, which had abstained, both declared their intentions to vote against partition. The hopes of Zionists and pro-partition delegations in the Assembly sank even lower when Haiti, which had first supported partition and then abstained

---

[43] Roll-call vote, *ibid.*, pp. 222-23. See Table 4.

[44] See the report of the *Ad Hoc Committee on the Palestinian Question*, document A/516.

[45] *Plenary Meetings*, 2nd sess. (1947), p. 1326.

TABLE 4. VOTING ALIGNMENTS ON THE PARTITION OF PALESTINE

State	Nov. 22 estimate	Committee vote	Plenary vote	State	Nov. 22 estimate	Committee vote	Plenary vote
Afghanistan	N	N	N	Iraq	N	N	N
Argentina	U	A	A	Lebanon	N	N	N
Australia	U	Y	Y	Liberia	U	A	Y
Belgium	A	A	Y	Luxembourg	U	A	Y
Bolivia	Y	Y	Y	Mexico	U	A	A
Brazil	U	Y	Y	Netherlands	U	A	Y
Byelorussia	U	Y	Y	New Zealand	A	A	Y
Canada	Y	Y	Y	Nicaragua	U	Y	Y
Chile	Y	Y	A	Norway	Y	Y	Y
China	Y	A	A	Pakistan	N	N	N
Colombia	U	A	A	Panama	Y	Y	Y
Costa Rica	U	Y	Y	Paraguay	U	—	Y
Cuba	N	N	N	Peru	Y	Y	Y
Czechoslovakia	Y	Y	Y	Philippines	U	—	Y
Denmark	A	Y	Y	Poland	Y	Y	Y
Dominican Republic	Y	Y	Y	Saudi Arabia	N	N	N
Ecuador	U	Y	Y	Sweden	Y	Y	Y
Egypt	N	N	N	Syria	N	N	N
El Salvador	A	A	A	Thailand	U	N	—
Ethiopia	U	A	A	Turkey	U	N	N
France	U	A	Y	Ukraine	U	Y	Y
Greece	U	A	N	South Africa	Y	Y	Y
Guatemala	Y	Y	Y	U.S.S.R.	Y	Y	Y
Haiti	Y	A	Y	United Kingdom	A	A	A
Honduras	U	A	A	United States	Y	Y	Y
Iceland	U	Y	Y	Uruguay	Y	Y	Y
India	N	N	N	Venezuela	Y	Y	Y
Iran	N	N	N	Yemen	N	N	N
				Yugoslavia	N	A	A

Y — Yes
N — No
A — Abstention
U — Uncommitted in committee debate
— — Absent

in committee voting, now joined the opposition. The gloom was only partially lifted when New Zealand, the Netherlands, and Belgium announced their conversion from abstention to support of partition as a less unsatisfactory course of action than no decision at all. With the balance apparently running against them, the partition forces rallied enough votes to defeat a proposal for a night meeting and thus postpone a decision until Friday, with opportunity over the Thanksgiving holiday to work on doubtful delegations. The vote was extremely close, 24-21, with the United States supporting postponement.[46]

[46] *Ibid.*, p. 1364. Remarks of Philippine, Greek, Haitian, New Zealand, Dutch, and Belgian delegations are found *ibid.*, pp. 1313-15, 1320-21, 1353-58, 1364-66. See com-

Having put the intervening hours to good use, the supporters of partition returned in a more confident mood to the Assembly when it reconvened on Friday, November 28. In the meantime it had been learned that Haiti, whose representative only two days before had announced opposition to partition, was now instructed to vote in favor of the resolution. Paraguay, which did not cast a vote in committee, would also vote for partition. But Chile, it was learned, had decided to switch from the affirmative to absention.[47] Other shifts in the voting alignment left the balance clearly on the side of partition. However, a postponement once again delayed the decision. The representative of France, grasping at a straw of hope for compromise which he found in comments of Arab representatives, proposed that a further twenty-four-hour respite be granted for an eleventh-hour attempt at conciliation. A majority was more than willing to let the hour of decision slide by once more. The proposal was adopted by a vote of 25-15, with the United States voting but not speaking in opposition to the postponement.[48]

On Saturday afternoon, November 29, when the Assembly met again in plenary meeting, the Arab delegations made a last desperate bid to stave off defeat. The Lebanese representative presented the outline of a plan for a single federal state which, he said, might provide a basis for a compromise between the two opposing points of view which had domi-

ments of the New York *Times,* Nov. 27, 1947, p. 1. "Black Wednesday," the day was dubbed by the group of Zionists at the General Assembly. At the close of the afternoon session, Horowitz reports, "Shertok, Silver, Neumann, Eban, and I, among others, sat in a corner of the corridor, grim-faced and dejected. One of our South American friends came up and said: 'Go home. The sight of your faces is demoralizing your friends.' " Horowitz, *op. cit.,* p. 299.

[47] New York *Times,* Nov. 28, 1947, p. 10, and Nov. 29, 1947, p. 1.

[48] For remarks of the French delegate see *Plenary Meetings,* 2nd sess. (1947), pp. 1401-4. The vote is recorded *ibid.,* p. 1410. See New York *Times* commentary, Nov. 29, 1947, pp. 1, 2. The French representative lamented the failure of the conciliation subcommittee: "The attempt at conciliation does not appear to have been carried very far; at all events, we were simply informed that it had not succeeded." *Plenary Meetings,* 2nd sess. (1947), pp. 1402-3. At the next meeting the rapporteur, who with the chairman and vice-chairman had composed the subcommittee, read into the record the verbatim text of Chairman Evatt's report on the work of the conciliation subcommittee. He defended the subcommittee's efforts and justified their failure by reason of the unbridgeable gulf between the two parties. *Ibid.,* pp. 1413-15. Later in the same meeting the Syrian representative alluded to the work of the subcommittee on conciliation. As far as he knew the only measure taken was a letter sent by Chairman Evatt to Prince Feisal, head of the Saudi Arabian delegation, suggesting private consultations between him and the United States Secretary of State George C. Marshall. Feisal sent a letter of acceptance, the Syrian representative said, but no reply was received nor any arrangements made for the suggested discussions. *Ibid.,* pp. 1419-20. Evatt himself had already left for Australia but members of his delegation later told the press that "he had made several fruitless efforts to reconcile the views of the two subcommittees." New York *Times,* Nov. 29, 1947, p. 2.

nated Assembly discussions. Since the new plan was submitted without details and was in essence similar to the minority recommendations of UNSCOP which had already been passed over, this last-minute proposal smacked strongly of a subterfuge aimed at further delaying Assembly action. Herschel Johnson rose to request that the partition resolution be put to the vote immediately. This was followed by an Iranian proposal that the Assembly adjourn until January 15. The president of the Assembly, however, gave precedence to the partition proposal. When the final count was taken the alignment stood at thirty-three in favor, thirteen opposed, and ten abstentions—an endorsement well over the required two-thirds. The opposition remained solid except for the Thai representative, whose credentials were cancelled on November 26 because of a revolution in Thailand. Greece, moving from abstention into the ranks of the opposition, maintained the figure at thirteen. The proponents of partition were joined by Paraguay and the Philippines, neither of which had voted in committee, although the Philippine representative had spoken against partition. Seven abstainers in committee voting—Belgium, France, Haiti, Liberia, Luxembourg, the Netherlands, and New Zealand—voted in the affirmative to give the resolution its comfortable margin of victory.[49]

PRESSURE AND COUNTER-PRESSURE

The exact influence of the United States upon the Assembly decision to partition Palestine has been subject to numerous conflicting estimates. García-Granados claims that there was no American pressure on other countries to obtain votes for partition. As late as seven days before the final plenary vote, he asserts, United States liaison officers had not been instructed to solicit votes from other delegations, and "not until three days before we brought the resolution to the Ad Hoc Committee did they begin to suggest mildly that partition was worthy of support. At no time did their campaign go over the heads of the delegates to the various governments involved."[50] General John H. Hilldring, political adviser to the United States delegation for the Palestine question, likewise denied that "pressure" was used. Speaking to members of the United Jewish Appeal in Atlantic City after the adjournment of the second Assembly, he stated:

The United States Government took the position that every member of the United Nations, large or small, interested or disinterested, was entitled to its own independent judgment on the merits of the problem. To this policy the U.S. Delegation subscribed wholeheartedly, not only out of a sense of loyalty, but even more so from deep conviction. Certainly, we tried as best we could to persuade other countries of the logic and justice of our position. I am

---

[49] For Lebanese proposals see *Plenary Meetings*, 2nd sess. (1947), pp. 1412-13. Johnson's statement is found *ibid.*, pp. 1415-17, and the proposal of the Iranian delegate, pp. 1417, 1423. The voting is recorded pp. 1424-25.

[50] García-Granados, *Birth of Israel*, p. 269.

glad that we succeeded. But we succeeded not because of threats, intimidation or pressure indulged in by any member of the U.S. Delegation or by any official of your government. I am sure that the cause of the new Jewish State is immeasurably more secure and that the hearts and minds of all Americans, Jews and non-Jews alike, will be comforted and reassured by the knowledge that its officials did not resort to sordid tactics in the Palestine dealings.[51]

A commentator in the *Foreign Policy Bulletin,* noting that the United States had been berated by one side for using pressure to line up votes for partition and by the other for failing to do so, concluded that specific evidence of American pressure was lacking.[52] Another writer distinguished between the use of "influence" and "pressure" by concluding that "the United States government itself did not use pressure to gain votes, though it used its influence." [53] Perhaps this distinction is implicit in the denials by García-Granados and General Hilldring that pressure was exerted, since both admit that the United States did in fact try to secure votes for partition. Freda Kirchwey in the *Nation,* far from speaking of American pressure, charged the United States with pursuing, until the last days before the vote, a policy of "deliberate ambiguity." [54]

The Arabs and their supporters were the first to cry "pressure" as the efficient determinant of the Assembly decision. The Soviet Union was included in the denunciation, but efforts of the United States, being more effective, received the larger portion of condemnation. On the opening day of plenary debate the representative of Lebanon urged the Assembly to hold fast to "democratic methods" and "freedom in voting." [55] He continued,

If we were to abandon this for the tyrannical system of tackling each delegation in hotel rooms, in bed, in corridors and ante-rooms, to threaten them with economic sanctions or to bribe them with promises in order to compel them to vote one way or another, think of what our Organization would become in the future. . . .

And if, to turn from the general to the particular, I may refer to that great nation, the United States, which throughout its history has represented for all peoples the ideals of liberty, justice and equity, I am forced to note that unfortunately that giant, the United States, is putting on the fatal shirt of Nessus.

Two days later, when the tide had clearly turned for partition, the Cuban representative stood to reaffirm his opposition to the resolution "despite the pressure which has been brought to bear upon us." The Iranian representative, whose address followed immediately, likewise declared it was

---

[51] Quoted in Hamilton, *op. cit.,* p. 291.

[52] Vernon McKay, "Success of Partition Hinges on Arab-Jewish Cooperation," *Foreign Policy Bulletin,* vol. 27 (Dec. 5, 1947), pp. 1-2.

[53] Eugene P. Chase, *The United Nations in Action* (1950), p. 151.

[54] Kirchwey, *op. cit.,* p. 610.

[55] *Plenary Meetings,* 2nd sess. (1947), p. 1341.

"no secret" that "some great powers" were bringing pressure to bear upon other members of the Assembly. Perhaps the most biting allegation of all was a statement of Pakistani delegate Sir Zafrullah Khan, prepared before his departure from New York and read by an aide to the Assembly just after the final vote was taken: "A fateful decision has been taken. The die has been cast. In the words of the greatest American, 'We have striven to do the right as God gives us to see the right.' We did succeed in persuading a sufficient number of our fellow representatives to see the right as we saw it, but they were not permitted to stand by the right as they saw it. Our hearts are sad but our conscience is easy. We would not have it the other way round." [56] In less elegant phraseology Sir Zafrullah later specifically charged the United States with coercing delegates into voting for partition.

Observers less likely to exaggerate American influence upon the Assembly decision also testified as to its exercise. Sumner Welles made a sweeping assertion of American pressure. By "direct order of the White House," he stated, "every form of pressure, direct and indirect, was brought to bear by American officials upon those countries outside of the Moslem world that were known to be either uncertain or opposed to partition. Representatives or intermediaries were employed by the White House to make sure that the necessary majority would at length be secured." [57] Even David Horowitz, intimately and actively associated with the world-wide Zionist propaganda campaign for partition, acknowledged that the way the final vote turned out must be ascribed to the weight of United States influence exerted almost at the last hour.[58]

Despite the variance in opinion, certain conclusions regarding the exercise of pressure by the United States government appear warranted. Until the last week or ten days before the final decision, the United States did try to avoid the use of pressure in any form, limiting its advocacy to arguing the merits of the partition proposal. Beginning about Saturday, November 22, the United States began actively to solicit votes in the conviction that a stalemate would otherwise result. Members of the American delegation went "down the line" with other delegations at the Assembly in an effort to persuade them to vote for partition. This is admitted by participants and even by those who claim that such action did not constitute the exercise of pressure. Within the definition accepted for purposes

[56] Remarks of Cuban, Iranian, and Pakistani delegates are found *ibid.*, pp. 1385, 1389, 1426.

[57] Welles, *op. cit.*, p. 63.

[58] Horowitz, *op. cit.*, p. 301. See also Fay, *op. cit.*, p. 271; Pitman B. Potter, "The Palestine Problem Before the United Nations," *American Journal of International Law*, vol. 42 (Oct., 1948), p. 861; remarks of Chesley Manly, Chicago *Tribune*, June 20, 1955, p. 8, and June 30, 1955, p. 16. Manly alleged "extraordinary pressure by the Truman administration upon countries receiving American aid."

of the present study, however, the activities of the delegation clearly entered the realm of pressure tactics. Without a doubt, the "heat" was turned on. It also appears reasonable to assume that at least some foreign governments were contacted, since this is a common practice with questions in which the United States has a deep interest. The switch of Haiti and the Philippines from a negative position to a vote for partition was doubtless influenced in some degree by pressure from official sources.

It is not likely, however, that pressure by the United States government extended as far as direct threats or bribes. In the first place, many officials in the State Department and the delegation, who supported partition out of deference to Presidential directives, would not go any further than absolutely necessary. Second, as has been set forth in a preceding chapter, the United States does not characteristically operate on this level. If pressure is equated with threats and bribes, then there was no pressure. But if pressure is insistence, and persuasion on bases other than the facts directly pertaining to the question, pressure was exerted by the United States and, without doubt, saved the partition resolution from defeat.

One factor which increases the difficulty of estimating the effect of United States influence was the exertion of parallel pressures by private persons in a non-official capacity. Many persons having official connections with the United States government worked actively to promote the Zionist cause. As a result the line between official and non-official pressure at times became extremely thin. The Zionists had a highly organized propaganda machine which enlisted support from every available source. As Horowitz reports, in the last days of the campaign, the Zionist delegation at Lake Success "was a nerve-center of Zionist diplomacy, its tentacles reaching to all parts of the world." Their representatives engaged in "explanations, cajolings, pressure and use of pull," employing every possible means to persuade and convince.[59] And some of the individuals who rallied to the standard of partition were very influential Americans. Reportedly Bernard Baruch, consultant to the administration on matters of economic policy and atomic energy control, David Niles, presidential administrative assistant, and Adolph A. Berle, former Assistant Secretary of State and at the time legal adviser to the Haitian government, were among those who lent weight to the Zionist campaign. A joint telegram signed by twenty-six pro-Zionist Senators was sent to the Philippines and

[59] Horowitz, *op. cit.*, pp. 287, 259. The entire Horowitz volume is a story of Zionist organization and efforts to influence the establishment of an independent Jewish state in Palestine. While the Palestine question was being debated, the Jewish Agency maintained an unofficial delegation at New York which lobbied incessantly among other delegations. At the height of negotiations the Zionists met with "tens of delegations" in one day, Horowitz testifies. At the same time, Zionist envoys abroad launched "intensive diplomatic action in world capitals, making strenuous efforts to mobilize world opinion in various countries." See *ibid.*, pp. 258-301.

several other members of the Assembly. At least two Supreme Court Justices, reportedly, importuned the Philippine delegate on behalf of partition. Harvey Firestone, with his extensive business interests in Liberia, personally telephoned the Liberian government to cast its vote for partition.[60] "How far our delegation was directly involved in the lobbying is hard to say," Kermit Roosevelt observed, "and it must have been even harder for the small nations and their representatives at the UN to put a true value on many of the tactics employed." [61] At any rate, the tactics were successful as the final voting record attests. The Philippines and Haiti, whose representatives had within a matter of hours spoken against partition, voted for the resolution,[62] and six members that had abstained in the committee vote also joined the majority. The one exception was Chile, which, presumably in protest at the pressure tactics being employed, changed its vote from affirmative to abstention.[63]

This discussion of efforts to influence the Palestine decision would not be complete without mention of the pressures applied by the Arabs and their supporters. For all their denunciations of pressure tactics used by pro-partition forces, the Arabs differed chiefly in their lack of success. The threats of war and of economic and political boycotts were certainly thinly veiled efforts at forcing a pro-Arab solution. The United States was subjected to repeated importunings by Arab representatives. Arab diplomatic representatives in foreign capitals pled their case directly with the governments concerned, and Arab delegates at New York lobbied as

---

[60] Alfred M. Lilienthal, op. cit., pp. 60-67, writes an extremely frank account of the extra-official pressures by persons in official positions and others presumed to have authoritative connections with the United States government. Although Lilienthal's anti-Zionist bias at times distorts the facts, the author is convinced that his account of Zionist pressures is very well informed and essentially accurate. See also Kermit Roosevelt, "The Partition of Palestine: A Lesson in Pressure Politics," The Middle East Journal, vol. 2 (Jan., 1948), pp. 1-16, and Millis, op. cit., pp. 345-46, 358.

[61] Roosevelt, op. cit., pp. 14-15.

[62] Lillie Shultz was inclined to minimize the influence of American pressure. "As far as I am aware," she states, "The United States produced perhaps one important vote, the vote of the Philippines, and then only when it became a matter of face saving." The Haitian government, far from being influenced by the United States to vote for partition, was persuaded "by liberal friends on moral grounds alone." Likewise, the intention of the Liberian delegation to cast a negative vote "was changed through the efforts of friendly, unofficial Americans." Op. cit., p. 677.

Regarding the Haiti vote, Sir Zafrullah Khan declared that the Haitian delegate, under pressure from the United States, voted for partition "with tears in his eyes." Another anti-partitionist claimed that the vote had been "bought" for a bribe of $10,000. Replying to these allegations in a letter to the New York Times, Haitian Ambassador Dr. Joseph D. Charles protested their falsity and asserted that at every international conference Haiti voted "consistently in all freedom and independence of mind." See New York Times, Dec. 5, 1947, p. 15; Dec. 11, 1947, p. 32; Hamilton, op. cit., p. 291.

[63] See comments of New York Times, Nov. 29, 1947, p. 1, and Ball, op. cit., pp. 10-11.

assiduously, if not as effectively, as the Zionists. That they failed in the execution of their own preferred policies was not from lack of trying.[64]

[64] See, e.g., New York *Times*, Sept. 25, 1947, p. 1; Sept. 9, 1947, sec. IV, p. 4; Oct. 10, 1947, sec. IV, p. 1; Oct. 14, 1947, p. 5; Nov. 28, 1947, p. 10; García-Granados, *Birth of Israel*, pp. 263-64.

CHAPTER FIVE

Labeling the Aggressor

Chinese Communist intervention in the Korean war placed members of the United Nations in a difficult dilemma. The Chinese troops had intervened at the orders of the Central People's Government, and their march across the thirty-eighth parallel into South Korea constituted a new case of aggression. Most members of the United Nations realized these facts. But fear that the Korean hostilities might spread to other parts of Asia, or even touch off a third world war, made many reluctant to take a firm stand against Chinese aggression. They hesitated to aggravate Chinese intransigence or further arouse Chinese antagonism by attaching to them the label of aggressor. And they shrank from action which the United States might interpret as a carte blanche authorizing any action it thought necessary, including use of atomic weapons and bombardment of targets across the Manchurian border. Some, too, were reluctant to condemn the Chinese action as aggression in view of India's prior warning that a United Nations crossing of the thirty-eighth parallel into North Korea would provoke Chinese intervention.

The United States did not share these misgivings. Convinced that firmness was the only answer to Chinese intervention, it was faced with the problem of persuading others. The possibility that a strong Assembly pronouncement might prolong or spread the conflict seemed less real to the United States. The Chinese, it was felt, would fight until there was no longer any military or political advantage to be won by fighting, with or without the aggressor label. As for American intentions, the Truman administration was just as concerned as the governments of other countries that hostilities be localized. Of this fact some friendly governments were unsure; but the United States government, knowing its own intentions, could press for a strong United Nations stand with the assurance that a third world war, if it came, would result from communist and not American initiative.

Chinese troops were first identified in Korea in late October at a time when United Nations forces were on the verge of completing their drive to the Manchurian border. Before many days the trickle of Chinese "volunteers" became a torrent of Chinese regulars against whose onslaught there was no alternative but retreat. On November 6 the United States appealed to the Security Council for action and, with Cuba, Ecuador,

France, Norway, and the United Kingdom, introduced a resolution noting the intervention of Chinese troops and calling for their immediate withdrawal. The resolution finally came to a vote on November 30, at which time the anticipated Soviet veto prevented its adoption.[1] The next court of appeal was the General Assembly.

THE CEASE-FIRE APPEAL

Four days after the Security Council vote the same six nations which had sponsored the resolution in the Security Council requested that the question of Chinese intervention in Korea be placed on the agenda of the General Assembly. From the beginning of Assembly debates the United States government was convinced that no appeal for troop withdrawal or cease-fire would be heeded by the Communists as long as their armies were pressing ahead and, consequently, that the authority of the United Nations must be vindicated by resistance and condemnation of the intervention.[2] Many non-communist nations, however, were not convinced of the wisdom of strong words which might bar the door to an early negotiated peace. Developments both in Korea and in the United States gave them cause for concern. United Nations military reverses evoked thunderings from MacArthur over his inability to strike across the Manchurian border. Even more ominous were reports of President Truman's press conference, held November 30, in which the President indicated that Manchuria might be subjected to air attacks and the atom bomb might be used if circumstances should warrant. The following day President Truman asked Congress for a special defense appropriation totalling nearly eighteen billion dollars.[3] World press reports bore accounts of grave and increasing apprehension over this new turn of events, and official spokesmen of foreign governments counseled caution. The imminent danger of a general Asiatic war crystallized the long-smoldering dissatisfaction of Britain, Western Europe, and the British Commonwealth countries with General MacArthur's handling of the military situation. In London Prime Minister Clement Attlee, in a surprise announcement to the House of Commons, declared his intention

---

[1] *Official Records of the Security Council,* 5th year, nos. 60-72, and document S/1894.

[2] The New York *Times* reported that the United States at that early date was considering a resolution to condemn Communist China as an aggressor and, possibly, to authorize General MacArthur to bomb Manchuria. Dec. 1, 1950, p. 1.

[3] *Ibid.,* Dec. 1, 1950, p. 1, and Dec. 2, 1950, p. 1. Reaction to the Truman press conference statement was so alarming that Charles G. Ross, Presidential press secretary, issued a statement the same afternoon that the atomic bomb would under no circumstances be used until the President gave express authorization. Some had been led to believe, apparently, that General MacArthur had been given authority to use his own discretion on the matter.

to fly to Washington to confer with President Truman on the threat to world peace in the Far East.[4]

The counsel of caution prevailed. For the sake of allies who were not yet ready to take more drastic action, the United States consented to the submission by the six powers of a resolution similar in important respects to the draft vetoed in the Security Council.[5] It noted the presence of Chinese armed forces in Korea, called for their withdrawal, reaffirmed the Assembly's October resolution concerning the unification and rehabilitation of Korea, affirmed the intention to withdraw United Nations forces as soon as possible and to hold the Manchurian frontier inviolate, and urged that no action be taken which might lead to the spread of the Korean conflict. This was not a measure that the United States would have formulated had its allies been willing to go further; it was only the first step toward securing a condemnation of Chinese intervention. Certain that the appeal would fall on deaf ears, the United States was only deferring to the wishes of others who felt that the Chinese Communists might yet be found willing to negotiate a settlement on terms acceptable to the United Nations. The process of policy execution required that milder alternatives first be proven ineffectual.[6]

While the United States and its close allies were attempting to reach agreement on a common course of action, thirteen Arab and Asian states under the leadership of India opened up a new avenue of approach. In a private meeting at the apartment of the Indian chief delegate, Sir Benegal Rau, the thirteen nations framed an appeal to the North Korean and Chinese authorities for a negotiated settlement, to be preceded by assurances that the communist forces would not advance south of the thirty-eighth parallel.[7] A reply from Mao Tse-tung, sent through the government of India, indicated willingness to negotiate with the United States, the United Kingdom, and the Soviet Union if the Central People's Government were granted a full and equal voice in the discussions as

[4] *Ibid.*, Dec. 1, 1950, pp. 1, 9, 16; Dec. 2, 1950, p. 1; Dec. 3, 1950, p. 34; Dec. 3, 1950, sec. IV, p. 5; Dec. 4, 1950, p. 4.

[5] Document A/C.1/638.

[6] The delay between the final action of the Security Council and the submission of the question to the General Assembly, some four or five days, was attributed by United States spokesmen to "procedural complications," while other delegates believed that it was to provide time for President Truman and Prime Minister Attlee to work out a common policy. New York *Times*, Dec. 1, 1950, p. 1. In actual practice, the transfer of an item from the Security Council to the Assembly often requires a good deal of preparation, including widening the circle of conferees from nine or ten to thirty or forty or more. Hence the delay of a few days would not have been remarkable even if there had been no special differences with the United Kingdom to patch up.

[7] *Ibid.*, Dec. 6, 1950, p. 1. The thirteen nations were Afghanistan, Burma, Egypt, India, Indonesia, Iran, Iraq, Lebanon, Pakistan, the Philippines, Saudi Arabia, Syria, and Yemen.

the government of China, and if Formosa and other Far Eastern problems were considered along with Korea.[8] Mao's conditions appeared impossible of fulfillment in view of the United States attitude toward the recognition of Communist China and its almost equally firm position that the Korean question must be settled prior to the consideration of other Far Eastern problems. However, the Arab-Asian group continued to probe the possibilities of a cease-fire and settlement by negotiation. After extensive consultations which included, among others, leading members of the American delegation, the group agreed upon a new proposal for Assembly action.[9]

On the morning of December 12 Sir Benegal Rau laid before the First Committee two draft resolutions. The first, sponsored by the thirteen Arab and Asian states, requested the president of the General Assembly "to constitute a group of three persons including himself to determine the basis on which a satisfactory cease-fire in Korea can be arranged and to make recommendations to the General Assembly as soon as possible." The second draft, sponsored by the same group except for the omission of the Philippines, recommended the convening of a conference for the settlement of Far Eastern problems. Participants were not named in the draft, but the Indian representative suggested that they include Communist China, France, the United Kingdom, the United States, the Soviet Union, Egypt, and India. Sir Benegal moved that priority of consideration be given to the thirteen-power draft because of its urgency and importance. With a minimum of debate, and protest only from the communist states, the Indian motion for priority was adopted by a vote of 48-5-4.[10]

The United States representative voted to give priority to the cease-fire resolution and subsequently supported its passage. However, he made plain his interpretation of the draft: that the cease-fire should be fully accomplished before any political settlement was considered. In agreeing to sidetrack the six-power resolution in favor of the Arab-Asian cease-fire draft, the United States was further deferring to the opinions of other members of the Assembly. The Soviet representative, however, saw it as an Anglo-American maneuver brought on by defeat in Korea, to gain time for the regrouping of forces.[11] The draft

[8] *Ibid.*, Dec. 10, 1950, p. 1.

[9] An American representative made clear to the press that the talks were upon Indian initiative, not that of the United States. Sir Benegal was described as busy from morning until night, engaged in numerous private talks with groups of delegations, sometimes leaving one conference for a few minutes to dash to another. *Ibid.*, Dec. 11, 1950, pp. 1, 5, and Dec. 12, 1950, pp. 1, 6.

[10] *First Committee*, 5th sess. (1950), pp. 434, 435, and documents A/C.1/641 and A/C.1/642.

[11] American and Soviet comments are found *First Committee*, 5th sess. (1950), pp. 437, 440-42. The absence of the Philippines from the list of sponsors of the

was approved by the committee the following day, and on December 14 the Assembly in plenary meeting endorsed the measure 52-5 with Nationalist China abstaining.[12]

Nasrollah Entezam, president of the Assembly, appointed Lester B. Pearson of Canada and Sir Benegal N. Rau of India to serve with him on the cease-fire group.[13] After enlisting the aid of the Secretary-General, the three attempted to make contact with General Wu Hsiu-Chuan, representative of the Peiping government who had come to New York some weeks previously to discuss Soviet charges in the Security Council and General Assembly of United States aggression against China. Wu refused to receive the group and told a press conference that the cease-fire proposal was a "trap" designed to give the American forces a breathing space before committing new aggression. He declared his intention to leave for China on December 19, since the Assembly refused to discuss the Soviet charges of American aggression.[14] While these overtures were being made to General Wu in New York, the cease-fire group sent a cable directly to Peiping with their proposal for cease-fire discussions. In the official reply, by cable dated December 23, the Chinese Foreign Minister Chou En-lai parroted Soviet charges of American aggression and refused to entertain any proposal involving cease-fire before negotiations. As essential pre-conditions to a peaceful settlement in Korea, Chou demanded withdrawal of all "foreign troops" from Korea, withdrawal of American "aggression forces"—that is, the Seventh Fleet—from Formosa, and a United Nations seat for Communist China. Since the Chinese conditions, as they stood, ruled out all hope of compromise, the group found itself unable to make any recommendation to the Assembly with regard to a cease-fire.

The Assembly adjourned over the Christmas holidays and met on January 3 to hear the report of the cease-fire group. By this time all were aware of its contents. To add to the seriousness of the situation,

---

second Arab-Asian draft was regarded by the Soviet delegate as significant. He claimed that pressure by the United States and Philippine representatives had impelled the other sponsors to accept two alternative resolutions, one acceptable to the United States and the other not, instead of a single composite draft.

[12] Resolution 384 (V). Committee voting was 51-5-1. *First Committee*, 5th sess. (1950), p. 451. For plenary vote see *Plenary Meetings*, 5th sess. (1950), p. 660. Nicaragua and Peru were absent.

[13] For account of activities and correspondence of the cease-fire group through January 2, 1951, see document A/C.1/643.

[14] New York *Times*, Dec. 17, 1950, pp. 1, 12, and Dec. 20, 1950, p. 1. President Entezam then sent a request through the Swedish embassy in Peiping that General Wu be instructed to remain in New York to discuss the possibility of arranging a cease-fire. A reply received on December 21 through the same channel declared the resolution on the cease-fire group illegal and reaffirmed the instructions for Wu to return home.

on December 31 the Chinese and North Korean troops launched a major offensive against United Nations lines just south of the thirty-eighth parallel. These new developments added strength to the American contention that intervention must be met with firmness. Consequently, in early January the United States initiated extensive negotiations to develop support for condemning Chinese aggression and instituting economic and diplomatic sanctions.[15] In the First Committee Warren R. Austin asked the Assembly to demonstrate that it would not "voluntarily reward aggression, nor stand aside in face of it." [16] After a month's delay the United States was girding for a decisive show-down on Chinese intervention.

THE SECOND CEASE-FIRE APPEAL

Many members of the Assembly were still not ready to concede the necessity of the steps advocated by the United States. The twelve Asian and Arab states, not including the Philippines, met to determine what their next move should be.[17] The delegation of Israel produced its own peace plan involving a settlement through a chronological sequence of stages, beginning with unconditional cease-fire and leading finally to consideration of all questions affecting the relations of the United Nations and Communist China. The course of action which gained the most general support, however, was another try by the three-man cease-fire group. This suggestion was made to the January 3 meeting of the First Committee by Norway and the United Kingdom.[18]

While the cease-fire group was engaged in preparing a new statement, a conference of Commonwealth Prime Ministers convened in London. During the eight-day conference from January 4 to January 12, Korea

[15] The New York *Times* reported that on January 4 a circular note was dispatched to Britain, France, and twenty other members of the United Nations giving the United States view that China should be condemned as an aggressor if it refused to agree to a cease-fire, and that the Collective Measures Committee should study further action to be taken. A number of other delegations were said to have received a somewhat longer note on the same question. Jan. 6, 1951, pp. 1, 3. See also *ibid.*, Jan. 2, 1951, pp. 1, 2, and Jan. 3, 1951, p. 6.

Regarding these consultations the President's report states: "As the year 1950 came to a close the six-power draft resolution seemed out of date and consultations were undertaken by the United States with other members with a view to the adoption of measures which would have wide acceptance by the General Assembly to meet the aggression by the Peiping regime. Negotiations revealed that a substantial number of states were prepared to support a resolution finding that the Peiping regime had violated the Charter and initiating a study of additional measures which might be taken to meet Chinese Communist aggression." *The U.S. and the U.N.*, report of President to Congress (1950), pp. 46-47. See also *ibid.*, (1951), pp. 28-32.

[16] Verbatim text in *U.S. Mission Press Release*, no. 1190, Jan. 3, 1951.

[17] New York *Times*, Dec. 29, 1950, p. 3.

[18] *First Committee*, 5th sess. (1950-51), p. 461. The Israel plan is found *ibid.*, pp. 464-65.

was the most urgent question on the agenda. Although the Commonwealth Prime Ministers were themselves so divided as to make virtually impossible the formulation of a common policy toward the Far East, all were in agreement on the need for new efforts to secure a cessation of Korean hostilities,[19] and their views were no doubt conveyed to the cease-fire group, two of whose members represented Commonwealth countries.[20] Senator Austin had meanwhile agreed to delay submission of a condemnatory resolution pending completion of the statement by the group.[21]

The supplementary report of the cease-fire group, presented to the committee on January 11, constituted an earnest attempt to satisfy communist demands without sacrificing United Nations principles. The principle of cease-fire before negotiations was not compromised. The report also insisted that withdrawal of all non-Korean armed forces should be followed by free elections for the establishment of a "unified, independent, democratic, sovereign state." But as a concession to the Chinese Communists, the cease-fire group suggested that immediately after agreement on a cease-fire was obtained the Assembly should set up an "appropriate body," including representatives of the United Kingdom, the United States, the Soviet Union, and Communist China, to discuss Formosa, representation for Red China in the United Nations, and other Far Eastern problems. When the report was presented, the delegates of Norway, France, India, and the United Kingdom quickly offered their endorsement.[22]

The crucial question was the attitude of the United States. In view of the American campaign for condemnation there was good reason to doubt that support would be given. However, the United States once more chose moderation. As Senator Austin stated to the committee, the United States government felt that the United Nations must face the

[19] See New York *Times*, Jan. 6, 1951, p. 5; Jan. 9, 1951, p. 7; Jan. 13, 1951, p. 3. Although sessions of the conference were closed the press reported the general outline of discussions. In a communiqué issued January 12 the Prime Ministers stated, "in the last few days we have directed our efforts to the securing of a cessation of hostilities in Korea, so that around the conference table the great powers concerned may compose their differences on a basis which will strengthen the United Nations and fulfill the purpose of the Charter." *Ibid.*, Jan. 13, 1951, p. 3.

[20] On January 10 the group was reported to be standing by awaiting the outcome of the Commonwealth talks in London. *Ibid.*, Jan. 10, 1951, p. 7. The British representative subsequently made it clear that the proposals had the backing of the Commonwealth Prime Ministers. *First Committee*, 5th sess. (1950-51), p. 507. F. H. Soward, "The Korean Crisis and the Commonwealth," *Pacific Affairs*, vol. 24 (June, 1951), pp. 115-30, discusses in some detail the relationship of the new cease-fire proposals to the Commonwealth conference.

[21] *First Committee*, 5th sess. (1950-51), pp. 467-68, and New York *Times*, Jan. 6, 1951, p. 3.

[22] *First Committee*, 5th sess. (1950-51), pp. 475-77, and document A/C.1/645.

fact of Chinese Communist aggression in Korea and demonstrate its united will to resist. But because the majority seemed to favor this new approach he would vote in favor of the statement of principles in the report. Approval by a wide margin was thus assured. On January 13 the committee approved the conclusions in the supplementary report by a vote of 50-7 with 1 abstention, and recommended that they be transmitted to the Peiping government for its consideration.[23]

United States support of the new cease-fire proposals, with their commitment to discuss Formosa and Chinese representation in the United Nations, created a furor among some members of Congress. Senator Robert A. Taft declared it a "shocking step" toward appeasement, while Senator Tom Connally, chairman of the Senate Committee on Foreign Relations, complained that the action had been taken by the State Department without consulting him and he had doubts as to its wisdom. Dean Rusk and John D. Hickerson, Assistant Secretaries of State, hastened to inform the Foreign Relations Committee that the Department had omitted consulting them on the matter because it involved no basic change of policy.[24] On January 17 the State Department issued a press release explaining in detail its reasons for supporting the measure. Although not sharing the belief of other members that the resolution would accomplish its purpose, the United States voted for the resolution to maintain the unity of the free nations and to demonstrate adherence to the principle of peaceful settlement.[25] State Department explanations apparently did not set the perturbed Congressmen at ease. Senator Walter F. George later remarked that "we in Foreign Relations were in consternation for fear they would accept the proposal," which he interpreted as offering Formosa and a seat in the United Nations to Communist China.[26]

[23] *First Committee*, 5th sess. (1950-51), p. 496. Vote on the motion to transmit the proposals to the Chinese Communist government, document A/C.1/651, was 45-5-8. *Ibid.*, p. 500. For Austin statement see *ibid.*, p. 477.

[24] New York *Times*, Jan. 15, 1951, p. 9, and Jan. 17, 1951, pp. 1, 3. When called some months later before the Senate Committees on Armed Services and Foreign Relations, Secretary of State Dean Acheson held that the United States action in supporting the resolution maintained the interpretation "that having restored peace and stopped the aggression in Korea, we were then reverting to the situation which existed before in which all questions could be and should be discussed in the United Nations." U.S. Senate, Committee on Armed Services and Committee on Foreign Relations, *MacArthur Hearings*, May 3-Aug. 17, 1951, 82nd Cong., 1st sess., pt. 3, p. 1968.

[25] Reprinted in *Department of State Bulletin*, vol. 24 (Jan. 29, 1951), pp. 164-65.

[26] *MacArthur Hearings*, pt. 3, p. 2004. Senator George continued: "Mr. Secretary, on that point, I thought we had very frankly made a mistake, and I thought the State Department had recognized its error, and prayed considerably during about three days that the Communists would reject it, and fortunately the Communists did reject the proposal. I think it is a fine illustration of the efficacy of prayer, Mr. Secretary. I may be wrong, but that is the impression I got at that time." *Ibid.*

The reply from Peiping Foreign Minister Chou En-lai came on January 17. Cease-fire before negotiations, it declared, would serve merely to give United States troops a breathing space. A "genuine and peaceful solution" of the Korean problem could only be achieved through a conference of Communist China, the Soviet Union, the United Kingdom, the United States, France, India, and Egypt, held in China, where arrangements might be made to put an end to hostilities in Korea. The United Nations must agree beforehand to the withdrawal of all foreign troops from Korea, "the settlement of Korean domestic affairs by the Korean people themselves," and immediate seating of the Peiping regime in the United Nations. Withdrawal of American armed forces from the Formosa area must be included among the subjects for negotiation.[27]

CONDEMNATION

Secretary of State Dean Acheson quickly termed the communist reply a "complete rejection" of United Nations proposals, and in the First Committee Warren Austin moved to secure condemnation of the Chinese Communist regime.[28] From the time the question was first placed upon the Assembly agenda the United States had been convinced that Chinese aggression ought to be condemned and strong action taken to meet it. But the long process of converting others to this point of view had involved acquiescence in efforts to obtain a negotiated cease-fire and settlement short of condemnation. The latest Chinese reply set the stage for a final American drive to get its views endorsed by the Assembly. In anticipation of this hour the United States had been conducting negotiations with members of the United Nations since early January. Even before the completion of the cease-fire group's supplementary report, the United States was pressing its case abroad. Reportedly American diplomatic representatives were instructed to inform foreign governments of the State Department's view that the fate of the United Nations might depend upon its reaction to Chinese intervention in Korea, and that American public opinion might swing sharply against the organization if it ignored Chinese aggression.[29] At the time that Senator Austin announced United States support of the second cease-fire proposal, on January 11, delegation officials made it clear that rejection by the Peiping government would lead the United States to "press strongly" its demands in the Assembly.[30]

[27] Document A/C.1/653.

[28] New York *Times,* Jan. 18, 1951, p. 1, and *First Committee,* 5th sess. (1950-51), pp. 501-3.

[29] New York *Times,* Jan. 7, 1951, pp. 1, 12, and Blair Bolles, "Will UN Members Follow U.S. on China Policy?" *Foreign Policy Bulletin,* vol. 30 (Jan. 26, 1951), pp. 2-3.

[30] New York *Times,* Jan. 12, 1951, p. 1.

Mr. Austin delivered the opening speech in the First Committee when it reconvened on January 18 to discuss the communist reply. Detailing the series of rebuffs which the Assembly had received, he asked the Assembly to label the Chinese as an aggressor, call for a cessation of hostilities, affirm the determination of the United Nations to resist aggression, and assign a committee to consider additional measures for future action. In order to reaffirm the peaceful intent of the United Nations, he said, the Assembly might also authorize the creation of a group to use its good offices whenever the Peiping government showed itself ready to consider a peaceful settlement. Two days later the United States sponsored a resolution to give effect to Austin's proposals.[31] In the two-day interim the American delegation had busily engaged in consultations with other delegations in order to secure an impressive list of co-sponsors. However, Britain and France refused to join in co-sponsorship unless the reference to further collective measures were modified or removed. Unwilling to emphasize the differences between the major Western powers by presenting a list of co-sponsors not including France and the United Kingdom, the United States chose to sponsor the measure alone. It was felt that those who now were reluctant to sponsor the draft would eventually give support when it came to a vote.[32]

If representations at the seat of the United Nations and through regular diplomatic channels were not sufficient to emphasize the importance of the resolution to the United States government, the President and both houses of Congress acted to remove all doubt. In a press conference on January 18, the day on which the First Committee reconvened, President Truman stated that the United States would press vigorously with everything it could bring to bear, to obtain condemnation of Communist China. The following day the House of Representatives by a near-unanimous voice vote resolved "that the United Nations should immediately act and declare the Chinese communist authorities an aggressor in Korea." On January 23 the Senate unanimously called on the United Nations to reject China's demand for membership and denounce the communist regime as an aggressor.[33] There could be no doubt that the full force of the United States government was behind the resolution.

Within the Assembly a number of Western European states and members of the Commonwealth still entertained the fear that condemnation

---

[31] Document A/C.1/654 and *First Committee*, 5th sess. (1950-51), pp. 501-3.

[32] New York *Times*, Jan. 20, 1951, p. 3, and Jan. 21, 1951, p. 1.

[33] *Ibid.*, Jan. 19, 1951, p. 3; Jan. 20, 1951, p. 1; Jan. 24, 1951, p. 3. A third motion calling on the United Nations to take all necessary measures against the aggressors was sent to the Foreign Relations Committee. At the same time the Senate Foreign Relations Committee voted to delay action on an urgent request from India for American wheat. See comments of James Reston, *ibid.*, Jan. 28, 1951, sec. IV, p. 3.

might indefinitely postpone a peaceful settlement and perhaps lead to the spread of hostilities. Nevertheless they appeared ready to give in. The majority of Arab and South Asian states, however, were unwilling to support the American resolution. Under the leadership of India, they bent their efforts toward keeping the transoceanic negotiations alive.[34] On January 22 the Indian representative announced to the First Committee that independent queries from the Indian government had led to new Chinese proposals for the Assembly's consideration. If the principle of withdrawal of all foreign troops were accepted, the Chinese government would assume the responsibility of advising the Chinese volunteers to return to China. This was an assurance not previously given. As a step toward cease-fire before negotiation, the Chinese suggested that the previously proposed seven-nation conference could at its first meeting agree upon a cease-fire for a "limited period," after which the conference would discuss arrangements for troop withdrawal, proposals for a settlement in Korea by the Korean people themselves, the withdrawal of United States forces from Formosa and the Formosa straits, and other Far Eastern problems. United Nations membership for Communist China must be "ensured" from the outset of negotiations but, presumably, need not be granted immediately. Upon presenting this new information the Indian representative suggested a forty-eight-hour adjournment so that delegates might study the latest communication from China and consider other possible steps. The committee appeared evenly divided on the question of an adjournment. The United Kingdom delegate, among others, supported the proposal, while the United States representative spoke against it. The proposal for adjournment was passed 27-23.[35]

The Arab-Asian states put the intervening hours to good use. On January 25 they presented a revised version of their own proposal for a seven-nation conference, which had been submitted but not acted upon in December when the cease-fire group was created. The revised version noted the official January 13 reply of the Central People's Government and recommended that the seven powers—France, the United Kingdom, the United States, the Soviet Union, Egypt, India, and Communist China —meet as soon as possible to secure clarifications of the Chinese reply and make "any incidental or consequential arrangements toward a peaceful settlement of the Korean and other Far Eastern problems."[36] In London Prime Minister Clement Attlee welcomed the initiative of the Asian and Middle-Eastern states and counseled giving "all weight in this Asian dispute to the views of the Asian countries."[37] The British

[34] See *ibid.*, Jan. 20, 1951, p. 3, and Jan. 24, 1951, pp. 1, 4.

[35] *First Committee*, 5th sess. (1950-51), pp. 525-32.

[36] Document A/C.1/642/Rev.1.

[37] New York *Times*, Jan. 24, 1951, p. 4.

representative in the First Committee urged priority for the Asian draft over the United States proposal. On January 26 the Canadian delegate suggested a plan for a last attempt at negotiations before condemnation: the convening of a seven-nation conference, agreement on a cease-fire in Korea, consideration of a peaceful settlement of the Korean problem in accordance with principles set forth in the January 13 cease-fire offer, and, finally, a discussion of other Far Eastern problems, beginning with the question of Chinese representation in the United Nations.[38]

In the face of this manifest sentiment for continued negotiations the United States stood unequivocally opposed to any action that might further delay passage of the condemnatory resolution. The Chinese message transmitted through India was termed another rejection of the United Nations peace overtures little different from the reply of January 18 and a "transparent effort to divide the free world." [39] Moreover, in the United States view, the United Nations could scarcely take as a basis for continued negotiations information which India claimed as special knowledge but which had not been communicated to the United Nations as a whole. President Truman once more added his personal influence by declaring in a press conference on January 25 that, for his part, he believed in "calling an aggressor an aggressor." He attempted to reassure those who feared that the United Nations Unified Command in Korea might be encouraged to take drastic action by stating that "the question of what can and should be done about the aggression in Korea of course must be discussed with all other friendly nations." [40] For the United States there was no turning back from the resolution condemning Chinese aggression in Korea.

Debate continued for another week, but in the final decision two factors proved decisive: one was United States insistence; the other was the undeniable fact of Chinese aggression.[41] Prime Minister Attlee, while praising Asian efforts for continued negotiation, said that his government recognized "the stark facts of the situation in Korea" and agreed in "condemning Chinese intervention in support of an aggressor." [42] The

[38] *First Committee*, 5th sess. (1950-51), pp. 545, 554-55.

[39] See *ibid.*, pp. 531-32, 537-39, 569-70; *U.S. Mission Press Release*, no. 1122, Jan. 22, 1951; New York *Times*, Jan. 23, 1951, pp. 1, 4, 5.

[40] *Ibid.*, Jan. 26, 1951, p. 1.

[41] Lebanese delegate Charles Malik gave just these two reasons in an address to the committee. His delegation was a sponsor of the Arab-Asian draft but would also vote for the American draft because aggression existed and because, in the paraphrased version of First Committee debates, "nothing must be done to discourage the people of the United States from taking vigorous interest in and giving leadership to the Organization." *First Committee*, 5th sess. (1950-51), pp. 568-69. See also comments of Norman J. Padelford, "The United Nations and Korea: A Political Resume," *International Organization*, vol. 5 (Nov., 1951), pp. 694-700.

[42] New York *Times*, Jan. 24, 1951, p. 4.

Canadian representative also, while regarding it as unwise to submit the American resolution to a vote as long as the possibilities for negotiation had not been exhausted, declared that he would support the resolution because of the fundamental fact of Chinese intervention.[43] Many governments balked at the provision for considering additional measures to meet the aggression,[44] but all took hope from the proposed good offices committee which, ostensibly at least, left the door open to further negotiations. The qualms of still-reluctant allies were partially removed by United States acceptance of Lebanese amendments authorizing the proposed committee on additional measures to defer its report if the good offices committee reported satisfactory progress.[45] The Arab-Asian powers, in a last-minute effort to make their proposition successful, amended the draft to provide for the conclusion of a cease-fire as the first act of the proposed seven-nation conference.[46] The Indian government issued a final warning that it had been advised "on the highest authority," presumably the word of Mao Tse-tung, that adoption of the American resolution would remove all chance of a peaceful settlement.[47] But the committee had been persuaded otherwise. On January 31 the Arab-Asian draft was rejected, and the committee voted to condemn Communist China. The resolution was formally adopted in plenary meeting 44-7-9.[48] United States policy had once more been adopted.

---

[43] *First Committee*, 5th sess. (1950-51), pp. 555-56.

[44] Attlee had stated in the address to the Commons previously cited, "we do not believe that the time has yet come to consider further measures. To do so implies that we have abandoned hope of reaching a peaceful settlement, and this we have not done." New York *Times*, Jan. 24, 1951, p. 4.

[45] Document A/C.1/656. The Lebanese amendments also modified the resolution to read that the Peiping government had "not accepted" instead of "rejected all" United Nations proposals.

[46] Document A/C.1/642/Rev.2.

[47] New York *Times*, Jan. 30, 1951, p. 1.

[48] Resolution 498 (V). For committee voting see *First Committee*, 5th sess. (1950-51), pp. 601-2; for plenary voting, *Plenary Meetings*, 5th sess. (1950-51), p. 696.

Part Two

The Extent of Influence

CHAPTER SIX

Harmony and Discord

The many political problems brought before the Assembly are not all so dramatic or highly charged as the partition of Palestine or the condemnation of Communist China. But the extent of American influence is not to be determined from a survey of one or two headline-making questions. This may illustrate much as to method but can prove little about the consistency with which the United States is able to win support in the Assembly on political questions. Another type of analysis is necessary to give depth and perspective to the picture. The method chosen is to consider each political question, item by item, in its relation to policies advocated by the United States. The present chapter outlines Assembly action upon general principles of cooperation, proposals submitted apparently for propaganda purposes only, and a group of questions which may be termed "disputes and irritating situations." [1]

EXERCISES IN COOPERATION

EXTRADITION AND PUNISHMENT OF WAR CRIMINALS

The first session of the Assembly witnessed a brave show of unanimity in the adoption of several resolutions dealing with principles to which all could subscribe, albeit with some reservations. Early in the first part of the session Byelorussia presented a draft resolution recommending the arrest and extradition of war criminals to the countries where their crimes were committed. No voice was raised against the principle but some delegations felt that the term "war crimes" and "war criminal" as used in the draft required clarification. A drafting subcommittee quickly produced a revised text which satisfied all criticism, and the resolution was adopted unanimously.[2]

PERSECUTION AND DISCRIMINATION RESOLUTION

This item, proposed by Egypt, failed to receive approval by the General Committee but was successfully championed by its supporters

---

[1] A brief description of Assembly procedure, including the manner in which questions are placed upon the Assembly agenda, is found in Appendix C.

[2] *First Committee*, 1st sess., 1st pt. (1946), pp. 21-22, and *Plenary Meetings*, 1st sess., 1st pt. (1946), pp. 469-70. For final text of resolution see Resolution 3 (I). Resolutions for each session of the General Assembly are compiled and published as a supplement to the Official Records. They are numbered serially and the session of adoption is indicated by a Roman numeral set off in parentheses.

on the floor of the Assembly. As originally presented the Egyptian draft resolution called for an end to religious and racial persecution, with particular reference to states of central Europe. The Soviet delegate objected to singling out one area for special censure, but even with the objectionable reference to central Europe removed the item could still secure only three affirmative votes in the General Committee. In the Assembly, however, the Egyptian proposal easily found a place on the agenda. Members found it difficult to oppose such a laudatory principle as the abatement of racial and religious persecution. With newly found enthusiasm both the Soviet and American delegates added their encomiums, and the proposal was adopted unanimously without reference to a committee.[3]

THE RIGHTS AND DUTIES OF STATES AND FUNDAMENTAL
HUMAN RIGHTS AND FREEDOMS

The question of issuing United Nations Declarations on the Rights and Duties of States and on Fundamental Human Rights and Freedoms had been broached at the San Francisco Conference by a number of the smaller powers. They had been put off, however, with the suggestion that these subjects might properly be considered at the first session of the General Assembly. Accordingly Panama took the initiative in placing the two items upon the agenda of the first session. In the First Committee there was agreement with the general principles involved, but detailed discussion of substance was reserved to more specialized bodies. The Declaration on the Rights and Duties of States was, on the suggestion of the United States, referred for study to a recently created committee on methods for the codification of international law; the Declaration on Human Rights and Freedoms was referred to the Commission on Human Rights of the Economic and Social Council. Both resolutions were approved by the General Assembly without dissent.[4]

APPEAL TO THE GREAT POWERS

In 1946 the Great Powers tried to maintain a semblance of unity by agreeing upon statements of general principle, even though fundamental problems remained unresolved. Before many months had passed even the pretense of unity was gone. The third session of the Assembly opened in Paris in an atmosphere of tension and uncertainty aggravated by the Berlin blockade. The concern of the smaller powers, made no less real by a sense of their own impotence to cope with the situation, was strikingly evident. One manifestation of this concern was the Mexican delegation's "Appeal to the great powers to compose their differences

---

[3] Document A/BUR/51; *General Committee*, 1st sess., 1st pt. (1946), pp. 92-93; *Plenary Meetings*, 1st sess., 1st pt. (1946), pp. 953-64, 973-75; Resolution 103 (1).

[4] Documents A/19 and A/148; *First Committee*, 1st sess., 2nd pt. (1946), pp. 271, 283; *Plenary Meetings*, 1st sess., 2nd pt. (1946), pp. 1134, 1140.

and establish a lasting peace." [5] Although the objective was unimpeachable, the Mexican supporting draft was not, and a subcommittee composed of the five Great Powers and six lesser ones was appointed to reconcile the varying points of view.[6] The result was a compromise resolution solemnly affirming allegiance to the cause of peace, the Atlantic Charter, the United Nations Declaration, and the Yalta Declaration. The resolution also contained a recommendation for the early conclusion of peace treaties, with the suggestion that the Big Five consult in this regard the states which had signed the United Nations Declaration of January 1, 1942. Some disappointment was expressed that the draft did not call for greater participation of smaller states in the treaty-making process, but as the Big Five had agreed on this draft in the subcommittee it was adopted unanimously.[7] There was no question of a strong United States stand on the matter. The American interest, other than placating the smaller states by approving the resolution, was to make sure nothing in its wording could possibly impose any new commitments. In this the Big Five had a common interest and as a result they were able to reach agreement.

A TWENTY-YEAR PROGRAM FOR PEACE

Secretary-General Trygve Lie took the initiative in recommending to the fifth session of the Assembly a ten-point Twenty-Year Program for Peace. While advocating little that was new, Mr. Lie attempted to outline in a unified, coherent fashion the various avenues through which the United Nations might work toward a stable peace. With the exception of the communist states the fifth Assembly accorded the Secretary-General a sympathetic hearing and commended the program to appropriate organs of the United Nations for further study.[8] At the sixth session the question was once again considered in plenary meeting. A draft essentially the same as the resolution adopted at the previous session was approved by another lopsided vote of 45-5.[9] Although the United States supported the Assembly action in both sessions, the unity

[5] Document A/662/Rev.1.

[6] In addition to the Mexican draft a French proposal, document A/C.1/342, and a Soviet text, document A/C.1/343, had been submitted.

[7] Resolution 190 (III). See *First Committee*, 3rd sess., 1st pt. (1948), pp. 222-37, and *Plenary Meetings*, 3rd sess., 1st pt. (1948), p. 373.

[8] Resolution 494 (V). The vote was 51-5-1. *Plenary Meetings*, 5th sess. (1950), p. 495. Lie's ten points included (1) the inauguration of periodic meetings of the Security Council attended if possible by the heads of governments; (2) international control of atomic energy; (3) regulation of armaments; (4) provision of armed forces for the use of the United Nations; (5) acceptance of the goal of universality in membership; (6) programs of technical assistance; (7) more vigorous use of the specialized agencies; (8) promotion of human rights and fundamental freedoms; (9) the peaceful advancement of colonial and semi-colonial peoples to a position of equality; and (10) development of international law.

[9] Resolution 608 (VI). *Plenary Meetings*, 6th sess. (1951), p. 434.

of the non-communist states on this issue sprang more from basic agreement on the principles involved than from any vigorous American prodding. This item was not discussed at subsequent sessions of the Assembly.

PROPAGANDA PROPOSALS

A number of questions have been pressed upon the General Assembly almost solely for propaganda purposes. Admittedly, members of the United Nations must consider any political question from the standpoint of its impact upon opinion at home and abroad. Nor can it be denied that the propaganda motive is present to some degree in questions treated in this study under other headings. However, some items are recognizable more clearly than others as instruments designed by their sponsors primarily to sway world opinion. The questions considered here are those which by their nature and the circumstances of their presentation could scarcely serve any other objective.

TROOPS OF UNITED NATIONS MEMBERS STATIONED ABROAD

In the months immediately following the end of the war the United States and other Western powers adopted a policy of rapid demobilization. Relatively large numbers of the troops remaining were maintained abroad to occupy former enemy states and to man a far-flung network of military installations in friendly countries. The Soviet Union, by contrast, retained millions of men under arms, the vast bulk of which were stationed within her own borders. Hoping to reap a propaganda harvest from this situation, the Soviet delegation presented to the first session of the Assembly a proposal that members of the United Nations make public the number of their troops currently stationed abroad.[10] The import of this maneuver was not lost upon the United States delegation, which took the position that any troop census, if census there should be, must include troops at home as well as abroad. With this object in view the United Kingdom proposed to amend the Soviet draft by requiring information on all military personnel, with an effective system of verification. When it became apparent that the British amendments had majority support, the Soviet delegation tried to expand the census to cover armaments, including atomic weapons, as well as troops. But even this was denied. In committee voting every Soviet move was defeated and every British amendment approved, with the exception of the provision for inspection and verification. This paragraph was deleted on a United States motion by a margin of six votes.[11]

---

[10] Documents A/103 and A/C.1/62. A similar proposal had previously been rejected by the Security Council.

[11] *First Committee*, 1st sess., 2nd pt. (1946), pp. 129-74. For committee voting see *ibid.*, pp. 168-74.

In plenary meeting, the committee recommendation was swamped by a deluge of amendments and sub-amendments raising anew the whole problem of disarmament and inspection. The Assembly finally took refuge in a suggestion of its president to delay the final vote until the First Committee reported on the question of disarmament which it was currently considering. The draft was sent to a subcommittee of the First Committee for further deliberation.[12] In the meantime the Assembly unanimously adopted a resolution relating to the regulation and reduction of armaments.[13] In view of this development the subcommittee recommended an entirely new text calling upon the Security Council to determine what information members of the United Nations should furnish in order to give effect to the disarmament resolution just adopted. The subcommittee draft was approved by the First Committee and adopted in plenary session by a vote of 36-6-4.[14]

PROPAGANDA OF WAR AND PEACE

During the second session of the General Assembly the Soviet Union advanced the first of its perennial war-mongering charges against the United States.[15] In the most provocative terms the Soviet representative called upon the Assembly to condemn war propaganda emanating from "certain circles" in the United States, Greece, and Turkey, and to endorse a Soviet blueprint for peace through Great Power disarmament and prohibition of atomic weapons.[16] The United States delegate responded by urging the committee to reject the Soviet draft and "go on with its work for the establishment of peace." [17] But the question was not thus shortly to be disposed of. The right of free and full debate could not be denied, and many delegations which deplored the communist charges did not regard it as politically wise to dismiss out-of-hand a principle involving opposition to war. The bitterest kind of debate, punctuated by charges and accusations covering a whole gamut of sinister activities, ran on through eight meetings of the committee. Instead of flatly rejecting the Soviet proposals the committee settled on a substitute resolution replacing specific charges with general statements which could

[12] See *Plenary Meetings,* 1st sess., 2nd pt. (1946), pp. 1062-1114.

[13] Resolution 41 (I). The final text of the draft earlier approved by the First Committee but not acted upon by the General Assembly is found in document A/203.

[14] Resolution 42 (I). See subcommittee report, document A/C.1/133; *First Committee,* 1st sess., 2nd pt. (1946), p. 314; *Plenary Meetings,* 1st sess., 2nd pt. (1946), p. 1320. The United States approved this action.

[15] Document A/BUR/86. The item was entitled "Measures to be taken against propaganda and the inciters of a new war."

[16] The Soviet delegate expounded at length upon the "threat of a new war resulting from the criminal war propaganda of a clique of magnates of the American capitalist monopolies." *First Committee,* 2nd sess. (1947), p. 179.

[17] *Ibid.,* p. 195.

offend nobody.[18] The sponsors accepted a United States amendment to single out for special condemnation "propaganda controlled by governments or their political agencies," and a second American-sponsored proviso that governmental action should be solicited only "within its constitutional limits" was adopted by the committee in a close vote of 22-17 with 14 abstaining. A third United States amendment was withdrawn when the sponsors offered a suitable compromise. As amended the draft was adopted unanimously.[19]

The Soviet Union was back in the fourth session with a proposal to condemn alleged war preparations by the governments of the United States and the United Kingdom. The nostrum was immediate prohibition of atomic weapons and strict international control of atomic energy, coupled with a Big Five "Pact for the Strengthening of Peace." Acrimonious debate proceeded as before with one significant exception: Yugoslavia, through a turn of circumstance not without irony and a certain grim humor, was caught between two stools—forced to castigate her former communist allies but unwilling to embrace the West. Taking a lesson from the 1947 experience, the United States collaborated with the British in preparing a counter-measure. The result was the "Essentials of Peace," a pretentious statement of platitudes designed to satisfy those who wished to reject Soviet charges without wavering even a hair's breadth from the principle of peace. The Soviet draft was rejected in committee by the magnificent majority of 5-52 with only Yugoslavia and Yemen abstaining, and the Assembly endorsed the "Essentials of Peace" 53-5, with a frustrated Yugoslavia the lone abstainer.[20]

Variations on the same theme were proffered by the Soviet delegation in the following session. Condemnation of war propaganda, prohibition of the atomic weapon, and the Big Five peace pact were all there. Thrown in was a Soviet proposal, previously rejected in disarmament discussions, for a one-third reduction in the armed forces of the Great Powers, and a phrase from the Stockholm Peace Appeal to brand as a "war criminal" the first nation using an atomic weapon. After lengthy discussion the Soviet draft was rejected paragraph by paragraph, but with numerous abstentions by delegations not wishing to go on record against the

---

[18] Document A/C.1/224. The draft called for the avoidance of war, the promotion of fundamental freedoms, the condemnation of propaganda which might threaten the peace or incite to aggression, and the promotion of friendly relations and peace among nations.

[19] See Resolution 110 (II); *First Committee*, 2nd sess. (1947), pp. 240-46; *Plenary Meetings*, 2nd sess. (1947), pp. 1550-52. The text of United States amendments is found in document A/C.1/228.

[20] Resolution 290 (IV). For record of voting see *Plenary Meetings*, 4th sess. (1949), p. 438, and *First Committee*, 4th sess. (1949), p. 337. The Soviet proposal is contained in document A/996.

apparently innocuous statements of principle embodied in various parts of the draft.[21] As before, the United States co-sponsored a counter-resolution with the suggestive title of "Peace through Deeds." [22] In an obvious reference to Korean hostilities the draft condemned aggression in any form, whatever the weapons, whether committed openly or by fomenting civil strife. Other provisions reaffirmed resolutions on disarmament and atomic energy previously adopted by the Assembly. With minor amendments the declaration of "Peace through Deeds" was adopted by a vote of 50-5, with Yugoslavia again a lone abstainer. A number of Soviet amendments were defeated but drew ten to fifteen abstentions in the voting.[23]

With unflagging zeal the Soviet Union forced upon the sixth session an array of "Measures to combat the threat of a new world war and to strengthen peace and friendship among the nations." The oft-rejected peace pact and disarmament proposals only slightly modified were united to fulminations against the "aggressive Atlantic bloc" and a recommendation for the withdrawal of all foreign troops from Korea. A revised version of the Soviet draft resolution, calculated further to embarrass the Western powers, contained a number of apparent concessions with regard to disarmament.[24] Wearied with the frequent restatement of platitudinous principles, the West responded with a joint Franco-Anglo-American proposal to refer the Soviet recommendations regarding disarmament and atomic weapons to the newly constituted Disarmament Commission. The joint draft was approved in committee by a vote of 53-5 with 2 abstentions and adopted 40-5-3 by a listless plenary assemblage.[25]

A similar item, same title and substance with the addition of germ warfare charges, appeared on the agenda of the seventh Assembly under the sponsorship of Poland. However, the question did not come up for discussion until a resumed meeting of the Assembly in April, 1953. The Assembly's attention was then fixed upon the break in the Korean impasse brought about by agreement upon the exchange of sick and wounded prisoners of war. Ignoring all of the communist propaganda proposals, the Assembly took hopeful cognizance of the new situation and provided for a resumption of the session should new developments

---

[21] *First Committee,* 5th sess. (1950), p. 237, and document A/C.1/595.

[22] Document A/C.1/597/Rev.1. Co-sponsors were Bolivia, France, Lebanon, Mexico, the Netherlands, the United Kingdom, and the United States.

[23] Resolution 380 (V). *Plenary Meetings,* 5th sess. (1950), p. 429.

[24] The various Soviet proposals are found in documents A/1944, A/1947, and A/C.1/698.

[25] Resolution 504 (VI). *First Committee,* 6th sess. (1951), p. 213, and *Plenary Meetings,* 6th sess. (1951), p. 379.

warrant it. The voting was unanimous for the first time since the beginning of the Korean war.[26]

When the issue was raised in the eighth session, the First Committee wearily batted it down without offering a substitute measure. Abstentions were numerous, however, and in the plenary voting twelve delegations abstained on the draft as a whole.[27] In the ninth Assembly the Czechoslovakian delegation was permitted to sponsor the propaganda-for-war proposal. Under American leadership the committee approved a ten-power amendment referring once again to earlier resolutions on the subject and urging the removal of barriers to the free exchange of information and ideas.[28] Although the previous declarations had been adopted almost unanimously, with the exception of the Soviet bloc, nine delegations on this occasion chose to abstain in plenary voting.[29]

UNITED STATES AGGRESSION

Beginning with the fifth session the Soviet Union supplemented its peace propaganda with specific charges of United States aggression and interference in the internal affairs of other states. The United States naval blockade of Formosa formed the basis for an accusation of aggression against the People's Republic of China. The charge of interference drew its substance from a rather unfortunately drafted passage in the Mutual Security Act of 1951 appropriating one hundred million dollars to assist refugees from iron curtain countries to form themselves into elements of military forces supporting NATO or "for other purposes." [30] A related question alleging United States violation of Chinese air space along the Manchurian border was raised in the fifth session.[31] On each occasion United States representatives vigorously denied the allegations and called for their rejection in terms understandably emphatic. Without exception the committee responded by sending to the plenary session a report containing no recommendation of any kind. However, the number of abstentions tended to increase from session to session. In the fifth session only three abstained on the charge of aggression in Formosa

[26] Resolution 705 (VII). *Plenary Meetings*, 7th sess. (1952), p. 710. See document A/2229 for original Polish proposal.

[27] The plenary vote was 5-39-12. *Plenary Meetings*, 8th sess. (1953), p. 344, and *First Committee*, 8th sess. (1953), p. 275. For text of draft see document A/2485/Rev.1.

[28] Document A/AC.76/L.17, sponsored by Australia, Brazil, Cuba, France, Honduras, Iraq, Pakistan, the Philippines, the United Kingdom, and the United States. Text of Czech draft is document A/AC.76/L.16.

[29] Resolution 819 (IX). *Plenary Meetings*, 9th sess. (1954), p. 473.

[30] *U.S. Statutes at Large*, vol. 65, pp. 373-74, 82nd Cong., 1st sess. See documents A/1968/Rev.1 and A/2224/Rev.1. The charge was twice made, in the fifth and the ninth sessions. See documents A/1382 and A/2756.

[31] See document A/1382.

and two with regard to the violation of Chinese air space. The allegation of interference in the internal affairs of other states won eleven abstentions when voted upon in the sixth session and fourteen the following year, principally from Arab and Asian states. When the accusation of American aggression in Formosa was exhumed in 1954 for presentation to the ninth session of the Assembly it drew eight abstentions, five more than in 1950.[32]

A similar communist complaint on the agenda of the ninth session dealt with "violation of the freedom of navigation in the area of the China seas." The charge was systematic Chinese Nationalist depredations, under the authority and protection of the United States, upon vessels bound for mainland ports.[33] There was little vocal support for the Soviet position. However, the Syrian delegation made an effort to replace specific allegations with general principles, as had been done so often in the past, by substituting a declaration on the whole regime of the high seas. Just prior to committee voting the Soviet delegate announced support of the Syrian proposal, but upon a motion of the United States, Cuba, and the Philippines, the Syrian draft was referred to the International Law Commission for further consideration. The committee recommendation was subsequently approved by the General Assembly.[34]

UNITED STATES PROPAGANDA

On occasion the United States has used the General Assembly for a counterattack on the propaganda front. To combat communist charges of germ warfare in Korea the United States turned to the seventh Assembly with the "Question of impartial investigation of charges of use by United Nations forces of bacteriological warfare." [35] The ensuing debate provided ample opportunity for refutation of the communist accusations, and the non-communist members were almost unanimous in supporting the United States request for the establishment of a commission to investigate the charges.[36] In the final General Assembly vote only

---

[32] *Plenary Meetings*, 5th sess. (1950), pp. 701, 705; 6th sess. (1951), p. 313; 7th sess. (1952), p. 696; 9th sess. (1954), p. 529.

[33] See remarks of Soviet delegate in General Assembly, *Ad Hoc Political Committee*, 9th sess. (1954), pp. 251-52, and Soviet draft resolution in document A/AC.76/L.24. Original complaint is detailed in document A/2741 and Add.1.

[34] Resolution 821 (IX). Vote in committee was 35-5-15. *Ad Hoc Political Committee*, 9th sess. (1954), pp. 271-72. Plenary vote was 39-5-14. *Plenary Meetings*, 9th sess. (1954), p. 535. Document A/AC.76/L.25 contains text of Syrian draft.

[35] See document A/2231. Security Council action to investigate the charges had been thwarted by the veto.

[36] Co-sponsors of the draft resolution, A/C.1/L.36/Rev.2, were Australia, Belgium, Canada, Colombia, Ethiopia, France, Greece, Luxembourg, the Netherlands, New Zealand, the Philippines, Thailand, Turkey, the Union of South Africa, the United Kingdom, and the United States.

Burma, India, Indonesia, and Saudi Arabia abstained.[37] At the following session the commission had nothing to report because North Korea and Communist China had refused to admit United Nations investigators. Not to miss a propaganda opportunity, the Soviet Union was ready for the item with a draft resolution calling on all states to accede to or ratify the Geneva protocol of June 17, 1925, relating to the prohibition of bacterial weapons. The United States delegation had hoped to present a resolution branding the communist accusations as lies but was deterred by the reluctance of a number of Asian and African countries to support such a measure.[38] Even though a majority could undoubtedly be obtained, a large number of abstentions would make the condemnation less than decisive. As a result the only action taken was to refer the Soviet draft on the Geneva protocol to the Disarmament Commission.[39]

The question of atrocities committed against United Nations prisoners of war in Korea, placed on the agenda of the eighth session at the request of the United States, can also be regarded as largely a propaganda maneuver. The United States decision to raise the issue came as a surprise to many delegations at the General Assembly, although other delegations were subsequently consulted with regard to the strategy for handling the item.[40] The restraining hand of cautious allies is evident in the relatively mild wording of the resolution ultimately adopted.[41] Without passing judgment upon Red China and North Korea, the draft expressed "grave concern" at the reports of atrocities and reserved its condemnation for "any governments or authorities" committing atrocities against prisoners of war or civilian populations. Even this watered-down draft drew ten abstentions from Arab and Asian states.[42]

---

[37] Resolution 706 (VII). *Plenary Meetings*, 7th sess. (1952), p. 716.

The Soviet Union subsequently presented countercharges alleging the "mass murder of Korean and Chinese prisoners of war by United States military authorities on the island of Pongam." After discussion the Soviet complaint was rejected by the Assembly without reference to a committee. Voting was 45-5 with 10 abstentions. *Ibid.*, p. 530, and document A/2355.

[38] New York *Times*, Oct. 29, 1953, p. 15.

[39] Resolution 714 (VIII). Plenary voting was 47-0-13. *Plenary Meetings*, 8th sess. (1953), p. 279. See document A/C.1/L.67 for Soviet draft.

[40] New York *Times*, Oct. 31, 1953, p. 1, and Nov. 1, 1953, p. 4. According to Thomas J. Hamilton, the announcement of the decision without consulting allies sprang from lack of coordination between the Defense and State Departments. The report of atrocities released by the Defense Department to the press appeared in the morning papers of October 29. As the narrative runs, "By noon there was a rising chorus of Senators and Representatives demanding that the United States do something about it in the General Assembly. Mr. Lodge himself requested the State Department for permission to place this item on the agenda of the Assembly that same afternoon." Having received permission, Lodge acted without consulting others because the need for speed was felt to be so great. *Ibid.*, Nov. 6, 1953, p. 6.

[41] Document A/L.169, sponsored by Australia, France, Turkey, the United Kingdom, and the United States. Cf. the original complaint, document A/2531.

[42] Resolution 804 (VIII). The final vote was 42-5-10. *Plenary Meetings*, 8th sess. (1953), pp. 417-18. There was no referral of the item to a committee.

DISPUTES AND IRRITATING SITUATIONS

THE SPANISH QUESTION

One of the thorniest problems to confront the United Nations through-out its early years was the question of Spain.[43] The end of World War II found a natural reluctance among most of the United Nations to embrace a former Axis collaborator. Fascism so lately crushed in Germany and Italy was still blatantly proclaimed in Spain. Cooperation with an openly avowed dictatorship posed a moral issue to many states. Mutual animosity, rooted in both idealogy and recent history, created an impassable gulf between Franco Spain and Communist Russia. On the other hand forces were working to meliorate the Spanish position. The common cultural, religious, and linguistic heritage of Spain and Latin America weighed heavily in Franco's favor upon some American states, though not at all upon others. Likewise, the increasing realization that exorcism was not enough to unseat the Franco regime was a growing factor. Short of forcible intervention in Spain, which almost no one but the Communists desired, the only reasonable alternative was to establish some modus vivendi. More important still, cold war developments gave Spain great strategic value to the West. War-nurtured antipathies ran deep, but time and circumstance conspired with Franco.

Anti-Franco sentiment found official expression as early as the San Francisco Conference. Caught up in the flush of victory over German and Italian fascism, the conference by acclamation approved a Mexican-sponsored declaration that membership in the organization should be barred to "states whose regimes have been established with the help of military forces belonging to the countries which have waged war against the United Nations, as long as those regimes are in power." [44] At Potsdam these sentiments were echoed in a pronouncement that the Spanish government did not possess the necessary requirements for admission to the United Nations. When the General Assembly met for the first time in January, 1946, the question of Franco Spain still rankled severely. Acting upon a Panamanian motion, the Assembly put its official seal upon the San Francisco and Potsdam pronouncements with a recommendation that members "act in accordance with the letter and the spirit of these statements in the conduct of their future relations with Spain." [45]

[43] An excellent review of the whole history of United Nations action with regard to Spain is found in John A. Houston, "The United Nations and Spain," *Journal of Politics*, vol. 14 (Nov., 1952), pp. 683-709.

[44] *Documents of the United Nations Conference on International Organization, San Francisco, 1945*, vol. 6, pp. 127, 136. The United States delegation was in complete accord with this declaration. *Ibid.*, p. 135.

[45] Resolution 32 (I). The voting was 46-2, El Salvador and Nicaragua voting in the negative. *Plenary Meetings*, 1st sess., 1st pt. (1946), p. 361. See also Article 9, *Protocol of Proceedings of the Berlin Conference, July 17-August 2, 1945* (Potsdam Declaration).

During the interim between the two parts of the first session the Security Council took the problem under consideration but was unable to find any affirmative course of action upon which the Soviet Union and the West could agree. The question was again brought to the General Assembly when it reconvened in November. In the First Committee the Polish delegation offered a resolution calling for severance of diplomatic relations and the exclusion of the Franco government from all United Nations organs. A Byelorussian amendment went beyond this to demand a break in economic as well as diplomatic relations, including all forms of communication. The United States delegation countered with a much weaker draft recommending only the exclusion of Spain from participation in the activities of the United Nations until the Spanish people should choose an acceptable form of government. The American delegation felt that the situation in Spain was not a direct threat to the maintenance of peace, and the severance of relations would only further burden the Spanish people without unseating Franco.[46] In the hope of reaching agreement the First Committee established a subcommittee to consider the numerous conflicting proposals which had been submitted. When the resulting subcommittee draft was put to a vote the American delegate spearheaded an unsuccessful effort to delete a recommendation for breaking off diplomatic contact with Spain and to nullify a provision for the Security Council to take action if the Spanish government should fail to be democratized within a reasonable period of time.[47] At the last minute the committee accepted a compromise calling only for withdrawal of Chiefs of Mission instead of a complete severance of diplomatic relations. The United States abstained in the voting on this amendment and on the draft as a whole.[48] Yielding to considerations of harmony and the greatest possible unanimity, the American delegation switched to the affirmative in plenary voting. The resolution was adopted 34-6 with 13 abstentions, six Latin-American states voting in the negative.[49]

In subsequent consideration of the question the United States position became one of increasing embarrassment. At one extreme position the Communists demanded more vigorous measures, while at the other a number of Latin-American states which had failed to withdraw their ambassadors from Spain opposed even a reopening of discussion. The United States government was in the delicate situation of not wishing to

---

[46] *First Committee*, 1st sess., 2nd pt. (1946), pp. 239-40. Documents A/C.1/24, A/C.1/35 and Corr.1, and A/C.1/100 contain Polish, Byelorussian, and United States drafts, respectively.

[47] See document A/C.1/128. The voting on these two paragraphs was 22-22-6 and 26-8-16. *First Committee*, 1st sess., 2nd pt. (1946), pp. 300, 302.

[48] *Ibid.*, pp. 303, 304. Vote on the whole was 23-4-20.

[49] Resolution 39 (I). *Ibid.*, p. 1222. Note comments of U.S. delegate, *Plenary Meetings*, 1st sess., 2nd pt. (1946), pp. 1217-18.

ostracize Spain further, yet desiring not to appear as a Franco apologist. In debate during the second session the American representative straddled the fence nicely by expressing utter distaste for the Franco regime while firmly opposing any measure involving economic sanctions or a change of regime by violence.[50] The drafting subcommittee, so omnipresent in earlier sessions of the Assembly as a device for the attempted reconciliation of conflicting proposals, was again resorted to. A compromise draft produced by the subcommittee merely reaffirmed the previous year's resolution and left the Security Council to decide upon the timing and nature of any action deemed desirable.[51] Even this was too strong for the United States delegation, which took the position that calling again upon the Spanish people to overthrow their government would serve only to consolidate Franco's domestic position. The United States representative in the First Committee further recalled that his government had never favored the recommendation in the 1946 resolution for the Security Council to take action if the Franco regime persisted. In committee the statement of reaffirmation was approved 30-14-11 over American protest, but the change of a few crucial votes left the provision just short of a two-thirds majority in plenary voting. The United States then joined the majority in approving the emasculated resolution.[52]

By the spring of 1949, when the question was next considered, a sharp reversal of sentiment was evident. A joint draft of Bolivia, Brazil, Colombia, and Peru to remove the diplomatic ban missed adoption only by invocation of the two-thirds rule.[53] The United States delegate abstained in the voting. Officially the American delegation took the stand that there were no new facts to justify the restatement of past declarations or to require fresh action. The delegation was willing, however, to sanction Spanish participation in the work of the specialized agencies of the United Nations.[54]

[50] *First Committee*, 2nd sess. (1947), p. 412.

[51] Document A/C.1/265. Members of the subcommittee were Belgium, Cuba, Guatemala, India, Luxembourg, Mexico, the Netherlands, Panama, Poland, Uruguay, and Yugoslavia.

[52] Resolution 114 (II). The final vote was 36-5-12. *Plenary Meetings*, 2nd sess., p. 1096. Argentina, Costa Rica, the Dominican Republic, El Salvador, and Peru again opposed. Plenary vote on the stronger proposal was 29-16-8, a majority but not two-thirds. *Ibid.*, pp. 1095-96. For U.S. position and committee voting see *First Committee*, 2nd sess. (1947), pp. 427, 430.

[53] Document A/925. The plenary vote was 26-15-16. *Plenary Meetings*, 3rd sess., 2nd pt. (1948-49), p. 501.

[54] *First Committee*, 3rd sess., 2nd pt. (1948-49), pp. 212-14.
Reports that the United States delegation was clandestinely seeking votes for the Latin-American draft were emphatically denied by a delegation spokesman who asserted that "our delegation has not taken an active part in the proceedings and does not intend to." New York *Times*, May 10, 1949, p. 20.
Unofficially, members of the American delegation and the State Department were

Some eighteen months later when the question appeared for a fifth and last time upon the Assembly agenda, American reluctance to repudiate the Assembly's original course of action had disappeared.[55] This time a move to grant members freedom of action in their diplomatic relations with Spain and open the door to Spanish participation in the work of the specialized agencies received warm support from the United States. The communist delegations gnashed their teeth; Mexico, Guatemala and Uruguay mourned; and a number of states voiced misgivings at this retreat from principle. But strong United States advocacy assured adoption by the adequate if not overwhelming margin of 38-10 with 12 abstentions.[56]

THE GREEK QUESTION

The presence of British troops in Greece at the end of the war staved off the immediate threat of communist domination. But a strong guerrilla movement, aided by the communist states bordering Greece, posed an increasingly potent threat to the stability of the Greek government. A Security Council investigation undertaken at the request of the Greek authorities substantiated the charges of border violation on the part of Albania, Bulgaria, and Yugoslavia, but a remedy was forestalled by lack of cooperation from the offending Balkan states and invocation of the Soviet veto in the Security Council. Following a pattern not then so familiar as it was soon to become, the United States carried the problem to the General Assembly.[57] There the United States delegation called for censure of the three communist states and the establishment of a

---

reported at odds on the issue of diplomatic relations. According to the report some officials of the Department were said to be sympathetic to the removal of the diplomatic ban but were prevailed upon by dissenters within the delegation to accept abstention. See Olive Holmes, "U.S. Hedges on Action Against Franco," *Foreign Policy Bulletin*, vol. 26 (Dec. 13, 1946), p. 3.

[55] Early in 1950 Secretary of State Dean Acheson laid down the lines of a new policy toward Spain. In a letter of January 18, 1950, to Senator Tom Connally, chairman of the Senate Foreign Relations Committee, Secretary Acheson termed the withdrawal of ambassadors a "mistaken departure from established principle" and declared that the United States was prepared to vote for a resolution leaving members of the United Nations free to send an ambassador or minister to Spain if they should choose. Text reproduced in *Department of State Bulletin*, vol. 22 (Jan. 30, 1950), pp. 156-59.

[56] Resolution 386 (V). *Plenary Meetings*, 5th sess. (1950), p. 381.

It is of more than passing interest to note that the Spanish triumph was complete with the unanimous acceptance of Spain as a member of the United Nations in December, 1955, along with fifteen other nations. Events of the tenth session, however, are beyond the period of this study.

[57] A brief summary of events preceding submission of the problem to the Assembly is found in *First Committee*, 2nd sess. (1947), pp. 12-15. For an excellent detailed review of both Security Council action and General Assembly proceedings during the second session see Harry N. Howard, "The General Assembly and the Problem of Greece," *Department of State Bulletin*, supplement, vol. 17 (Dec. 7, 1947), pp. 1097-1147.

special Balkan commission to assist in the peaceful settlement of differences. When a number of delegations showed reluctance to pass such a strong judgment, the United States representative offered to omit the condemnatory phrases if all of the governments concerned would agree to cooperate with the special Balkan commission. No such assent was forthcoming from the three communist states but the United States delegation nevertheless found it politic to accept a modified draft which took note of the findings of the Security Council Commission of Investigation without necessarily implying censure of the three communist states. Except for this amendment the United States proposal was adopted essentially in the form in which it was introduced.[58]

The reports of the United Nations Special Commission on the Balkans (UNSCOB) to the third Assembly confirmed the finding of the earlier Security Council investigatory commission that Yugoslavia, Albania, and Bulgaria were illegally aiding communist guerrillas in Greece. Because of the non-cooperation of the communist states, however, the commission was unable to carry out its mandate to assist in a settlement of the dispute.[59] Buttressed by the factual findings of UNSCOB, the United States, together with China, France and Britain, encountered little difficulty in pushing through the Assembly a draft resolution containing a clear implication of censure and continuing UNSCOB as an observation group for another year. Only the six communist members voted in the negative, and there were no abstentions. At the same time the Assembly adopted the remnant of a contentious Soviet draft reduced by amendment to a plea for the re-establishment of diplomatic relations and a negotiated settlement of questions at issue. A third resolution called for the return of Greek children taken from their homes in Greece and sequestered in the satellite countries—an aspect of the Greek problem which was to demand increasing attention in subsequent Assemblies.[60]

Due to the defection of Yugoslavia from the Soviet East European bloc, UNSCOB was able to report improvement in the Greek border situation when the fourth Assembly convened.[61] The Assembly was presented with two draft resolutions, sponsored jointly by the United States, Britain, China and Australia, prescribing much the same action as in the past session. Before the First Committee could consider these proposals, several meetings were given to spirited discussion of communist resolutions demanding that the Greek government stop executing Greek

[58] Resolution 109 (II). The plenary vote was 40-6-11. *Plenary Meetings*, 2nd sess. (1947), pp. 461-62. See document A/C.1/191 for original proposal and document A/C.1/207/Corr.1 for text of amendment, sponsored by Britain and France. U.S. shifts of position are indicated *First Committee*, 2nd sess. (1947), esp. pp. 82, 108.

[59] Documents A/574, A/644, and A/692.

[60] Resolutions 193 A, B, C (III). Plenary voting on Resolution 193 A was 47-6-0. No member opposed the other two. *Plenary Meetings*, 3rd sess. (1948), p. 661.

[61] Documents A/935 and A/981.

"patriots"—communist guerrillas and collaborators—which in turn evoked debate on the desirability of abolishing capital punishment.[62] When the committee finally reached the central problem, it approved the two joint drafts—one continuing the life of UNSCOB for another year and the other calling again for repatriation of the Greek children kidnapped and illegally held in neighboring countries. With modifications the draft concerning the Greek children was adopted unanimously by the Assembly in plenary meeting. The other was approved essentially unchanged by a vote of 50-6 with 2 abstentions.[63]

During the following year the problem of guerrilla activity supported from neighboring states continued to decrease in intensity, but the Greek children, except for those held in Yugoslavia, remained unrepatriated. As in preceding sessions the fifth Assembly was compelled to debate the execution of Greek patriots and the abolition of capital punishment, after which the usual resolutions relating to UNSCOB and the return of the children were adopted.[64] A third resolution protested the forcible detention by the Communists of captured Greek military personnel.[65] The Greek question appeared again on the agenda of the sixth session, but by this time nearly all that could be done had been done. At the instance of the United States representative the United Nations Special Commission on the Balkans was discontinued with a vote of commendation, and in its stead a subcommission of the Peace Observation Commission was authorized to send observers on request of the Balkan countries concerned, without the need of further decisions by the General Assembly.[66] The Assembly also issued a final call for repatriation of the missing children.[67] Except for Yugoslavia this appeal again fell on barren ground. When the seventh Assembly convened there was no alternative but to condemn the satellite states for their failure to cooperate and suspend further activities until changed conditions might make practical action possible.[68]

[62] See, e.g., documents A/C.1/483 and A/C.1/508.

[63] Resolutions 288 A and B (IV). *Plenary Meetings*, 4th sess. (1949), p. 263. Documents A/C.1/513 and A/C.1/514/Rev.1 contain original proposals. Committee action is noted *First Committee*, 4th sess. (1949), pp. 183, 186.

[64] Resolutions 382 B and C (V). Voting on the resolutions was 53-6-0 and 50-0-5, respectively. *Plenary Meetings*, 5th sess. (1950), p. 510.

[65] Resolution 382 A (V). Voting was 53-5-1. *Ibid.*

[66] Resolution 508 (VI). Plenary voting was 48-5-1. *Plenary Meetings*, 6th sess. (1951), p. 218.
The Peace Observation Commission was established by the "Uniting for Peace" resolution, 377 (V), as a standing body to investigate and report to the Assembly on potential threats to international peace.

[67] Resolution 517 (VI). *Ibid.*, p. 488.

[68] Resolution 618 (VII). Voting was 46-5-6. *Plenary Meetings*, 7th sess. (1952), p. 389. The Greek delegation, backed by the United States, persuaded the Assembly to endorse one more effort to secure repatriation of captured Greek troops still held by the Communists. Resolution 702 (VII). The vote was 54-5. *Ibid.*, p. 554.

RIGHTS AND FREEDOMS IN EASTERN EUROPE

The spectacular trial and confession of Cardinal Mindzenty in the Hungarian courts provided the incident which catapulted the question of violated human rights and fundamental freedoms into the General Assembly. Behind this dramatic development lay a picture of communist repression in Eastern Europe which for some time had engaged the concern of the Western democracies. Although the request presented by Bolivia and Australia to the third Assembly made special reference to recent trials of church leaders in Hungary and Bulgaria, the basic issue was the whole pattern of communist seizure of power and forcible repression of human rights in the states of Eastern Europe.[69] The legal basis for action against Hungary and Bulgaria resided in the peace treaties signed at the conclusion of World War II, in which the former Axis allies had undertaken obligations to respect religious and civil liberties.[70] After lengthy debate in which the American representative assumed a vigorous role, the Assembly expressed its concern with the accusations lodged against Bulgaria and Hungary and called upon them to cooperate with the Western powers in the fulfillment of their treaty obligations. Meliorating amendments opposed by the American delegation were rejected, and the resolution was adopted 34-6 with 9 abstentions.[71]

When the problem came under review during the fourth session Rumania was included with the two states previously arraigned for violation of human rights.[72] In view of the refusal of Hungary and Bulgaria even to consider the charges against them, the prospects for a settlement were not bright. Hoping at least to bolster the legal position of the West, the American representative submitted a draft resolution requesting the International Court of Justice to give an advisory opinion as to the obligations of Bulgaria, Hungary, and Rumania to settle the current dispute through procedures laid down in the peace treaties. Verbal changes in the American text suggested by Brazil, Lebanon, and the Netherlands, and termed unobjectionable by the United States representative, were adopted with more abstentions than affirmative votes, but an Australian amendment of substance opposed by the United

---

[69] Benjamin Cohen, the American representative, made this clear in his address to the committee. *Ad Hoc Political Committee*, 3rd sess., 2nd pt. (1948-49), pp. 88-96. Complaints of Bolivia and Australia are found in documents A/820 and A/821.

[70] The United States as a treaty signatory had already protested to the Eastern European countries. See, for example, the text of notes to Rumania and Hungary reproduced in the *Department of State Bulletin,* vol. 17 (Aug. 17, 1947), pp. 329-32. Also pertinent is Isaac A. Stone, "American Support of Free Elections in Europe," *ibid.* (Aug. 17 and 31, 1947), pp. 311-23, 407-13.

[71] Resolution 272 (III). *Plenary Meetings,* 3rd sess., 2nd pt. (1948-49), pp. 272-73.

[72] Documents A/985 and Corr.1, and A/990.

States delegation was overwhelmingly rejected. The resolution was ultimately adopted 47-5.[73]

The subsequent opinion of the International Court was not too comforting to the West. In essence the court replied that Bulgaria, Hungary, and Rumania were legally bound to appoint representatives to commissions prescribed by the peace treaties for the settlement of disputes, but if they failed to do so there was legally nothing the other signatories to the treaties could do about it. Confronted at the fifth session with the court's decision, the Western powers realized that the Assembly could not gracefully prescribe further action. Accordingly the Assembly loosed a parting blast of condemnation upon the treaty violators and dropped the item from further consideration.[74]

SOVIET VIOLATION OF THE SINO-SOVIET TREATY

In the fall of 1949, when the remnants of Nationalist strength on the Chinese mainland were fast crumbling, the Nationalist delegation laid before the General Assembly an allegation of Soviet aid to the Chinese Communists in violation of the Sino-Soviet Treaty of August 14, 1945.[75] At this time United States policy with respect to China was in a state of flux. The State Department could not overlook the threat of Soviet imperialism in the Far East. Yet the recently issued China White Paper had attributed the collapse of the Nationalist regime to its own internal unsoundness.[76] And the non-communist Western nations were split on the question of recognizing the Chinese Communist regime.[77] When the item came under consideration in the First Committee, a Nationalist motion of censure encountered heavy opposition and was withdrawn. However, there was strong support for a proposal of three Latin-American states directing the Interim Committee of the General Assembly to study the question of Soviet treaty violation and report to the next session. The United States, hoping to subordinate the Nationalist complaint to more general considerations less likely to involve embarrassment for the free world, collaborated with Australia, Mexico,

---

[73] The vote was 47-5-7. *Plenary Meetings*, 4th sess. (1949), p. 150. Committee action on proposed amendments, documents A/AC.31/L.2 and A/AC.31/L.3, is found *Ad Hoc Political Committee*, 4th sess. (1949), pp. 65-66. For original American draft and comments see *ibid.*, pp. 27-29, and document A/AC.31/L.1/Rev.1.

[74] Resolution 385 (V). The vote of condemnation was 40-5-12. *Plenary Meetings*, 5th sess. (1950), p. 368. See document A/138 for court's decision.

[75] Document A/1000.

[76] *United States Relations with China, 1944-1949*, Department of State Publication 3573, Far Eastern Series 30, esp. pp. vii, x, xiii-xv.

[77] The United States delegation was hesitant to take the initiative because "it was seen that as the topic progressed there might be sharp cleavage between members of the free world, as it necessarily involved the difference between those who recognize the Communists and those who recognize the Nationalists." *The U.S. and the U.N.*, report of President to Congress (1950), p. 60.

Pakistan, and the Philippines in preparing a declaration of principles for the "Promotion of stability of international relations in the Far East." [78] At the same time the United States delegation supported Philippine amendments to the Latin-American draft which would authorize the Interim Committee to consider any threat to Far Eastern stability without specifically requiring it to discuss the charge of Soviet treaty violation. In close committee voting the Philippine amendments were rejected, and the Latin-American resolution won out over American opposition by four votes.[79] The American-sponsored draft declaration was approved overwhelmingly.[80] In plenary meeting the Latin-American resolution obviously could not command the necessary two-thirds majority. Bowing to the inevitable, its supporters accepted a Cuban amendment designed to do almost precisely what the Philippine amendments in the committee would have accomplished. The United States, having won its point, voted with the majority in approving the amended draft.[81]

Despite the repeated urgings of the Chinese representative, the Interim Committee postponed discussion of the Far Eastern question until September 15, 1950. Since the opening of the fifth session was then only a few days away, the committee decided to reserve debate for the General Assembly.[82] At this session the United States delegation was more bellicose but the Chinese were more moderate in their demands. They asked only for the appointment of a United Nations commission of inquiry to gather facts and report to the sixth session. Even with United States support the proposal met determined opposition. A number of delegations felt that the proposed inquiry would tend further to embitter the situation by culling over facts already well known. Others, while opposed to the creation of a new investigatory body, were willing to support a Syrian draft referring the question once again to the Interim

[78] Document A/C.1/552. With the customary obeisance to the Charter the draft called on all states to respect the political independence of China; to respect the right of the Chinese people to choose freely their own political institutions and establish a government independent of foreign control; to respect existing treaties with China; and to refrain from seeking spheres of influence and special privileges or from setting up foreign-controlled regimes.

Documents A/C.1/551 and A/C.1/553 contain the respective Chinese and Latin-American drafts.

[79] Voting on the Philippine amendments, document A/C.1/554, was 19-24-14 and 15-25-17. The Philippine delegation had no doubt collaborated closely with the United States delegation in the preparation of the amendments. On the Latin-American draft as a whole the vote was 23-19-14. *First Committee*, 4th sess. (1949), pp. 370-71. Fourteen Latin-American states voted with the majority and the Soviet bloc joined the United States in opposing the measure.

[80] Resolution 291 (IV). The vote in committee was 47-5-5 and in plenary meeting 45-5-0. *Ibid.*, p. 372, and *Plenary Meetings*, 4th sess. (1949), p. 571.

[81] Resolution 292 (IV). Voting on the Cuban amendment, document A/1221, was 33-5-14, and on the draft as a whole, 32-5-17. *Ibid.*

[82] Documents A/AC.18/SR.36—SR.45.

Committee. Bending with the wind the American delegation expressed its willingness to settle for the Syrian proposal. On the strength of twenty Latin-American votes the measure received a bare two-thirds majority.[83] With a somewhat greater show of unanimity, the Assembly reaffirmed the declaration of the preceding session on the "Promotion of stability of international relations in the Far East." [84]

The Interim Committee was unable to meet before the opening of the next session because the fifth Assembly was in continuous session throughout the year. The Chinese complaint was inscribed on the agenda of the sixth Assembly. By this time the question had become a source of extreme embarrassment to the West. Lack of unity among the Western nations made it imperative that the Assembly issue some final pronouncement and be rid of the question. Accordingly the Chinese delegation proposed a draft resolution expressing the sentiment of the Assembly that the Soviet Union had violated the terms of its treaty with China. This being a little too harsh for many delegations to accept, a Thai amendment replaced the word "violated" with the expression "failed to carry out." With this modification, and strong United States support, the resolution managed to carry by the inconclusive margin of 25-9 with 24 abstentions. Voting with the United States and China were sixteen Latin-American states, Greece, Iraq, Lebanon, Liberia, the Philippines, Thailand, and Turkey.[85]

A YUGOSLAV COMPLAINT

In 1951 the cold war between Yugoslavia and the Soviet Union found its way into the General Assembly through a Yugoslav complaint of "aggressive pressures" and enumeration of "hostile activities" on the part of the Soviet Union and her Eastern European satellites.[86] The United States representative in the Ad Hoc Political Committee strongly endorsed the Yugoslav protest and urged adoption of a resolution calling for abatement of the situation. Rising to the occasion the Assembly voiced its disquietude, noted Yugoslavia's declared willingness to comply with a recommendation of the Assembly, and admonished all parties concerned to conform in their mutual relations to the accepted practices of diplo-

---

[83] Resolution 383 A (V). The vote was 35-17-7. *Plenary Meetings,* 5th sess. (1950), p. 519. The original Syrian draft and the sidetracked Chinese draft are documents A/C.1/632 and A/C.1/631/Rev.1, respectively. For comments of American representative see *First Committee,* 5th sess. (1950), pp. 349-50, 363.

[84] Resolution 383 B (V). Voting was 39-6-14. *Ibid.*

[85] Resolution 505 (VI). *Plenary Meetings,* 6th sess. (1951), p. 455. Documents A/C.1/711 and A/C.1/715 contain the Chinese draft and Thai amendments.

[86] Document A/1946. The indictment included the establishment of an economic blockade, incitement of revolt, organization of subversive and terroristic activities, diplomatic discrimination, unilateral abrogation of agreements, and the increasing of military forces beyond treaty limits.

matic intercourse and settle their differences peacefully. Only the Soviet bloc dissented.[87]

ALL-GERMAN ELECTIONS

The question of holding free elections in Germany was placed before the sixth session of the General Assembly as the Western response to a heightened communist campaign for German unity. In November of the preceding year the East German government had submitted to the government of the Federal Republic of Germany a new proposal for the unification of Germany and the drafting of a peace treaty. The offer was renewed in September, 1951, by an East German appeal for consultations on the holding of all-German elections. In reply the West German parliament set forth its own proposals for the unification of Germany, which included the establishment of a neutral international commission to determine whether free elections were possible under existing conditions. Pursuant to this declaration the West German Chancellor requested that the Allied High Commission for Germany submit the matter to the General Assembly.[88]

In the Ad Hoc Political Committee the representatives of Britain, France, and the United States tendered a draft resolution to create the desired investigatory commission, which, with amendments suggested by friendly delegations, was subsequently adopted by the Assembly.[89] Throughout the debate the Soviet delegation disputed the authority of the United Nations to act on the matter, maintaining that such an investigation should be by the German people themselves under supervision of the four occupying powers.[90] No practical results were obtained through the resolution since the communist-controlled areas refused entry to the investigatory commission.

AN AUSTRIAN TREATY

The conclusion of an Austrian peace treaty, unaccomplished despite virtual agreement among the Great Powers on the principles of a settlement, was made an issue in the seventh session by Mexico and Brazil.[91] Although related in spirit to the Mexican "Appeal to the great powers" in the third session, the move coincided with efforts of the West outside

[87] Resolution 509 (VI). The plenary vote was 47-5-2. *Plenary Meetings,* 6th sess. (1951), p. 274. The U.S. position is stated *Ad Hoc Political Committee,* 6th sess. (1951), pp. 52-54.

[88] See document A/1938.

[89] Resolution 510 (VI). In the final voting Israel joined the five communist states in opposing the resolution, and eight nations abstained. *Plenary Meetings,* 6th sess. (1951), p. 287. Israel opposed the measure for reasons stemming from anti-Nazi sentiment. See *ibid.,* pp. 287-88.

[90] See, e.g., *Ad Hoc Political Committee,* 6th sess. (1951), p. 82.

[91] Documents A/2160, and A/2166 and Add.1.

the United Nations to achieve an Austrian settlement and was made with the blessing of the United States if not, as alleged by the Soviet representative, its connivance. When the draft proposal on Austria came under discussion the United States delegate took occasion to deliver a spirited defense of the Western position. The draft itself was quite innocuous. It merely took note of the Moscow Declaration of November 1, 1943, and the "Appeal to the great powers" as having present applicability, and called for an early Austrian settlement as a step toward the solution of other problems contributing to international tension. With the Soviet bloc refusing to participate in the voting, the resolution was adopted without dissent.[92]

CHINESE NATIONALIST AGGRESSION IN BURMA

The delegation of Burma appeared before the seventh Assembly to protest the aggressive activities of some twelve thousand Chinese Nationalist troops which had taken refuge in Burma from the Chinese Communist armies. Refusing internment, the Nationalist forces had established a military headquarters near the Burma-Thailand border and constituted a constant threat to Burma's peace and security. Acting on the assumption that the Chinese forces in Burma maintained close contact with the Kuomintang government on Formosa, the Burmese government had enlisted the good offices of the United States to obtain their withdrawal or internment. When these efforts over a period of two years proved ineffectual, Burma asked the Assembly to condemn the Kuomintang government and take action to end Nationalist aggression in Burma.[93] In committee discussion the American delegate took the position that the troops ought to be withdrawn—the United States was even then working on a solution involving troop withdrawal—but the Burmese draft would scarcely be conducive to an agreement. Calmer counsels prevailed and Burma reluctantly settled for a proposal approved by the United States, which, after much amendment and revision, condemned the presence of hostile troops in Burma and advocated their withdrawal but imputed no guilt to the Formosa government. The resolution was approved with but a single abstention.[94]

At the following session Burma reported no improvement in the situation. Early in the year representatives of Burma, China, Thailand, and the United States had met at Bangkok in a Joint Military Committee to

[92] Resolution 613 (VII). Afghanistan and Pakistan abstained. *Plenary Meetings,* 7th sess. (1952), p. 455. For Soviet and U.S. comments see *First Committee,* 7th sess. (1952), pp. 321-22, 331-32. The question did not again come before the Assembly. Agreement on a treaty was finally achieved in the spring of 1955.

[93] Documents A/2375 and A/C.1/L.42.

[94] Resolution 707 (VII). *Plenary Meetings,* 7th sess. (1952-53), p. 718. See U.S. comments, *First Committee,* 7th sess. (1952), p. 673.

consider the possibilities for troop withdrawal, but Burma later withdrew in dissatisfaction with the lack of progress. Before the end of the eighth Assembly, however, the Joint Military Committee, acting without Burma, was able to complete arrangements for the evacuation of about two thousand of the twelve thousand Chinese irregulars. Although the Burmese delegation continued to grumble, the Assembly was pleased to commend the progress which had been made and urged continued efforts "on the part of those concerned" in the spirit of the previous year's resolution. As before, the resolution was adopted without objection and with but one abstention.[95] The United States had hoped to confer United Nations status upon the Joint Military Committee by directly naming it in the resolution, but settled for an oblique reference to the committee's activities and reports.[96]

At the end of another year the Burmese delegation was able to report that nearly half of the Kuomintang troops had been evacuated and their principal bases restored to control of Burma. Upon completion of this stage of the evacuation, the Nationalist government announced that all the forces within its effective command had been withdrawn. The activities of the Joint Military Committee thereupon ceased, and Burma and Thailand were left to make arrangements for the disposal of the troops remaining. Taking note of the improved situation, the Assembly adopted a draft resolution once more assuring Burma of its full moral support. The United States delegation supported the draft without reservation.[97]

THE AMERICAN AIRMEN

Perhaps the most dramatic question considered by the ninth session of the General Assembly was that of the eleven American airmen detained by Communist China in violation of the Korean Armistice Agreement. The men were the crew of a B-29 bomber shot down in January, 1953, in the course of Korean hostilities. Their fate suddenly became an explosive international issue when on November 24, 1954, the Peking government announced that the men were alive and serving sentences in China for espionage. The announcement raised a storm of protest in the United States and led to a complaint in the General Assembly that the Chinese had violated the provisions of the Armistice Agreement relating to repatriation of prisoners of war.[98] The question was debated

[95] Resolution 717 (VIII). *Plenary Meetings*, 8th sess. (1953), p. 449. For report of interim developments see documents A/2468 and A/C.1/L.69.

[96] Cf. documents A/C.1/L.92 and A/C.1/L.92/Rev.1.

[97] *Plenary Meetings*, 9th sess. (1954), p. 265. The voting was without dissent or abstention, but China did not cast a vote. For statement of United States delegate see *Ad Hoc Political Committee*, 9th sess. (1954), p. 16. Burmese report and record of developments between eighth and ninth sessions are found in documents A/2739 and A/2740.

[98] Documents A/2830 and A/2843.

in the Assembly without reference to a committee, in this case an indication of the urgency with which the United States regarded the matter. After three days of acrimonious debate the Assembly adopted an American draft condemning the Chinese action and requesting the Secretary-General to seek the release of the prisoners "by the means most appropriate in his judgment." The vote was 47-5 with 7 abstentions.[99]

SUMMARY

The questions treated in the preceding pages were for the most part decided in a manner acceptable to the United States. In all but one instance the American delegation was with the majority in the final plenary voting. The one exception was an abstention on the Spanish question during the third session. However, nearly every question on which the United States took a strong position required some degree of compromise. And on one or two occasions the United States abstained or voted against parts of a resolution which it supported as a whole. If the broad outlines of the resolutions were conformable to American policies, the details were shaped to meet the demands of other states. Not all questions, of course, were of particular and vital interest to the United States. Questions considered under the heading of international cooperation, most of which were raised by small powers and eventuated in a unanimous decision, did not evoke strong exertion of American influence. Of these only the Secretary-General's Twenty-Year Program for Peace involved a strong clash of interests. Even there the noncommunist unanimity appears to have been largely spontaneous.

The United States had an understandably deep interest in the various propaganda proposals, since they either originated with the United States or were directed against it. The American delegation uniformly voted with a large majority, whether in rejecting Soviet charges or adopting counter-resolutions. However, plans for a strong denunciation of the communist germ warfare charges, contemplated during the eighth session, were abandoned when preliminary soundings indicated the lack of a sufficiently impressive majority. In the second session, too, the United States received something of a rebuff when the Assembly chose to adopt a substitute resolution instead of simply rejecting the Soviet proposals as the American representative had asked. This experience led the United States to initiate its own counter-propaganda measures in following years.

---

[99] Resolution 906 (IX). *Plenary Meetings,* 9th sess. (1954), p. 442. Representatives of Costa Rica, El Salvador, and Syria, unavoidably detained elsewhere at the time of the Assembly vote, later made a special request that their votes on the resolution be recorded, the first two in the affirmative and Syria abstaining. *Ibid.,* p. 462.

The United States assumed a role of active leadership in the consideration of questions arising from international disputes and irritating situations, three of which—the questions of Greece, German elections, and the imprisoned airmen—were originally placed on the agenda at American request. Heavy opposition was occasionally encountered in this area. In the early debates on the Spanish question the United States voted with the minority time and time again in an effort to secure sufficiently moderate resolutions. Support of the December, 1946, resolution came with great reluctance, following an original abstention in committee. At the second session the United States obtained a satisfactory resolution on the Spanish question only because the two-thirds rule prevented the incorporation of certain objectionable provisions favored by a majority. It was not until the fifth session that the United States spearheaded a movement to lift the diplomatic ban which it had so hesitantly approved in the first session. Defeat was also met in skirmishes over the Chinese Nationalist complaint of Soviet treaty violation. No final vote was lost, but proposals were weakened by amendment and majorities were relatively small. To emphasize opposition and concession, however, is to distort the picture. Despite occasional setbacks the American record on this category of questions is impressive indeed. Except for the instances specifically mentioned, the Assembly adopted resolutions conforming to United States policy in important respects.

CHAPTER SEVEN

Disarmament and Collective Security

DISARMAMENT AND ATOMIC ENERGY CONTROL

Nearly every session of the General Assembly has grappled with disarmament and atomic energy control,[1] and the elusiveness of a solution has in no way diminished concern with these questions. During the first Assembly the Great Powers reached agreement on both. In the case of atomic energy this was the result of prior agreement. At the Moscow Conference in December, 1945, the United Kingdom, Soviet Russia, and the United States had decided upon the text of a resolution dealing with atomic energy to be submitted to the Assembly when it convened the following month.[2] The draft provided for the establishment of an Atomic Energy Commission accountable to the Security Council and authorized to study methods for the control of atomic energy and the elimination of atomic weapons from national armaments. Its membership was to be the same as the Security Council, with an additional permanent seat for Canada. Although the smaller powers posed a number of objections, amendment of the Great Power text was futile. In what was as much a gesture of faith as of unanimity, the Assembly adopted the draft without a dissenting vote.[3]

No such prior Great Power agreement had been reached concerning disarmament. When the question came under discussion in the second part of the session, the Soviet Union, which had no atomic bombs, produced a disarmament program aimed primarily at the United States supply of atomic weapons. The United States, while recognizing the need to regulate atomic weapons, stressed the importance of controlling troop levels and other weapons of mass destruction as well. The role of the Security Council was another bone of contention. The United States insisted that the functions of inspection and regulation were to

[1] The second session is the only exception.

[2] Subsequently Canada, China, and France were invited to join in sponsorship of the measure. See *First Committee*, 1st sess., 1st pt. (1946), p. 7.

[3] Resolution 1 (I). *Plenary Meetings*, 1st sess., 1st pt. (1946), p. 267. The New York *Times* commented, "Thus one of the most complex and difficult questions before the Allied coalition passed through all stages of the General Assembly without even a serious attempt to analyze what it meant. The general attitude of the Assembly was that members could not change it without antagonizing the powers that controlled the atomic secrets, so they did not try." Jan. 25, 1946, p. 1. See also committee discussions, *First Committee*, 1st sess., 1st pt. (1946), pp. 6-13.

be performed by a body not subject to the Great Power veto, whereas the Soviet delegate contended that any control system must be subject to the Security Council with its unanimity rule.[4] A drafting subcommittee was called into action. In 1946 there was still room for compromise and an acceptable formula was found: plans for disarmament would embrace all major weapons but give special consideration to atomic armaments. Agreement was also obtained, at least on the verbal level, with regard to the Security Council. The organs of inspection and control were to be established "within the framework of the Security Council" but would "derive their powers and status from the convention or conventions under which they are established." The General Assembly adopted the draft unanimously.[5]

At the first meeting of the Atomic Energy Commission the United States presented the so-called "Baruch plan," the key feature of which was the establishment of an international atomic energy authority to own and control all fissionable materials in dangerous amounts. The control system, with appropriate licensing and inspection, was to become operative by stages, culminating in the disposal of all existing atomic bombs and the discontinuance of their manufacture when the program was in full operation. A rival Soviet proposal offered a much simpler alternative: destruction of all atomic bombs within three months and the negotiation of a draft convention as the first step toward international control of atomic energy. The United States plan was approved by the Atomic Energy Commission, vetoed in the Security Council, and brought to the third session of the General Assembly. In consequence of the impasse the commission had suspended its activities.[6]

In the First Committee the United States representative took the lead in defending the Atomic Energy Commission report and urged adoption of a Canadian draft embodying the essentials of the Baruch plan. The Soviet Union, which had advanced a step from its position in the Atomic Energy Commission, now suggested that the Security Council and the commission prepare a plan under which international control of atomic energy and prohibition of atomic weapons would take effect simultaneously. The two drafts, along with other proposals which had been submitted, were referred to a drafting subcommittee, but the day of compromise on basic issues was past. The subcommittee reported out a modified form of the Canadian draft, endorsing the Atomic Energy Commission report and requesting the six permanent members to make

---

[4] Relevant Soviet and U.S. comments and proposals are found *First Committee,* 1st sess., 2nd pt. (1946), pp. 189-91, 198-99, 221-22, and documents A/BUR/42, A/C.1/ 83, and A/C.1/90 and Corr.1.

[5] Resolution 41 (I). *Plenary Meetings,* 1st sess., 2nd pt. (1946), p. 1316.

[6] For review of developments precipitating the impasse, see *First Committee,* 3rd sess., 1st pt. (1948), pp. 13-16.

an effort to reach agreement among themselves. The United States made one significant concession on the issue. It had early gone on record against reviving the activities of the full commission under existing conditions but conceded to the dominant sentiment for continuing discussions on this level. Thus amended the resolution was adopted 40-6 with 4 abstentions.[7]

Deadlock in the Security Council and its Commission for Conventional Armaments, established by the Security Council pursuant to the Assembly resolution on disarmament,[8] thrust the problem of disarmament also upon the third Assembly. The initiative in this instance came from the Soviet Union. Early in the session the Soviet delegation presented a draft resolution calling for prohibition of atomic weapons and reduction by one-third in the armed forces of the five Great Powers. After several days of debate in the First Committee a subcommittee was commissioned to seek out a basis for agreement. With the United States supporting the majority in each instance the subcommittee voted down the Soviet draft and recommended that the Security Council continue its efforts through the Commission for Conventional Armaments, giving first priority to methods for obtaining authenticated information. The recommendation was approved in committee and adopted by the Assembly with opposition only from the Soviet bloc.[9]

Neither the Atomic Energy Commission nor the six permanent members of the commission meeting privately were able to report any real progress to the fourth session.[10] Yielding to United States insistence that any substantive recommendations might inspire false hopes of a solution, the Assembly adopted a Franco-Canadian draft suggesting nothing more positive than continued consultations among the six permanent members.[11] At the same time it rejected the Soviet proposal for the simul-

[7] *Plenary Meetings*, 3rd sess., 1st pt. (1948), p. 470. Comments of U.S. delegate are found *First Committee*, 3rd sess., 1st pt. (1948), pp. 16-21, 195-96. For Canadian, Soviet, and subcommittee drafts see documents A/C.1/308, A/C.1/310, and A/C.1/333.

[8] See text of Security Council resolution creating the commission in document S/268/Rev.1. The commission, consisting of representatives of the members of the Security Council, was authorized to prepare specific proposals for regulation and reduction of armaments.

[9] Resolution 192 (III). *First Committee*, 3rd sess., 1st pt. (1948), p. 626, and *Plenary Meetings*, 3rd sess., 1st pt. (1948), p. 564. Plenary voting was 43-6-1. Document A/658 contains text of Soviet proposal. Following a customary course of action, the communist delegation resubmitted to the First Committee the proposals rejected by the subcommittee and put them up for rejection a third time in plenary meeting.

[10] Documents A/993, A/1045 and Corr.1, and A/1050. The most significant development during the year was the detonation of an atomic bomb in the U.S.S.R., dramatically announced by President Truman on September 23. *White House Press Release*, Sept. 23, 1949, reproduced in *Department of State Bulletin*, vol. 21 (Oct. 3, 1949), p. 487.

[11] Resolution 299 (IV). The vote was 49-5-3. *Plenary Meetings*, 4th sess. (1949), p. 358. For comments of U.S. representative see *Ad Hoc Political Committee*, 4th sess. (1949), pp. 194-95.

taneous institution of atomic energy control and the prohibition of atomic weapons. As with atomic energy control no agreement was in sight on the general question of disarmament. A plan for verification and publication of information relating to troops and conventional armaments, adopted by the Commission for Conventional Armaments, had been vetoed in the Security Council. Following a familiar pattern of action, France and Norway then asked the Assembly to endorse the commission's proposals and request the Security Council to struggle on with the problem of disarmament despite the lack of unanimity. The Soviet Union in turn submitted its own proposal for the submission of information on atomic weapons as well as conventional armaments. The United States delegation was not sanguine as to the prospects for effective disarmament but supported the Franco-Norwegian draft against the possibility that the Soviet attitude might change. In the usual manner the Assembly adopted the measure by a vote of 44-5 and rejected the Soviet proposal 6-39.[12]

The deadlock showed no signs of relaxing with the passage of another year. Nor was the situation improved by the Soviet decision not to participate in the discussions of the Atomic Energy Commission as long as the Nationalist representative occupied the Chinese seat. After abbreviated plenary discussion the fifth Assembly endorsed a draft, cosponsored by the United States, which recommended the appointment of a committee to study the advisability of establishing a new combined agency to better coordinate the work of the Atomic Energy Commission and the Commission for Conventional Armaments.[13] The oft-rejected Soviet proposal for simultaneous establishment of atomic energy control and atomic weapons prohibition was again voted down.

New life was infused into the twin questions of disarmament and atomic energy control during the sixth Assembly. Seizing the initiative, the United States, Britain, and France issued a public tripartite statement setting forth an all-embracing program for regulation and reduction of armaments, prohibition of atomic weapons, and atomic energy control. The one really new feature of the program, as embodied in a three-power draft resolution, was a provision for the establishment of a Disarmament Commission to supersede the Atomic Energy Commission and the Commission for Conventional Armaments. Otherwise it merely drew together in one piece the substance of previous Western proposals, unmodified in any essential by a few drafting concessions to the Soviet Union. Even the system of atomic energy control, long anathema to

---

[12] Resolution 300 (V). The vote on the Franco-Norwegian draft, document A/AC.31/L.33/Rev.2, was 44-5-5, and on the Soviet proposal, document A/AC.31/L.35, 6-39-9. *Plenary Meetings*, 4th sess. (1949), p. 522. For views of United States see *Ad Hoc Political Committee*, 4th sess. (1949), pp. 222-23.

[13] Resolution 496 (V). Voting was 47-5-3. *Plenary Meetings*, 5th sess. (1950), p. 652.

the Soviets, was commended to the Assembly as the best plan yet pro-posed.[14] Once again the question was referred to a subcommittee in the hope of a compromise solution. Unable to prepare a draft acceptable to all, the subcommittee confined itself to delimiting the areas of agree-ment and disagreement between the West and the Soviet Union.[15] While some agreement was reported, the gap still remaining was unbridgeable. The outcome in the Assembly was to be expected. With a few modifi-cations apparently designed to demonstrate that the three sponsoring powers still possessed a spirit of conciliation, the Franco-British-American proposal was adopted by a substantial majority.[16]

The reports of the Disarmament Commission to the seventh session boasted numerous proposals but no substantial agreement among the six permanent members. Under the circumstances Assembly discussion of substantive programs appeared useless. The United States joined with thirteen other powers in presenting a recommendation that the Dis-armament Commission continue its search for an acceptable plan and report to the next session of the Assembly. The fourteen-power draft reaffirmed the resolution of the previous year and praised the commission for its efforts. In a gratuitous slap at the Soviet Union it further com-mended those members of the commission whose proposals had been constructive. At the suggestion of a number of Arab states, however, the sponsors agreed to forego this ill-disguised rebuke to the U.S.S.R. As amended the draft was approved in committee with five dissenting votes and five abstentions. Communist demands that the commission be required to consider the Soviet proposals for disarmament and atomic energy control were rejected.[17] In plenary meeting the Soviet Union announced its willingness to support the draft if the Assembly would

[14] Document A/C.1/667 and tripartite statement of November 7, 1951, reproduced in document A/1943.

[15] Subcommittee report, document A/C.1/677. There were three fundamental areas of disagreement: (1) The West asked balanced reduction of armaments and armed forces, with prohibition of atomic weapons to follow the establishment of an ef-fective control system; the Soviet Union demanded a flat one-third reduction of armed might and prohibition before control. (2) The West adhered to the United Nations plan for atomic energy control, while the Soviets argued that it would in-fringe on the domestic jurisdiction of members, create a monopoly trust under American control, and permit indefinite postponement of the prohibition of atomic weapons. (3) The West insisted upon progressive disclosure of information by agreed stages and continuing verification of information reported. The Soviet Union asked for a one-shot disclosure of all relevant information, with subsequent inspection and verification to take place infrequently, preferably only for probable cause.

[16] Resolution 502 (VI). The voting was 42-5-7. *Plenary Meetings*, 6th sess. (1951), p. 295.

[17] The vote was 50-5-5 on the amended draft and 5-41-13 on the Soviet proposals. *First Committee*, 7th sess. (1952), pp. 502-3. See documents A/C.1/L.30 and A/C.1/ L.32.

strike out the commendation of the commission and omit reaffirmation of the previous year's resolution. The Assembly obliged to the extent of accepting the first amendment, but the West refused to retreat further even for the sake of unanimity. The amended draft was adopted 52-5 with 3 abstentions.[18]

The Disarmament Commission met only once during 1953 pursuant to this fresh mandate and at that time postponed discussion in the hope that the conclusion of a Korean armistice might provide an atmosphere more conducive to agreement. Consequently, debate on disarmament during the eighth session was just another re-digging of old ground. The initial Western draft, co-sponsored by the United States, merely noted the desirability of disarmament with adequate safeguards and continued the Disarmament Commission for another year. In the usual fashion the Soviet delegation moved an amendment to incorporate its own shop-worn disarmament program into the text. This forced the United States, Britain, and France to submit an amendment reiterating the principles of disarmament laid down in past Assembly resolutions. Additional modifications suggested by other delegations substantially increased the length of the draft and so softened its tone that the Soviet bloc condescended to abstain instead of voting in the negative.[19]

During the succeeding year the members of the Disarmament Commission met and disagreed. They met again in the ninth General Assembly and again disagreed. However, the sense of urgent concern in the Assembly provided a strong incentive for the Great Powers to reach unanimity on some kind of statement regarding disarmament. In this spirit the American representative in the First Committee set forth what were termed the four basic ideas animating the United States in its approach to disarmament: the desire for peace, disarmament, elimination of nuclear weapons, and a willingness to explore more than one path to disarmament. Moved by a like compulsion, the Soviet delegation announced itself ready to discuss Western proposals previously rejected in meetings of the Disarmament Commission. Debate quickly revealed that the fundamental differences so carefully delineated in the sixth session were by no means reconciled. However, through the intermediary efforts of the Canadian delegation a draft was finally pieced together which both the United States and the Soviet Union could accept without abandoning any strongly defended positions. With the two Great Powers

---

[18] Resolution 704 (VII). *Plenary Meetings,* 7th sess. (1952), p. 692. See Soviet comments, *ibid.,* p. 682, and document A/L.149.

[19] Resolution 715 (VIII). The vote was 54-0-5. *Plenary Meetings,* 8th sess. (1953), p. 331. Note original Western draft, document A/C.1/L.72, and Soviet amendments, document A/C.1/L.75 and Rev.1-Rev.3.

in accord on a disarmament resolution for the first time since 1946, unanimity was a foregone conclusion.[20]

The ninth Assembly witnessed a change of direction in the discussion of atomic energy control stemming from President Eisenhower's proposal to the eighth Assembly for international cooperation in the development of peaceful use of atomic energy. The United States came to the ninth session with a draft resolution designed to effectuate the atoms-for-peace program.[21] The two essential features of the draft were the establishment of a permanent international agency to facilitate cooperation in the development of atomic energy for peaceful uses, and the convocation of a conference to discover the fields in which development was most urgent and technically feasible. After two weeks of committee debate and extensive consultations outside committee chambers the United States and other co-sponsors produced a draft modified to take account of objections raised by other members of the Assembly, most notably India and the Soviet Union. To reassure India, the revised draft reiterated the urgency of developing atomic energy for peaceful purposes only, expressed the hope that the international agency might be established without delay, and made clear that the proposed conference was to be one of "Governments," rather than individuals or private agencies. In the hope of winning Soviet support the sponsors offered a tacit retraction of their earlier allegations of Soviet non-cooperation in the preliminary negotiations for instituting the program. At the instance of the Soviet delegation the draft was further modified to delete all reference to the future relationship of the proposed international agency to the United Nations.[22] The Soviet representatives had opposed the suggestion that it be similar to other specialized agencies, contending that the Security Council should have a greater role in its supervision. Beyond this point, however, the United States delegation refused to go, and other Soviet efforts to amend the draft were defeated. The Soviet bloc

---

[20] Resolution 808 A (IX). *Plenary Meetings*, 9th sess. (1954), p. 280. See Soviet and U.S. comments, *ibid.*, p. 136, and *First Committee*, 9th sess. (1954), p. 32. The Assembly also directed the Disarmament Commission to consider an Indian proposal for an "armaments truce" pending agreement on disarmament and to prepare a documentary statement of the present positions of the Great Powers with respect to disarmament. Voting on the two propositions was 57-1-0 and 56-0-2, respectively. *Plenary Meetings*, 9th sess. (1954), p. 280. See Resolutions 808 B (IX) and 808 C (IX). The latter directive was approved in committee by the narrow margin of 24-23 with 11 abstentions in preference to a proposal that the commission prepare an account of the various positions taken by the Great Powers throughout the entire history of disarmament debates in the United Nations. *First Committee*, 9th sess. (1954), p. 267. The United States and the Soviet Union both voted in favor of the report on present positions only.

[21] Document A/C.1/L.105 and Rev.1. For Eisenhower message see *Plenary Meetings*, 8th sess. (1953), pp. 450-52.

[22] Cf. drafts A/C.1/L.105 and A/C.1/L.105/Rev.1.

nevertheless found it possible to join with other delegations in adopting the resolution unanimously.[23]

THE KOREAN QUESTION

With the outbreak of hostilities in the summer of 1950 Korea suddenly became the focus of United Nations activity. This was, however, a culmination rather than a beginning of the Korean question. The problem had been placed upon the agenda of the General Assembly three years before at the request of the United States, when efforts to agree upon a plan for the unification of Korea through bilateral negotiations with the Soviet Union had ended in failure. At that time the United States proposed a plan for the unification of Korea involving free elections—within separate Soviet and American zones—of a Korean national assembly, organization of a government for the whole of Korea, and subsequent withdrawal of foreign troops. The responsibilities of the United Nations were to be discharged by a Temporary Commission for Korea instructed to observe the elections and offer advice to the new Korean authorities.[24] At the suggestion of India the proposal was altered to specify adult suffrage, the secret ballot, and elections on a national rather than a zonal basis. The Indians also insisted upon specific provision for the dissolution of all military or semi-military forces not included in the security forces of the new Korean government. With these modifications and others of less practical significance, the United States draft was adopted in plenary meeting by a vote of 43-0 with 6 abstentions. The communist states refused to participate in the voting.[25]

Developments in the next two years were characteristic of other United Nations attempts to mediate in areas of East-West conflict. Elections to a Korean national assembly were held in South Korea in cooperation with the Temporary Commission for Korea, but the Soviet zone refused even to grant entry to the commission. Returning the rebuff, the First Committee invited representatives of South Korea to participate in discussions of the third session but refused similar consideration to

[23] Resolution 810 (IX). *Plenary Meetings,* 9th sess. (1954), pp. 347-48. Plenary voting on the Soviet amendments was 5-43-12 and 6-36-18. See U.S. comments, *First Committee,* 9th sess. (1954), pp. 385-86.

[24] Document A/C.1/218. Before taking a decision on the American draft the First Committee engaged in a long and fruitless wrangle over a Soviet proposal to invite the elected representatives of the Korean people to participate in committee discussion of the question. Since representatives had already been chosen in North Korea but not in the South, this would have entailed postponing discussion for another year or proceeding with North Korean spokesmen only. The proposal was ultimately rejected. See *First Committee,* 2nd sess. (1947), pp. 255-81.

[25] Resolution 112 (II). *Plenary Meetings,* 2nd sess. (1947), p. 858. The Communists argued that a valid decision on the future of Korea could not be taken without consulting the elected representatives of the Korean people. *First Committee,* 2nd sess. (1947), p. 305.

the Soviet zone.[26] While the communist states fumed and protested the third Assembly adopted unmodified a proposal of the United States, Australia, and China to recognize the government of South Korea and create a United Nations commission to assist in the unification of Korea.[27] The next year witnessed a further solidification of differences in Korea and the General Assembly. The North Korean government still refused to deal with the United Nations commission, and the authorities of both parts of Korea were unwilling to cooperate in the establishment of a representative government based on the freely expressed will of the whole people. Tension existing on both sides of the thirty-eighth parallel was reflected in the fourth Assembly's mandate to the commission to watch out for developments that might eventuate in military conflict.[28] As in the preceding session the United States co-sponsored a measure to continue the United Nations Commission for Korea as a consultative and observational body. Two Guatemalan amendments of a textual nature were incorporated into the draft with American approval, but a third amendment, opposed by the United States delegation, was defeated in committee. The resolution was adopted with opposition only from the communist members.[29]

The communist invasion of South Korea on June 25, 1950, shed an entirely new light on the Korean question. What had been essentially a disagreement between the United States and the Soviet Union now became the first major challenge to the United Nations as an instrument of collective security. Absence of the Soviet representative and readiness of the United States to take immediate military action enabled the Security Council to act decisively against communist aggression. With the return of the Soviet member in August the Security Council was once more reduced to impotence by lack of Great Power unanimity, and the initiative in dealing with the Korean struggle fell to the General Assembly. When the Assembly met in the fall of 1950, early United Nations reverses had been nullified by the military developments which followed rapidly upon the surprise landing behind communist lines at Inchon. United Nations forces, apparently in full control of the situation, awaited only a signal from the General Assembly to advance north of

[26] *First Committee*, 3rd sess. (1948), p. 955. Note report of United Nations Temporary Commission for Korea, document A/575 and Adds. 1, 2, and 3, and Interim Committee report, document A/583.

[27] Resolution 195 (III). *Plenary Meetings*, 3rd sess. (1948), p. 1042. Voting was 48-6-1.

[28] Resolution 293 (IV). See document A/936.

[29] The vote was 48-6-3. *Plenary Meetings*, 4th sess. (1949), p. 130. Vote on the rejected Guatemalan amendment was 10-28-11. *Ad Hoc Political Committee*, 4th sess. (1949), pp. 24-25. Co-sponsors of the measure with the United States were Australia, China, and the Philippines.

the thirty-eighth parallel. Members of the Assembly were dazzled by the prospects for a free and unified Korea which this sudden turn of events had unexpectedly thrown up before them. Amid Soviet demands for the cessation of hostilities and immediate withdrawal of foreign troops, the Assembly adopted a program for the unification and rehabilitation of the whole of Korea under the supervision of a United Nations Commission for the Unification and Rehabilitation of Korea (UNCURK). The United States was not included among the sponsors of the resolution, which was originally drawn up by the United Kingdom, but gave the resolution its full support.[30]

The action of the Assembly proved premature. The outlook so sanguine in October took on darker tones in November and December with the mass intervention of Chinese Communist "volunteers." As the extent of the reverses became apparent, six members of the United Nations with armed forces in Korea appealed to the Security Council to take a firm stand against this new aggression. Thwarted by the Soviet veto, the same powers, with the United States in the van, placed the question of Chinese Communist intervention before the General Assembly. Even in the Assembly there was reluctance to act decisively. To many members the vindication of United Nations objectives in Korea was a small thing as against the possibility that the conflict might touch off a third world war. Recognizing though not sharing these apprehensions, the American delegation acquiesced in a number of conciliatory overtures to the Chinese Communist regime.[31] Only after efforts to negotiate a settlement proved futile was the United States able to marshal a substantial majority for a resolution finding the Peiping government guilty of aggression in Korea. When subsequent attempts to negotiate with Peiping ended in failure, the Assembly was further persuaded to endorse American demands for a limited embargo against the Chinese Communists.[32]

Events finally accomplished what words had failed to do. Battle lines in Korea became stabilized in the area of the thirty-eighth parallel with little prospect of further communist advances, and the Chinese and North Korean military authorities agreed to talk about a peaceful settle-

[30] Resolution 376 (V). The plenary vote was 47-5-7. *Plenary Meetings*, 5th sess. (1950), p. 232. Subsequently the Assembly adopted a resolution for the establishment of a United Nations Korean Reconstruction Agency (UNKRA), by a vote of 51-0-5, on the report of the Joint Second and Third Committee. See Resolution 410 (V) and *ibid.*, p. 525.

[31] See Resolution 384 (V) and documents A/C.1/643, A/C.1/645, and A/C.1/651. For a fuller account of the question of Chinese Communist intervention see Chapter Five.

[32] Resolutions 498 and 500 (V). Plenary voting was 44-7-9 and 47-0-8, with five communist members not participating in the latter vote. *Plenary Meetings*, 5th sess. (1950-51), pp. 696, 742.

ment. The sixth Assembly met while negotiations in the border town of Panmunjom were still in their early, hopeful stages. Desiring not to precipitate a debate of political issues which might hinder a settlement of military questions at Panmunjom, the United States delegate recommended postponement of discussion for the current session. The Assembly responded by overwhelmingly adopting a draft sponsored jointly by Britain, France, and the United States authorizing the Secretary-General to convene a special session if the conclusion of an armistice or other developments in Korea should make consideration of the problem desirable.[33]

There was no occasion during the ensuing year for the Secretary-General to convene a special session. At Panmunjom the negotiators finally hammered out an armistice agreement mutually acceptable in all but one important particular—the repatriation of prisoners of war. The Communists demanded full repatriation by force if necessary, while the United States insisted upon leaving each prisoner the option as to whether he would return home. On this issue the talks hung motionless when the seventh session convened. Contrary to its position of the previous year the United States now favored discussion of the Korean problem out of a conviction that the talks in Korea had reached the point of negative returns. In the preceding Assembly the United States delegation had favored postponing discussion of the Korean question in order not to hinder armistice negotiations then in progress. Convinced now that every possibility for agreement in Korea had been exhausted, it asked for an affirmation of the principle of non-forcible repatriation.[34] Twenty delegations joined the United States in sponsoring a draft resolution to this end. A number of delegations were not certain that unequivocal endorsement by the Assembly of a principle already flatly rejected by the Communists would contribute to an agreement. India proposed a substitute draft which affirmed the principle of non-forcible repatriation but provided for machinery of repatriation that might or might not operate in accordance with the principle. In the interests of greater unanimity the United States delegation agreed to accept the Indian proposal with certain amendments to assure greater impartiality and workability. In particular the United States sought binding assurance that all unrepatriated prisoners would be released unconditionally within a reasonable period of time. A second revision of the Indian draft met the minimum United States demands and was approved by the

---

[33] Resolution 507 (VI). The plenary vote was 51-5-2. *Plenary Meetings*, 6th sess. (1951-52), p. 523. See U.S. comments, *First Committee*, 6th sess. (1951-52), pp. 174, 290-91.

[34] *The U.S. and the U.N.*, report of President to Congress (1952), p. 25, and *First Committee*, 7th sess. (1952), p. 27.

Assembly in the most impressive display of free world unity since the beginning of the Korean war.[35]

When the seventh Assembly was resumed in the spring of 1953 the United States took the position that no additional resolution concerning the Korean Armistice was either necessary or desirable. However, the agreement in Korea for the exchange of sick and wounded prisoners of war created strong sentiment in favor of officially acknowledging the improved situation. Unwilling to oppose majority feelings in such a matter, the American delegation agreed to support a Brazilian proposal to take note of the encouraging developments and authorize a further resumption of the seventh session should events in Korea warrant.[36]

The Armistice Agreement was signed July 27 and the session was resumed August 17. The principal business of the Assembly was to act upon a proposal in paragraph 60 of the Armistice Agreement for a high-level political conference on Korea. Four draft resolutions lay before the Assembly when it convened.[37] The first, co-sponsored by the United States and fourteen other members with troops in Korea, set forth terms of reference for the proposed political conference. Among other things the draft provided that the United Nations should be represented at the conference by the members whose troops had fought in Korea and that each participant should be bound only by the decisions to which it agreed. A second measure, sponsored by Australia, Denmark, New Zealand, and Norway, recommended that the U.S.S.R. participate in the conference in addition to the Korean combatants. The third draft proposed the participation of India in the conference, and the fourth offered a tribute to the armed forces which had fought under the United Nations flag in Korea. With minor modifications the fifteen-power proposal relating to the political conference was adopted by a vote of 43-5. Likewise the tribute to the United Nations armed forces was endorsed 53-5.[38] By virtue of a carefully framed change of wording, the proposal

[35] Resolution 610 (VII). The plenary vote was 54-5-1, with China the only abstainer. *Plenary Meetings*, 7th sess. (1952), p. 301. Cf. original U.S. and Indian drafts, documents A/C.1/725 and A/C.1/734. For elaboration of U.S. position see *First Committee*, 7th sess. (1952), pp. 139-41; *The U.S. and the U.N.*, report of President to Congress (1952), pp. 28-31; New York *Times*, Nov. 23, 1952, pp. 1, 4.

[36] Resolution 705 (VII). This action was earlier discussed in connection with Soviet propaganda proposals. The reversal of the United States position is noted in *The U.S. and the U.N.*, report of President to Congress (1953), pp. 20-22.

At the spring meeting the Assembly appealed for continued support of the United Nations Korean Reconstruction Agency, created by the fifth session to assist in the reconstruction of war-devastated Korea. See Resolutions 410 (V), 507 (VI), and 701 (VII).

[37] Documents A/L.151, A/L.152, A/L.153, and A/L.154 and Rev.1.

[38] Resolutions 711 A and 712 (VII). *Plenary Meetings*, 7th sess. (1952-53), pp. 735, 749. The Assembly also voted to send records of the resumed session to the governments of Communist China and North Korea. *Ibid*. See Resolution 711 C (VII).

for Soviet representation at the conference won almost unanimous approval. The United States opposed Soviet participation in the conference as a neutral or as a representative of the United Nations, so the sponsors worked out a formula to invite the Soviet Union "provided the other side desires it." With this alteration the resolution was adopted with only one negative vote and one abstention.[39] American objections to the participation of India were not to be thus easily circumnavigated. Unmoved by the manifest will of the majority or the pleas of its closest allies, the United States stood its ground to the end. With support only from China, Greece, Pakistan, and seventeen states of Latin America, the United States lost the committee battle on a vote of 27-21 with 11 abstaining. In plenary session, however, the two-thirds rule stood as an insurmountable obstacle to India's participation in the conference. While some vestiges of dignity still remained the Indian representative magnanimously suggested to the Assembly that the question not be put to a division, in order not "to add to the heat of any battle." Needless to say the American representative quickly took the rostrum to laud the Indian delegate for his statesmanlike action.[40]

The General Assembly had now decided upon the nature and composition of the political conference, but securing the assent of Communist China and North Korea was yet to be accomplished. With wounds still fresh from the battle over Indian participation, the Western nations secured postponement of discussion of the Korean question until the end of the eighth session on the ground that Assembly debate would kill any chance of reaching an agreement with the Communists for the prompt convening of the political conference. At the end of the session the United States representative used the same argument in support of further postponement. The Assembly adopted the proposal, sponsored jointly by Brazil and India, that the eighth Assembly recess without discussing Korea and reconvene should developments in Korea warrant.[41]

The eighth session never reconvened. The political conference on Korea, held at Geneva in conjunction with efforts to reach an Indochina settlement, uncovered no new basis for compromise, and the problem was held over for the ninth Assembly.[42] When the Assembly met for its ninth regular session the Soviet Union was ready for another try at a political conference. The American representative, however, as spokes-

[39] Resolution 711 B (VII). The plenary vote was 55-1-1. *Ibid.*, p. 735.

[40] See *ibid.*, pp. 724-26, and *First Committee*, 7th sess. (1952-53), p. 768.

[41] Resolution 716 (VIII). The vote was 55-0-5. *Plenary Meetings*, 8th sess. (1953), p. 446. See comments of American and British representatives, *ibid.*, pp. 76-78, and *First Committee*, 8th sess. (1953), pp. 5, 7, 295.

[42] The report of the fifteen nations representing the United Nations at Geneva ascribed the failure of the conference to communist intransigence. Document A/2786.

man for the sixteen members who had fought in Korea, opposed continued negotiations as fruitless without evidence of a change in the communist position. The Communists, he said, must first recognize the right of the United Nations to take collective action against aggression in Korea and agree to the free election of a Korean national assembly under United Nations supervision, with representation according to population. Until they accepted these principles any consideration of the Korean question would court new failure and be damaging alike to the prestige of the United Nations and the morale of the Korean people. Rejecting the communist proposals and sidestepping the attempts of India to secure a more equivocal statement of the United Nations position, the Assembly placed its seal of approval upon the sixteen-power principles.[43]

UNITING FOR PEACE

The war in Korea with all its implications for the future of collective security forced the Assembly to consider methods to strengthen its own capacity to deal with aggression when the Security Council was deadlocked. A program to accomplish this purpose was vigorously urged upon the fifth Assembly by the United States delegation. Secretary of State Dean Acheson devoted nearly two-thirds of his opening address in the Assembly to the problem of providing defense against communist aggression. His plea for action to "save the hope of peace, of security, of well being and of justice for generations to come" was accompanied by a specific program to make the Assembly a more effective instrument of collective security.[44] During the committee process verbal changes and minor alterations were accepted by the sponsors in a spirit of accommodation, but none affected the major purposes or objectives of the resolution.[45] As finally approved, the resolution laid down procedures for convening a special session upon twenty-four hours' notice to deal with threats to world peace, created a Peace Observation Commission to report on potential threats to peace, requested members to earmark forces

[43] Resolution 811 (IX). The plenary vote was 50-5-4. *Plenary Meetings*, 9th sess. (1954), p. 468. For Soviet and Indian proposals see documents A/C.1/L.16 and A/C.1/L.18, respectively. Comments of U.S. representative are found *First Committee*, 9th sess. (1954), pp. 10-16.

[44] *Plenary Meetings*, 5th sess. (1950), pp. 23-27, and document A/C.1/576. Canada, France, the Philippines, Turkey, the United Kingdom, and Uruguay joined the United States in sponsoring the measure.

[45] Compare the original proposal, document A/C.1/576, with the final text of Resolution 377 (V). According to the New York *Times*, spokesmen for the United States delegation emphasized the fact that the resolution was open to amendment and that suggestions "consistent with the objectives of the plan" would be welcomed. Oct. 8, 1950, p. 3. The State Department later acknowledged that the major features of the program originally proposed were maintained. *The U.S. and the U.N.*, report of President to Congress (1950), p. 100.

for an international army, and established a Collective Measures Committee to study methods and resources available to the United Nations for the maintenance of international peace and security. A concluding section, added in the course of discussion, enjoined the observance of human rights and fundamental freedoms and the maintenance of economic and social well-being.[46] While the United States took a dominant role in promoting the "Uniting for Peace" program, many of the smaller states were more than pleased to see the sphere of the General Assembly thus expanded at the expense of the Security Council. For the United States the "Uniting for Peace" resolution marked a complete reversal from its position at San Francisco that collective military action should be undertaken only at the behest of the Security Council, where the unanimity rule prevailed.

In subsequent Assemblies the Collective Measures Committee three times reported upon "Methods which might be used to maintain and strengthen international peace and security in accordance with the purposes and principles of the Charter," and three times the Assembly registered its approval of the committee's conclusions. Advocates of the committee reports kept abstentions at a minimum of two or three by accepting reasonable modifications in the resolutions of endorsement.[47] The United States championed the activities of the Collective Measures Committee but likewise showed willingness to compromise on details for the sake of achieving near-unanimity among the non-communist nations.

Another problem in collective security was raised by Yugoslavia in the fifth session with a proposal relating to "Duties of states in the event of the outbreak of hostilities." Essentially the Yugoslav delegation sought the adoption of a formula for designating the aggressor in a case of armed conflict. On the surface the procedure suggested was exceedingly simple. Its success hinged on the good faith of combatants in making a public avowal of their willingness to stop fighting and withdraw all armed forces to their own borders within a period of twenty-four hours. Any state

[46] Plenary voting was 52-5-2. The Soviet bloc stood as usual in isolated opposition, while only Argentina and India abstained on the final vote. *Plenary Meetings*, 5th sess. (1950), p. 347.

[47] Resolutions 503 (VI), 703 (VII), and 809 (IX). The plenary vote was 51-5-3 in the sixth session, 50-5-3 in the seventh, and 48-5-2 in the ninth. *Plenary Meetings*, 6th sess. (1951), p. 326; 7th sess. (1952), p. 554; 9th sess. (1954), p. 281. Committee studies included possible collective measures under three headings—political, economic, and military. They were designed to provide a catalog of alternative and complementary courses of action, proceeding from an appeal to the parties concerned, severance of diplomatic relations, and suspension of United Nations membership privileges, through the imposition of economic sanctions and use of actual military force. The objective was to survey in advance the methods and resources available for collective action and, insofar as possible, obtain advance commitments from member nations to cooperate in collective political, economic, and military action, whenever the need should arise. See documents A/1891, A/2215, and A/2713.

not making the public declaration or not honoring it would automatically be declared an aggressor. The chief United States interest in the proposal was to render it harmless without offending anyone's sensibilities. Both Britain and the United States voiced serious objections to the draft resolution as it stood but offered suggestions for its improvement. The Yugoslav delegation subsequently presented a completely revised draft which, through all its verbiage, said little more than that each case of aggression should be judged on its own merits. Although scarcely recognizable as the original Yugoslav proposal, it possessed the virtue of meeting all of the British and American objections. The measure was approved 49-5.[48]

SUMMARY

The record of the United States with regard to questions of disarmament, atomic energy control, Korea, and other problems of collective security is one of overall success, concession in detail, and a few major setbacks. With notable exceptions the United States worked closely with its allies, particularly Britain, France, and Canada, in order to present a common policy to the Assembly. The essentials of the Baruch plan for the control of atomic energy were repeatedly endorsed by the Assembly, as were Western disarmament proposals based on the principles of balanced reduction of armaments, prohibition of atomic weapons after the institution of a control system, and an effective system of inspection and verification. On these major principles the United States was never forced to compromise. In the first session, and again in the eighth and ninth, the United States assented to the statement of disarmament aims in terms vague enough to win Soviet agreement, but this involved no compromise of principle. During discussion of the third session the United States made what was, in the light of the position originally taken, a substantial concession to majority sentiment by agreeing to the continuation of discussions of the whole Atomic Energy Commission. This was not, however, a concession on the principle of disarmament but on the best method of reaching agreement. Similarly, the United States supported a disarmament resolution favored by the majority in the fourth session without any real conviction that it represented a step toward Great Power accord. There were also the inevitable textual revisions, of more or less significance, in preferred resolutions. But on the whole the United States had little reason to be displeased with Assembly action on disarmament and atomic energy control.

Except for the seventh session, the United States record on Korea is

---

[48] Resolution 378 (V). Plenary voting was 49-5-1. *Plenary Meetings,* 5th sess. (1950), p. 427. Cf. original Yugoslav proposal, documents A/1399 and A/C.1/604. U.S. and British comments are found *First Committee,* 5th sess. (1950), pp. 249-50, 261-62.

equally good. Prior to the Korean war the United States obtained, without substantial concessions, commanding majorities on its recommendations for United Nations action in Korea. Upon the outbreak of hostilities new problems emerged. The fifth Assembly initially gave strong support to the American-led United Nations action in Korea and early approved a program for the unification and rehabilitation of Korea. Responding to American leadership, the non-communist members, with only two abstentions, adopted the Uniting for Peace resolution through which they hoped to make the Assembly an effective instrument of collective security. But with the intervention of Communist China and the consequent threat of a third world war, American leadership was seriously challenged by a vocal Asiatic neutralist bloc and divisions among the Western nations. By dint of much persuasion the United States finally secured a resolution condemning the Chinese intervention. But this was possible only after efforts at negotiation, tolerated but not encouraged by the United States, had failed, and sixteen states either abstained or voted in the opposition. During the sixth session the Assembly readily consented to the American proposal for postponement of discussion pending the outcome of negotiations for an armistice in Korea. The seventh session was notable more for American retreat and defeat than victory on the Korean question. The United States was forced by majority sentiment to abandon its own proposal relating to prisoner-of-war repatriation and accept instead a compromise Indian measure. In the spring the United States first opposed any new resolution on Korea, then relented when agreement on the exchange of sick and wounded prisoners created demand for a new Assembly pronouncement. Retreat turned into defeat at the August meeting, when the United States actually voted with a minority in opposing Indian representation at the proposed political conference on Korea. The majority of non-communist nations once more closed ranks, however, on other aspects of the Korean question considered at the resumed session, and in the two succeeding Assemblies the United States, as spokesman for the sixteen members fighting in Korea, had little trouble finding large majorities.

CHAPTER EIGHT

Legacies of Colonialism

Treatment of Indians in the Union of South Africa

Of all the political questions appearing perennially on the agenda of the General Assembly, no other showed such monotonous sameness of issues and arguments from session to session or such a complete lack of progress toward a solution as India's complaint concerning the treatment of Indians in the Union of South Africa. Year after year the Indian delegation produced its harping accusations and insistent demands that discrimination cease forthwith, while Arab and Asian delegations sympathized, Communists cheered, and American delegates squirmed. Just as consistently the Union of South Africa stubbornly maintained that the question involved domestic matters beyond the jurisdiction of the United Nations. Throughout the annual debates the United States delegation tried desperately to take a stand upon middle ground. It had to acknowledge the factual basis of the Indian complaint and, in fact, deplored the situation in South Africa, but at the same time it regarded any attempt to coerce the South African government as both undesirable and futile. The outcome of each debate was happy for no one but the Communists, whose propaganda machines joyfully exploited South Africa's laggard social conscience.

The problem was one of long standing, stemming from the immigration of large numbers of Indians in the late nineteenth century to meet the demand for cheap labor in the mines and plantations of South Africa. The immigrants and their descendents, except for a few who were repatriated, became citizens of the Union of South Africa, albeit second- and third-class citizens as policies of racial discrimination were tightened in South Africa. From time to time the Indian government had sought by agreement to improve their condition but with little practical result. In 1946 India broke off diplomatic relations with the Union of South Africa as a protest against the imposition of new legal restrictions on occupation and residence.

The establishment of the United Nations offered new hope for redress, and India placed her complaint upon the agenda of the first session. An accompanying draft resolution declared South Africa's treatment of Asiatics to be in contravention of the Charter and requested the government of South Africa to bring its policy respecting Asiatics into conformity with the Charter.[1] Claiming interference in domestic affairs, the South African delegate urged the Assembly to request an opinion of the International Court of Justice as to its jurisdiction before acting on the substance of the Indian charges. This course of action appealed strongly to the United States delegation, but the Assembly majority demanded a stronger stand against the violation of human rights. While the American delegate protested that the case was being prejudged, the committee approved a modified draft which made no reference to Charter violation but stated that "treatment of Indians in the Union should be in conformity with the international obligations under the agreements concluded between the two governments, and the relevant provisions of the Charter." Despite American opposition, the committee recommendation received two votes more than the necessary two-thirds majority in plenary meeting.[2]

As might have been expected, the South African government totally disregarded the recommendations of the Assembly. Undaunted, the Indian delegation returned to the second Assembly with a new draft resolution calling for a round-table conference between the two governments on the basis of the previous year's resolution. The United States delegation was willing to support the proposal for a conference but maintained that reaffirmation of the earlier resolution was likely to prevent the parties from finding common ground for negotiation. Nevertheless, the First Committee approved the Indian draft after first deleting an invidious reference to the failure of South Africa to carry out the recommendations of the first Assembly. In plenary meeting, however, the two-thirds rule proved too formidable an obstacle and the draft failed of adoption. Brazil, Cuba, Denmark, and Norway rushed to the breach with a resolution urging the parties to confer without reference to the 1946 resolution. Although the United States lent its support, the new draft fell short even of a simple majority.[3] Deadlocked, the Assembly was forced to remain silent on the issue.

Frustrated by the two-thirds rule in the second session, the Indian delegation tried to sell the question to the third Assembly as a threat to international peace. The United States delegation, among others, re-

---

[1] Document A/C.1 & 6/3. See also the comments of the Indian and South African representatives, *Joint Committee of the First and Sixth Committees*, 1st sess. (1946), pp. 1-4.

[2] Resolution 44 (I). The vote was 32-15-7. *Plenary Meetings*, 1st sess., 2nd pt. (1946), p. 1061. The committee vote was closer—24-19-6. *Joint Committee of the First and Sixth Committees*, 1st sess. (1946), p. 51. For comments of U.S. representative see *ibid.*, pp. 15-16.

[3] The vote was 24-29-3. *Plenary Meetings*, 2nd sess. (1947), p. 1170. For text see document A/496. Vote on the defeated Indian draft, document A/C.1/244, was 31-19-6 in plenary meeting and 29-15-5 in committee. *Ibid.*, p. 1169, and *First Committee*, 2nd sess. (1947), p. 481. Remarks of U.S. delegate are found *ibid.*

mained unconvinced, but the committee approved an Indian draft providing for a three-man commission to investigate conditions in the Union of South Africa relative to the Indian charges. As the proposal was still not free from implication of censure, the American delegation again joined the opposition. With only a four-vote majority in committee the measure was obviously destined to create a situation in the Assembly similar to that of the preceding year. To avoid a complete stalemate the committee approved a second draft calling upon India, Pakistan, and the Union of South Africa to undertake round-table discussions in the spirit of the United Nations Charter and the Universal Declaration of Human Rights. This measure was adopted in plenary session with only South Africa voting in the negative, and the Indian delegation judiciously chose not to press for a final vote on the more controversial proposal.[4]

The question of Indians in South Africa was omitted from the agenda of the fourth session, and preparation for a round-table conference reached the stage of preliminary talks in February, 1950. At home, however, the South African government continued to implement its policies of racial segregation by the enactment of a "Group Areas Act" setting aside areas for the exclusive occupation or ownership of a single racial group. India, incensed, demanded suspension of the act as a prerequisite to further negotiations. The South African government refused, and there the situation stood when the fifth Assembly convened.[5] In the Ad Hoc Political Committee, India, Burma, Indonesia, and Iraq presented a draft resolution bristling with condemnation of South African racial policies, with special reference to the Group Areas Act, and urging the Union of South Africa to bring its treatment of Indians into conformity with the Charter of the United Nations and the Universal Declaration of Human Rights. The United States delegation at first supported a milder five-power draft recommending further negotiations but announced its intention to abstain when it was amended to include reference to the Group Areas Act. India accepted the amended five-power proposal and the committee approved it 26-6 with 24 abstentions. For reasons unexplained in the record the United States changed its vote from abstention to affirmative when the resolution was adopted in plenary meeting.[6]

---

[4] Resolution 265 (III). The vote in committee was 39-2-9 and in plenary meeting 47-1-10. Committee vote on the Indian draft, document A/C.1/461/Rev.1, was 21-17-12. *First Committee*, 3rd sess., 2nd pt. (1948-49), pp. 321-24, and *Plenary Meetings*, 3rd sess., 2nd pt. (1948-49), p. 455.

[5] Document A/1289 contains resumé of events.

[6] The vote was 33-6-21. *Plenary Meetings*, 5th sess. (1950), p. 534. See document A/AC.38/L.35, sponsored by Bolivia, Brazil, Denmark, and Norway, and amendment thereto, document A/AC.38/L.39. For comments of American delegate see *Ad Hoc Political Committee*, 5th sess. (1950), pp. 275, 287-88. Document A/AC.38/L.33 contains original Indian proposal.

The pattern of action was now well established. In every subsequent session India submitted a report that the South African government had refused to carry out the previous year's recommendations. Just as consistently the South African delegation pleaded interference in domestic affairs and took its stand on the basis of the formula for negotiations agreed upon in February, 1950, which India had irrevocably repudiated. Each year the Assembly adopted a resolution modeled on those previously adopted, with variations in the suggested procedures for negotiation and mediation.[7] In like manner the American representative each year drew attention to the difficulty of the problem, expressed concern at the direction of South Africa's racial policies, and cautioned against trying to force a solution on South Africa. In committee discussion of proposed draft resolutions, the United States delegation made a similar effort to lean as far as possible in both directions. It invariably questioned the wisdom of censuring national legislation, opposed provisions for automatically including the question on the agenda of the next session, and then took a stand against racial discrimination by voting for the resolution as a whole.[8] After eight years the problem was no closer to a solution than when first presented to the Assembly.

THE PROBLEM OF *Apartheid*

Beginning with the seventh session thirteen Asian and African states attacked South African racial policies on a wider front. Their target was the program of *apartheid*, or total segregation of whites from non-whites, which the Union government was attempting to institute.[9] Five additional African and Latin-American delegations joined the thirteen in sponsoring a draft resolution to condemn the South African government for its policies and establish a United Nations commission to study the racial situation there. Pointing out that a fact-finding commission was not a practical means of influencing the South African government, the United States representative exhorted the Assembly to accept instead a Scandinavian draft which set forth the obligation of all states to conform to the principles of the Charter in the whole area of human rights

---

[7] Resolutions 511 (VI), 615 (VII), 719 (VIII), and 816 (IX).

[8] For comments of American representatives see *Ad Hoc Political Committee*, 6th sess. (1951), pp. 172-73; 7th sess. (1952), pp. 48-49; 8th sess. (1953), pp. 91-93; 9th sess. (1954), p. 39. The record of plenary voting is found in *Plenary Meetings*, 6th sess. (1951), p. 330; 7th sess. (1952), p. 330; 8th sess. (1953), p. 288; 9th sess. (1954), p. 281.

[9] See document A/2183. Alleging that *apartheid* implied the permanent superiority of whites over non-whites, the thirteen nations detailed the discriminatory actions, including implementation of the Group Areas Act, segregation in public services and facilities, use of a Suppression of Communism Act to suppress democratic movements, debarment of non-whites from combat services, restrictions upon the movement of non-whites, exclusion of certain classes from skilled work, and toleration of deplorable living conditions among the non-white groups.

and fundamental freedoms. The Assembly compromised by adopting both resolutions. Those delegations like the United States, which could not support both, registered their disapproval by abstention rather than a negative vote.[10]

As with the treatment of Indians in South Africa, Assembly pronouncements on *apartheid* left the South African government wholly unmoved from its stand on the principle of domestic jurisdiction. The Commission on the Racial Situation reported its findings and recommendations to the eighth and ninth Assemblies, noting that the government of South Africa had refused to cooperate in the work of the commission. The United States declared its concern at this disturbing trend in United Nations treatment of domestic policies. But the Assembly on both occasions reestablished the investigatory commission and curtly admonished South Africa to bring its policies into conformity with the principles of the Charter. The United States delegation demurred at the harsh words and opposed the continuation of the commission, but out of concern for the flagrant disregard of human rights it abstained in the final voting on each resolution.[11]

THE PROBLEM OF PALESTINE

PARTITION

The war's end found the Holy Land seething with accumulated dissatisfactions born of frustrated national ambitions during a quarter century of British rule under its League of Nations mandate. Arab demands for an independent state in Palestine had proved incompatible with Zionist conceptions of the requirements for the Jewish "National Home" promised in the much controverted Balfour Declaration of 1917. Under pressures generated by the existence in Europe of hundreds of thousands of Jewish displaced persons desiring to immigrate to Palestine, an explosive situation reached the crisis stage in the spring of 1946. Manifestly unable to please either Arab or Jew, the United Kingdom declared its mandate unworkable and appealed to the General Assembly to find some remedy for the clash of nationalisms in the Holy Land.

---

[10] Resolutions 616 A and B (VII). The plenary vote on the harsher draft was 35-1-23, and on the statement of general principles, 24-1-34. *Plenary Meetings*, 7th sess. (1952), pp. 333-34. Remarks of U.S. representative are found *Ad Hoc Political Committee*, 7th sess. (1952), pp. 90-91.

[11] Resolutions 721 (VIII) and 820 (IX). The plenary vote in the eighth session was 38-11-11 and in the ninth 40-10-10. *Plenary Meetings*, 8th sess. (1953), p. 437, and 9th sess. (1954), pp. 490-91. See comments of United States representatives in committee debate, *Ad Hoc Political Committee*, 8th sess. (1953), pp. 191-92, and 9th sess. (1954), pp. 212-13. Some of the features of the second report of the commission, document A/2719, were particularly objectionable to the United States, one of which was a reference to the Soviet Union as an example which South Africa might emulate in solving its racial problems. In support of his objections the American representative cited extensively evidence of racial discrimination in the U.S.S.R. *Ad Hoc Political Committee*, 9th sess. (1954), pp. 212-13.

At British request a special session was convened to appoint a preliminary fact-finding committee on Palestine. The early days of the
session were marked by near-violent procedural wrangles. The United
States delegation, unwilling at this time to be committed to any substantive policy, helped to beat down an Arab attempt to force a substantive
discussion of Palestinian independence.[12] On a second preliminary issue
—the participation of Jewish and Arab non-governmental organizations
in committee discussions—the United States had to accept less severe
limitations than it thought desirable.[13] However, the United States had
little reason to be displeased with the manner in which the Assembly
discharged its principal task of establishing an investigatory commission.
The final draft which emerged from the committee and subcommittee
process was similar in broad outline to an American text proposed at
the beginning of the session. The American delegation had asked for a
commission of seven neutral states, not including permanent members
of the Security Council, with the widest possible powers of investigation
and recommendation. The Assembly departed from these suggestions to
the extent of including representatives of four additional disinterested
states. The final resolution was adopted with seven Near Eastern states
voting in the opposition.[14] The Assembly adopted without objection,
but with thirteen abstentions, a Norwegian proposal calling upon all
governments and peoples to refrain from any action that might create
an atmosphere prejudicial to an early settlement of the Palestine problem.[15]

The United Nations Special Committee on Palestine presented the
second Assembly with two alternative plans for the future government
of Palestine. The majority plan, endorsed by seven of the eleven members of the Special Committee, prescribed partition of Palestine into
Arab and Jewish states with economic union of the two. Three committee members supported a plan for a single federal state. Representatives
of the Arab states in the United Nations refused to accept either alternative, demanding that the people of Palestine be permitted to form their
own independent Arab government. Jewish spokesmen, with an alacrity
that belied the reluctance in their words, quickly announced acceptance
of partition. An increased sense of urgency was added to the bitter
partisanship of discussion by the announcement that, in the absence of
a settlement, the Assembly must anticipate an early withdrawal of

[12] See documents A/287, A/288, A/289, A/290, A/291; *General Committee*, 1st spec.
sess. (1947), p. 81; *Plenary Meetings*, 1st spec. sess. (1947), pp. 59-60. The plenary
vote on the Arab proposal was 15-24-10.

[13] See documents A/BUR/81 and A/305; *General Committee*, 1st spec. sess. (1947),
pp. 101-27; *Plenary Meetings*, 1st spec. sess. (1947), pp. 65-98.

[14] Resolution 106 (S-I). Cf. document A/C.1/150. The vote was 45-7-1. *Plenary
Meetings*, 1st spec. sess. (1947), pp. 176-77.

[15] Resolution 107 (S-I). The vote was 40-0-13. *Ibid.*, pp. 174-75.

British forces and of British administration from Palestine. Feelings ran high and controversy was heated, but the collaboration of the United States and the Soviet Union enabled the Ad Hoc Political Committee and its subcommittee to forge a plan for partition capable of surmounting the two-thirds majority barrier in the Assembly. Disregarding Arab accusations of "pressure" and threats of forcible resistance, the Assembly decreed partition for Palestine by a vote of 33-13 with 10 abstentions.[16]

Implementation of the partition resolution depended upon the acquiescence of both Arabs and Jews or, alternatively, willingness on the part of the United States and the Soviet Union to enforce compliance. Since neither of these conditions could materialize, the Assembly was called into special session in April, 1948, at the instigation of the United States to deal with the Palestine problem for the third time in twelve months.[17] Meanwhile, the British government had announced that, come what may, its mandate would be terminated on May 15. The United States, having decided that partition was unworkable under the circumstances, and no longer able to rely upon the British to preserve a modicum of order in Palestine, now urged a temporary settlement in the form of an international trusteeship. Zionists and Communists flatly rejected the idea of a temporary trusteeship. No one was enthusiastic, although the Arab delegates indicated a willingness at least to consider the United States plan. As debate wore on objections loomed so formidable that the plan was finally buried in a subcommittee.[18] To preserve face the Assembly had to take some affirmative course of action. An American-inspired attempt to secure a trusteeship for the limited area of Jerusalem and its environs foundered upon the two-thirds rule in listless voting.[19] But at

[16] *Plenary Meetings,* 2nd sess. (1947), pp. 1424-27. Document A/364 contains UNSCOP report and recommendations. For committee discussion see *Ad Hoc Committee on the Palestinian Question,* 2nd sess. (1947). The events of this session with respect to the partition of Palestine are treated in detail in Chapter Four.

[17] The request was made by the Security Council at the instigation of the United States. Document A/530 and *Department of State Bulletin,* vol. 18 (Mar. 28 and Apr. 4, 1948), pp. 408, 451.

[18] See documents A/C.1/277 and A/C.1/292, and *First Committee,* 2nd spec. sess. (1948), esp. pp. 17-20, 25-26, 192-97, 217-28.

[19] Plenary voting was 20-15-19. *Plenary Meetings,* 2nd spec. sess. (1948), p. 36. The vote in committee to forward the plan without passing on its substance was indicative of the enthusiasm the measure evoked—15-0-26. *First Committee,* 2nd spec. sess. (1948), p. 274.
  The Assembly had earlier requested the Trusteeship Council to study and report on suitable measures for the protection of Jerusalem. Acting upon the report of the Trusteeship Council, the Assembly recommended that Britain appoint before May 15 a neutral person, acceptable to both Arabs and Jews, as special Municipal Commissioner to administer essential public services. The problem of protecting Jerusalem was thrown back to the First Committee and acted upon as indicated above. See Resolutions 185 (S-II) and 187 (S-II). Voting on the request to the Trusteeship Council was 46-0-7, and on its report, 35-0-17. The United States supported both propositions. *Plenary Meetings,* 2nd spec. sess. (1948), pp. 10-27.

length a common denominator was found in the appointment of a United Nations Mediator for Palestine. With opposition only from Cuba and the six communist states, the Assembly commissioned the Mediator to arrange for necessary public services in Palestine, assure the protection of the shrines and Holy Places sacred to three world religions, and promote a peaceful adjustment to the new situation by all parties concerned.[20]

The Assembly, which had convened to recant its earlier decision for partition, was not yet formally ended when events made retreat from partition impossible. On May 15 a new State of Israel was proclaimed, and to the astonishment of many delegations and the chagrin of American representatives who had just been telling the Assembly that partition was at present impracticable, *de facto* recognition was immediately extended by the President of the United States.[21] The United States thus completed the circle from partition to trusteeship to partition. Arab troops from neighboring countries, making good the threat to meet partition with forcible resistance, marched against the new Jewish state. Acting upon its responsibility to preserve international peace, the Security Council intervened to secure a cease-fire, but not before the underrated armies of Israel had repulsed the Arab attack and seized territories well beyond the bounds allotted in the original partition plan. During the uneasy truce that ensued the United Nations Mediator acted to carry out his mandate from the Assembly. In mid-September the world was shocked by news of the assassination of the Mediator, Swedish Count Folke Bernadotte, but his successor, Ralph Bunche, continued with the task of mediation and submitted to the third Assembly a report based upon recognition of Israel as a viable entity.[22]

The United States approved the report of the Mediator, with a few reservations, and in subsequent Assembly discussions supported a British draft resolution to implement it. The draft provided for a three-member Conciliation Commission to assume all functions previously conferred upon the Mediator, facilitate a settlement of outstanding differences between Israel and her Arab neighbors, and present to the fourth Assembly a detailed proposal for a permanent international regime for Jerusalem. The draft endorsed the Mediator's proposal for cession of the non-Jewish portions of Palestine to Transjordan, provided for the protection of Jerusalem and its environs, and recommended repatriation or compensation of refugees at the refugees' option. In a sense, the draft was an attempt to make a fresh approach to a settlement, since every suggestion that the commission should be bound by previous resolutions was carefully omitted. The United States was able to persuade the

---

[20] Resolution 186 (S-II). The plenary vote was 31-7-16. *Ibid.*, pp. 44-45.

[21] See New York *Times* comment, May 15, 1947, p. 1.

[22] Document A/648.

British to accept desired revisions, but securing committee approval was another thing. After wrangling and maneuvering, supporters of the British proposal won the right for the Conciliation Commission to seek a settlement without any necessary reference to the two previous resolutions on the question. However, the provision for merging the Arab portions of Palestine with the Kingdom of Transjordan, strongly urged by Britain and the United States, was defeated by eight votes. Even with this and other extensive amendments, the United Kingdom draft had only three votes to spare in committee voting.[23] Faced with the certainty that the measure could never get a two-thirds majority, its supporters reluctantly permitted deletion of the entire preamble with its commendatory references to the Mediator's report. This, with certain minor changes to please individual delegations, finally rallied the necessary majority and the resolution was adopted 35-15 with 8 abstentions. France, Turkey, and the United States were subsequently chosen to be members of the Conciliation Commission.[24]

JERUSALEM

Partition was now a fact. A national state of Israel was established in the Holy Land, and King Abdullah of Jordan was proceeding with his plans for merger with the Arab portions of Palestine in defiance of the Assembly's refusal to authorize the annexation.[25] But the question of Palestine was far from closed. Of the many problems still remaining, the determination of the future status of Jerusalem was one of the most difficult and highly charged. From the outset of Assembly discussions, some form of international regime had been contemplated as the best means to protect the religious interests of Christian, Jew, and Moslem, as well as the rights of the city's mixed Arab and Jewish population. Against these considerations lay the respective claims of Israel and Jordan, bolstered by *de facto* control, to Jewish and Arab zones of a partitioned Jerusalem. The attempt to find a viable solution to this many-sided problem overshadowed all other activities of the United Nations Conciliation Commission for Palestine during the first two years of its existence.

Recognizing the difficulties inherent in any disposition not acceptable to the Jordanian and Israeli governments, the Conciliation Commission

---

[23] The vote was 25-21-9. *First Committee*, 3rd sess., 1st pt. (1948), pp. 923-24. Vote on the paragraph relating to merger with Transjordan was 18-26-12. *Ibid.*, p. 890. For final text as approved in committee see document A/776. Cf. original draft, document A/C.1/394/Rev.2. Note U.S. comments, *First Committee*, 3rd sess., 1st pt. (1948), pp. 680-83, 779-80.

[24] See Resolution 194 (III). *Plenary Meetings*, 3rd sess., 1st pt. (1948), p. 996. For text of amendment see document A/789. Voting on the amendment was 35-6-5. *Ibid.*, p. 994.

[25] New York *Times*, Dec. 19, 1948, sec. IV, p. 5; Jan. 3, 1949, p. 9; Apr. 25, 1950, p. 1.

recommended to the fourth Assembly a plan which, in its essentials, meant partition of Jerusalem between Israel and Jordan, with special provision for United Nations supervision over the Holy Places and other specified matters of international concern. The United States delegate, as a member of the commission and co-sponsor of the measure, earnestly but unavailingly argued the merits of the proposal before the committee.[26] Other delegations, firmly committed to a more completely internationalized regime than the commission plan offered, proceeded with the preparation of a draft resolution to make of Jerusalem a *corpus separatum*, administered as a trusteeship by the Trusteeship Council. Heedless of the United States warning that the Trusteeship Council was not equipped to implement such a program against determined opposition, the Assembly adopted the resolution by a substantial majority of 38-14.[27]

Events fully justified American doubts concerning the practicability of the trusteeship plan. The Trusteeship Council was forced to report failure due to non-cooperation of the peoples and governments involved.[28] This admission spelled the end of bold Assembly efforts to dictate a settlement for Jerusalem. As with partition, events overruled deliberations. In the Ad Hoc Political Committee the Swedish delegation submitted a draft conceding the right of Jordan and Israel to control their respective areas of Jerusalem in return for pledges to observe human rights and fundamental freedoms, maintain free access to the Holy Places, and cooperate with a United Nations commissioner in the supervision and protection of the Holy Places. The United States endorsed this proposal with certain textual modifications.[29] The majority in the committee, however, were not yet ready so unashamedly to admit defeat. Although the United States delegate protested that past negotiations had already been exhaustive, the committee approved a Belgian proposal for further consultations with Israel and Jordan regarding the protection of the Holy Places. The twelve-vote margin of victory in the Ad Hoc Committee was gratifying but insufficient to carry the day in plenary meeting. No resolution was adopted, and the decision went to Israel and Jordan by default.[30]

---

[26] *Ad Hoc Political Committee*, 4th sess. (1949), pp. 247-50, and document A/973 and Add.1.

[27] Resolution 303 (IV). The final vote was 38-14-7. *Plenary Meetings*, 4th sess. (1949), p. 607.

[28] Document A/1286. See also the report of the United Nations Conciliation Commission for Palestine, document A/1367, Corr.1 and Add.1.

[29] *Ad Hoc Political Committee*, 5th sess. (1950), pp. 495-96. For text of amendments, sponsored by Britain, Uruguay, and the United States, see document A/AC.38/L.73/Rev.2. Cf. original draft, A/AC.38/L.63.

[30] Plenary voting was 30-18-9. *Plenary Meetings*, 5th sess. (1950), p. 684. Committee voting on the Belgian proposal, document A/AC.38/L.71, was 30-18-11. *Ad Hoc Political Committee*, 5th sess. (1950), pp. 521-22. See comments of United States representative, *ibid.*, pp. 495, 519.

CONCILIATION

The problem of Jerusalem did not drop completely out of sight after the fiasco of the fifth session, but in subsequent Assembly debates it was merged with the questions of refugees, boundaries, and frozen assets in the problem of a general settlement. The Conciliation Commission, established in 1948, continued in its thankless efforts to assist Arabs and Jews to reach agreement in Palestine. Supporters of the commission's activities experienced harrowing times in attempting to pilot acceptable resolutions safely through the Assembly. In the sixth session a draft proposal urging agreement "in a spirit of justice and realism and on the basis of mutual concession," sponsored jointly by France, Turkey, Britain, and the United States, underwent severe mutilation before final adoption. The United States delegation opposed most of the changes but voted with the majority in approving the amended document.[31] Differences less easily compromised emerged in the seventh session. The Arab delegations, who complained bitterly of the Conciliation Commission's failure to implement Assembly resolutions pertaining to Palestine, demanded that the United Nations exert greater effort to make Israel comply with Assembly directives. The United States delegation contended that the questions at issue could best be settled by direct negotiations between Israel and the Arabs, with United Nations assistance through the Conciliation Commission where appropriate. A resolution in conformity with American views successfully weathered Arab opposition in committee by a vote of 32-13 and came before the plenary session with an apparently safe majority.[32] There, however, the lines wavered, then broke. An amendment designed to placate the Arabs and opposed by the United States was defeated only by the two-thirds rule. Seven Latin-American states which had supported the resolution in committee voted "no" in plenary meeting, and it too failed of adoption.[33] The problem of a general settlement in Palestine was not made the subject of discussion in the eighth and ninth Assemblies.

[31] Cf. original draft A/AC.53/L.22 with Resolution 512 (VI). The final vote was 48-5-1. *Plenary Meetings*, 6th sess. (1951), p. 404. For voting on the various amendments in committee, see *Ad Hoc Political Committee*, 6th sess. (1951), pp. 231-33.

[32] The vote was 32-13-13. *Ad Hoc Political Committee*, 7th sess. (1952), p. 237. Comments of U.S. delegate are found *ibid.*, pp. 161-62. See document A/AC.61/L.23/Rev.4.

[33] The vote was 24-21-15. *Ibid.*, pp. 413-14. It should be noted that the United States, while supporting direct negotiations between the parties, did not take such an active lead in the discussions as in former years. See *The U.S. and the U.N.*, report of President to Congress (1952), p. 79.

The defeated amendment, document A/L.134, proposed that the parties to negotiations be bound by previous Assembly resolutions and that they give special consideration to the internationalization of Jerusalem. Voting on the separate parts of the amendment was 26-24-10 and 28-20-12. *Plenary Meetings*, 7th sess. (1952), p. 413.

REFUGEES

The internationalization of Jerusalem might be postponed indefinitely; conciliation could await a happier day; but the problem of some nine hundred thousand Arab refugees from Jewish-held territories, made homeless during the Palestine war, could not be ignored nor its consideration postponed to some future date. The question found place on the agenda of the third session and was still a matter of urgent concern in the ninth. Two lines of approach were marked out for the Assembly. From the Arab viewpoint the most satisfactory solution was repatriation of the refugees to their homes in Israel or, at their option, compensation by the government of Israel for abandoned property holdings. The Assembly agreed on the principle of repatriation or compensation, but the reluctance of Israel either to accept the expatriates or to compensate them made some other course of action imperative. This took the form of a United Nations Relief and Works Agency for Palestine Refugees in the Near East (UNRWA), established in 1949 to provide immediate relief assistance and to cooperate with Near Eastern governments in developing long-range projects for the permanent rehabilitation of the refugees. Debate on measures to relieve the condition of the refugees was relatively free from the bitter controversy that marked other phases of the Palestine question. France, Turkey, the United Kingdom, and the United States, as members of the advisory board of UNRWA, annually sponsored measures dealing with its activities, and on each occasion the proposals were accepted by the Assembly without a dissenting vote.[34] The absence of opposition was due in part to the nature of the problem and in part to the willingness of the four sponsors to modify their proposals in response to criticism from other delegations. In this regard the four powers were especially solicitous of the Arab delegations.[35] But as year after year went by with little Arab initiative in the establishment

[34] Resolutions 302 (IV), 393 (V), 513 (VI), 614 (VII), 720 (VIII), and 818 (IX). The communist states abstained in the voting and were usually joined by two or three others.

[35] In the sixth session the original four-power draft, document A/AC.53/L.34, was modified extensively to meet Arab complaints that the language of the resolution infringed upon their sovereign rights by linking the refugee problem to their internal policies. See comments of Arab delegates, *Ad Hoc Political Committee*, 6th sess. (1951), p. 236, and the revised text, document A/AC.53/L.36.

When, in connection with the fifth Assembly's discussion of the refugee problem, the four powers offered a resolution dealing with the whole question of a Palestine settlement, they encountered determined opposition. The resolution was ultimately adopted but only after a key paragraph relating to settlement through direct negotiation was amended over the protest of the sponsors. See Resolution 394 (V). Plenary voting on the amended draft was 48-5-4. *Plenary Meetings*, 5th sess. (1950), p. 678. The vote on the amendment in committee was 33-13-9. *Ad Hoc Political Committee*, 5th sess. (1950), p. 467. For text of original proposal see document A/AC.38/L.57.

of the reintegration projects, the United States was forced to issue a
warning that further delay might result in the withdrawal of American
financial support from the relief and reintegration programs.[36] The admonition had no apparent effect on the voting pattern in the Assembly,
and its effect upon the policies of the Near Eastern governments remained to be seen.

THE FORMER ITALIAN COLONIES

The disposal of the former Italian colonies presented the General
Assembly with an opportunity unique in its history. For once the Assembly was asked to make a decision upon a major political problem
which the Great Powers were committed in advance to accept and implement. Through an undertaking in the peace treaty with Italy, the governments of France, the Soviet Union, the United Kingdom, and the United
States had agreed to transfer the right of determination to the Assembly
if they could not agree among themselves on the future status of Libya,
Eritrea, and Italian Somaliland by September, 1948. Agreement was not
reached by the stipulated time, and the question was placed on the
agenda of the third session.[37]

When the topic came under consideration in the First Committee, the
United States indicated support of a British proposal to establish an international trusteeship system for Libya and Somaliland and to divide Eritrea
between Ethiopia and the Sudan. Of the three Libyan provinces, Cy-
renaica was to be administered by the United Kingdom, and the governments of Egypt, France, Italy, the United Kingdom, and the United
States were to make recommendations to the fourth Assembly for the
temporary disposition of Tripolitania and the Fezzan. The whole of
Libya was to receive independence after ten years if the Assembly should
decide it was ready. The plan contemplated Italian administration of
Somaliland.[38]

Other delegations vigorously objected to the British draft and disagreed with one another. The communist delegations demanded administration of trusteeships through organs of the United Nations rather than
by individual states. A number of Latin-American states were determined
to press Italian claims, while Arab members opposed continued Italian
administration for any part of the former colonies and urged a solution
involving independence at the earliest practicable moment.

[36] *Ad Hoc Political Committee,* 9th sess. (1954), pp. 131-32.

[37] For summary of events leading to submittal of the question to the General Assembly see *First Committee,* 3rd sess., 2nd pt. (1948-49), pp. 7-10. Provisionally, the
Fezzan in Libya was under French military administration, with British military administration for the other areas.

[38] See document A/C.1/446 and *First Committee,* 3rd sess., 2nd pt. (1948-49), pp.
158-59.

Despite the sharp conflict of incompatible views, a drafting subcommittee reported out a draft very much like the original British proposal. There were significant differences, however. Instead of postponing action on the Fezzan and Tripolitania, the administration of the one was awarded to France and the other to Italy. Libya was slated to achieve independence automatically within ten years unless the Assembly should decide it was not ready. Somaliland was left to be administered by Italy with a view to its ultimate independence. Provision for the western province of Eritrea was entirely omitted.[39]

In committee the subcommittee draft was approved by a vote of 34-16.[40] The United States was not wholly satisfied with the measure but supported it in preference to postponing a decision. In plenary meeting, however, the carefully constructed coalition in favor of the draft fell apart. While the proposal, as one package, had commanded a greater than two-thirds majority in committee, the separate parts would not bear the same weight. The provisions for Italian administration of Tripolitania and Somaliland fell short, though by the slenderest of margins, and bereft of this leg the proposition collapsed with the mass shift of Latin-American votes. Only fourteen delegations, including the United States and Britain, voted for the resolution in the final balloting. Having no better course of action the Assembly voted to postpone further consideration until the fourth session.[41]

The American and British delegations returned sadder but wiser to the fourth Assembly. Declaring that Libyan trusteeship was no longer feasible, they now advocated almost immediate independence for Libya. Both delegations still supported an Italian-administered trusteeship for Somaliland and division of Eritrea between Ethiopia and Sudan.[42] The United States sponsored a draft resolution to implement these views, including statehood for Libya after a three-year transition period. The proposal did not find unanimous acceptance, and the end product of committee and

---

[39] Document A/C.1/476.

[40] *First Committee*, 3rd sess., 2nd pt. (1948-49), p. 394.

[41] Resolution 287 (III). The vote on postponement was 51-0-6 after the subcommittee draft had been defeated 14-37-7. *Plenary Meetings*, 3rd sess., 2nd pt. (1948-49), pp. 595-96, 608. U.S. comments are found *ibid.*, pp. 549-51. A recommendation that the Economic and Social Council consider the problems of economic progress and social development of the former colonies was adopted 44-0-7. *Ibid.*, p. 596. See Resolution 266 (III).
For insight into the underlying clash of interests and the backstage negotiations which characterized the third Assembly's attempt to deal with the former Italian colonies see Rivlin, *op. cit.*, pp. 459-70.

[42] *First Committee*, 4th sess. (1949), pp. 19-25. *The U.S. and the U.N.*, report of President to Congress (1949), p. 53, observed that the United States "had modified its position in the light of the earlier Assembly discussion and the developing facts bearing on the matter, and in an effort to meet what appeared to be the trend of opinion generally."

subcommittee deliberations was a distinct compromise: full independence for Libya by January 1, 1952; independence for Somaliland after ten years with an Italian-administered trusteeship in the interim; and postponement of an Eritrean settlement pending the report of a five-member commission appointed to study the question. The compromise was adopted in plenary meeting with only the Ethiopian delegation objecting. The United States delegate voted for the resolution but expressed disappointment at the failure to take a decision on Eritrea.[43]

At the next session the United States co-sponsored a measure to assist Libya in its progress toward self-government. The draft called for the convocation of a representative Libyan national assembly by January 1, 1951, and requested ECOSOC and the specialized agencies to extend technical and financial aid to the new state. In plenary meeting the sponsors had to fight off an Egyptian attempt to require that the Libyan assembly be "elected" as well as "representative." The sponsors explained that this omission had been made in conformity with the wishes of Libyan political leaders. The Egyptian amendment won a majority of votes cast but fell short of the necessary two-thirds. The resolution then passed without a dissenting vote.[44]

When the question of Libyan independence came before the seventh Assembly, the Western powers did not fare so well. Their draft resolution encountered a number of Egyptian amendments designed to lessen Libya's dependence upon France, Britain, and the United States by channeling economic and financial assistance to the new Libyan government exclusively through organs of the United Nations.[45] The amendments were subsequently modified in an effort to meet American objections, but two amendments opposed by the United States even in revised form were incorporated into the draft in extremely close committee voting. In plenary meeting the committee recommendation was adopted unani-

---

[43] Resolution 289 A (IV). Cf. U.S. proposal, document A/C.1/497. Plenary voting was 48-1-9. *Plenary Meetings*, 4th sess. (1949), p. 302. See U.S. comments, *ibid.*, pp. 268-69. The Assembly in separate resolutions nominated a United Nations Commissioner for Libya and authorized the Interim Committee to study the delimitation of the boundaries of the former colonies. See Resolutions 289 B and C (IV).

[44] Resolution 387 (V). The vote was 50-0-6. *Plenary Meetings*, 5th sess. (1950), p. 423. Vote on the Egyptian amendment was 24-20-15. See *ibid.*, pp. 420-23. A companion resolution concerning technical and financial assistance to Libya was adopted unanimously at a subsequent meeting. *Ibid.*, p. 686. See Resolution 388 (V).

[45] For original text of Western draft, see document A/AC.53/L.39. Egyptian amendments are found in document A/AC.53/L.41. Libya, as one of the world's poorest countries, "approached independence in 1951 facing the prospect of relatively large budget deficits and an adverse balance of payments. It was clear that the new state would require outside help to survive." The United Kingdom and France offered the necessary financial aid, as distinct from technical assistance, and by agreement both were given a voice in naming Libyan financial and economic advisers. See *The U.S. and the U.N.*, report of President to Congress (1951), pp. 97-98.

mously after an unsuccessful American attempt to delete the two objectionable paragraphs.[46]

The settlement for Eritrea proved almost equally controversial. The five-member commission appointed to study the problem presented to the fifth Assembly no less than three different recommendations, including independence, federation with Ethiopia, and outright annexation. The United States, while acknowledging preference for Ethiopian annexation of all but the western province of Eritrea, supported federation as an equitable compromise solution.[47] The Soviet bloc, most of the Arab states, and a few Latin-American delegations banded together in support of alternative proposals, but their combined voting power was not enough to prevent committee approval of a plan for federation of Eritrea and Ethiopia. Just prior to plenary voting the delegate of Iraq announced that the Arab delegations would support federation in consequence of assurances received of equal treatment for all inhabitants of Ethiopia. This switch in alignments assured overwhelming approval of the resolution.[48] Two years later the Assembly was able to note with satisfaction the consummation of its recommendations.[49]

INDONESIA

The Security Council assumed a much more active role than the Assembly in assisting Indonesia along the stormy road to independence, although the question was twice on the Assembly agenda. In the spring of 1949 the continuation of hostilities between Dutch and Indonesian forces in disregard of Security Council orders prompted India and Australia to place the problem before the third session. The appeal to the General Assembly proved premature. Before Assembly discussion was

[46] Resolution 515 (VI). See *Plenary Meetings*, 6th sess. (1951), p. 476. The Assembly decided on a vote of 29-17-5 that a two-thirds majority was not required for the adoption of the two paragraphs. The paragraphs were then approved 30-16-5 and 30-12-5. Committee voting on the two amendments was even closer, 23-22-3 and 23-20-5. *Ad Hoc Political Committee*, 6th sess. (1951), pp. 291-92, 305.

[47] *Ad Hoc Political Committee*, 5th sess. (1950), p. 246. Prior to the convening of the fifth session the British and American delegations had private discussions with representatives of countries most directly concerned in order to reach an equitable compromise on Eritrea. *The U.S. and the U.N.*, report of President to Congress (1950), p. 87. For report of the five-member commission on Eritrea see document A/1285.

[48] Resolution 390 (V). The committee vote was 38-14-8 but voting in plenary meeting was 46-10-4. *Ad Hoc Political Committee*, 5th sess. (1950), p. 361, and *Plenary Meetings*, 5th sess. (1950), p. 546. At the same session the Assembly also approved the report of the Interim Committee, document A/1388, on the boundaries of the former colonies, with opposition only from five communist members. See Resolution 392 (V) and *ibid.*, p. 683.

[49] Resolution 617 (VII). The plenary vote was 51-0-5, the communist members abstaining. *Plenary Meetings*, 7th sess. (1952), p. 384.

under way the Security Council was able to initiate discussions between the two parties. Not wishing to interfere with this auspicious development, the Assembly expressed its hope for a lasting settlement and deferred consideration until the fourth session. Only the Soviet bloc opposed the postponement.[50] By the time the question was again discussed in the Assembly, participants in a Round-Table Conference at the Hague had reached substantial agreement upon the establishment of an Indonesian Republic. With the Communists again offering the sole protest, the Assembly tendered its congratulations and best wishes for a speedy consummation of the Hague arrangements.[51]

One of the major issues left unsettled at the Hague Round-Table Conference of 1949 was the status of West Irian in Western New Guinea, claimed by both the Dutch and the Indonesians. Over the protest of Indonesia the Dutch government subsequently incorporated West Irian into the Netherlands kingdom. Unable to effect a reconsideration of this action through direct negotiation with the Netherlands, the Indonesian government put the question to the ninth Assembly. An Indonesian draft calling for a resumption of negotiations without delay, in terms objectionable to the Dutch, was bypassed by the First Committee, but a substitute text almost equally objectionable was approved 34-14.[52] The United States delegation was one of ten who abstained and took no part in the discussion. During the week's pause between committee voting and plenary consideration a number of the abstainers, not including the United States, moved into the ranks of the opposition. As a result the proposition failed to carry the necessary two-thirds vote.[53]

TUNISIA AND MOROCCO

The collision of emergent Arab nationalism with French colonial policies in North Africa created a situation which was certain sooner or later to have reverberations in the General Assembly. The situation was not without embarrassment for the United States which had to find some middle course between rejection of self-determination and abandonment of its French ally. At the insistence of thirteen Asian and African delegations the twin questions of Tunisia and Morocco were included on the

---

[50] Resolution 274 (III). The plenary vote was 43-6-3. *Plenary Meetings*, 3rd sess., 2nd pt. (1948-49), p. 348. Complaints of India and Australia are detailed in documents A/826 and A/827.

[51] Resolution 301 (IV). The plenary vote was 44-5-2. *Plenary Meetings*, 4th sess. (1949), p. 563. Note comments of the Indian delegate, *Ad Hoc Political Committee*, 4th sess. (1949), p. 330.

[52] Cf. documents A/C.1/L.109 and A/C.1/L.110. The vote was 34-14-10. *First Committee*, 9th sess. (1954), pp. 457-58.

[53] Voting on two key paragraphs was 34-23-3 and 33-23-4. *Plenary Meetings*, 9th sess. (1954), pp. 120-21.

agenda of the seventh session.[54] The problems were discussed separately in view of the somewhat different conditions prevailing in the two French protectorates, but the basic issues in each case were essentially the same. The Asian and African delegations wanted the Assembly to affirm the right of Tunisia and Morocco to full independence in the immediate future. Opposing them stood the United States and other delegations with a more sympathetic view of the French position, which favored instead an expression of confidence in the ability of France, Morocco, and Tunisia to negotiate a mutually satisfactory settlement. The French delegation refused to participate in the discussion of either question, claiming the matter was solely one of French domestic concern.

As a *pièce de résistance* in the Tunisian question the thirteen Afro-Asian delegations introduced a measure censuring French policies and urging resumption of negotiations to implement the Tunisian right to self-determination. Eleven Latin-American states countered with an expression of confidence in the good intentions of the French government. The draft went so far as to suggest continued negotiations leading to eventual self-government for the Tunisians. The United States supported this proposal as a moderate, helpful approach to a delicate situation. The thirteen-power draft was rejected by a three-vote margin, and the delegations of Africa and Asia, lacking the strength to secure a measure more to their liking, voted for the half loaf which the more moderate draft offered.[55]

Action on Morocco followed a similar pattern, with a few noteworthy variations. The thirteen African and Asian states submitted a resolution similar in import to their earlier draft on Tunisia, and the eleven Latin-American delegations presented a counter-resolution. Instead of recommending progress through negotiation toward self-government for Morocco, however, the Latin-American draft called for the development of "free political institutions" with "due regard to legitimate rights and interests under the established norms and practices of the Law of Nations." Speaking in support of the Latin-American proposal the United States delegate justified the variation in wording on the basis of differing conditions in Tunisia and Morocco. The thirteen-power text was

---

[54] See documents A/2175 and Add.1, and A/2405 and Add.1. The thirteen states were Afghanistan, Burma, Egypt, India, Indonesia, Iran, Iraq, Lebanon, Pakistan, the Philippines, Saudi Arabia, Syria, and Yemen. The question of Morocco had been broached to the sixth Assembly, but its consideration was indefinitely postponed. The United States voted for the postponement. The Arabs had also tried unsuccessfully to place Tunisia on the Security Council agenda in the spring of 1952. The United States abstained on the Security Council vote.

[55] Resolution 611 (VII). Cf. the Arab draft, document A/C.1/736. The plenary vote was 44-3-8. *Plenary Meetings*, 7th sess. (1952), p. 382. Vote on the thirteen-power draft was 24-27-7. *First Committee*, 7th sess. (1952), p. 270. Remarks of U.S. delegate are found *ibid.*, pp. 206-8.

defeated but its supporters were not willing to acquiesce in the alternative draft. Arguing that what was good for Tunisia was good for Morocco, they rallied sufficient votes in committee to substitute "self-government" for "free political institutions" as the ultimate goal in Morocco, using the same wording as in the Tunisian resolution. In plenary meeting the moderates had the last word. Without their votes the amended paragraph would be deleted altogether through failure to obtain a two-thirds majority. Faced with this situation the Afro-Asian delegations abstained while the controversial passage was restored to its original form, then resignedly approved the resolution as a whole.[56]

Morocco took precedence over Tunisia on the agenda of the First Committee in the eighth session. Internal disorders climaxed by the forcible deposition of the Sultan of Morocco added cogency to the arguments of the African and Asian delegations and urgency to their demands.[57] In a resolution more adamant than before the thirteen states demanded an end to French repression in Morocco and called for full independence within five years. The Bolivian delegation ventured a competing draft similar to those of the preceding session, although chiding France to the extent of noting that free political institutions had not yet been established. As before, the thirteen-power draft was defeated.[58] But the Bolivian proposal was not approved until its operative paragraph had been amended to make the establishment of free political institutions a matter of right and necessity rather than a desirable possibility. The amended draft was endorsed by the committee 31-18 with the United States voting in the negative. This majority was not sufficient for plenary voting and the draft failed of adoption.[59]

Discussion of the Tunisian question ended in a similar stalemate. Alleging French dereliction in the establishment of conditions suitable for free negotiations in Tunisia, the thirteen delegations presented a resolution similar in essence to the rejected Moroccan draft. No one offered an alternative proposal, and the draft was approved in committee after two

---

[56] Resolution 612 (VII). The plenary vote on the controversial paragraph was 29-8-22, and 45-3-11 on the resolution as a whole. *Plenary Meetings*, 7th sess. (1952), pp. 425-26. In committee the Afro-Asian amendment, document A/C.1/L.14, had been adopted by the narrow margin of 28-23-4, while the original Arab proposal, document A/C.1/L.12, was rejected by two votes, 25-27-3. *First Committee*, 7th sess. (1952), p. 218. U.S. comments are found *ibid.*, pp. 291-92.

[57] Document A/2406 and Add.1. The French delegation again charged interference in domestic affairs and absented itself from committee discussions.

[58] The committee vote was 22-28-9. *First Committee*, 8th sess. (1953), p. 77, and document A/C.1/L.60.

[59] Voting on the sole operative paragraph, which had been amended in committee to strengthen the plea for free institutions, was 33-22-5, far short of the required two-thirds. The United States voted against the paragraph. *Plenary Meetings*, 8th sess. (1953), pp. 265-67. Committee vote on the Bolivian proposal, document A/C.1/L.61 as amended, was 31-18-9. See *First Committee*, 8th sess. (1953), pp. 77-78.

of its more objectionable directives to the French government were removed. The United States delegation tried unsuccessfully to dismember the resolution and voted against the draft as a whole. The draft resolution could not command support of a two-thirds majority in plenary meeting and fell short on a vote of 31-18 despite the incorporation of moderating amendments.[60]

In the ninth session the United States reiterated its position that the interests of France, Morocco, and Tunisia, as well as the principles of the United Nations Charter, would be best promoted through the cooperative efforts of the peoples and governments directly concerned. In view of the steps being taken by the government of Mendès-France the United States regarded the passage of any resolution inadvisable at the moment. The Arab delegations were not content thus to let matters rest and, with their supporters, again submitted draft proposals on Morocco and Tunisia. Both drafts were much more conciliatory than those of previous years and the United States delegation indicated willingness to relent if the proposals were made sufficiently moderate. Current negotiations between France and Tunisia augured such a favorable outcome that the United States and the Afro-Asian delegations were able to reach agreement. A revised twelve-power draft was approved in committee and adopted by the Assembly without a dissenting vote.[61] Since an acceptable compromise on Morocco was not reached in the committee stage, the United States felt bound to oppose the proposed draft. In plenary meeting, however, a spirit of conciliation prevailed. An amendment expressing confidence that a satisfactory solution would be achieved, rejected in committee voting, was approved by the Assembly without a single opposing vote. The United States then voted with the majority in adopting the amended draft 55-0.[62]

Cyprus

The long-standing Anglo-Greek dispute over Cyprus arose to plague the free world in the ninth session of the General Assembly. Disgruntled by the persistent refusal of the British government even to consider re-

---

[60] See documents A/C.1/L.64 and A/L.166. The vote was 31-18-10. Vote on the amendments was 32-16-11. The United States abstained on the amendments and voted "no" on the resolution. *Plenary Meetings*, 8th sess. (1953), p. 293. The committee vote on the proposal was closer, 29-22-5. *First Committee*, 8th sess. (1953), p. 112.

[61] Resolution 813 (IX). Cf. original draft, document A/C.1/L.128. The plenary vote was 56-0-3. *Plenary Meetings*, 9th sess. (1954), p. 538. For comments of American representative see *ibid.*, p. 537, and *First Committee*, 9th sess. (1954), pp. 571, 577.

[62] Resolution 812 (IX). Cf. original draft, document A/C.1/L.122/Corr.1. Vote on the amendment was 57-0-1, and on the draft as a whole, 55-0-4. *Plenary Meetings*, 9th sess. (1954), pp. 536-37. The committee vote was 39-15-4. *First Committee*, 9th sess. (1954), p. 541. For U.S. comments see *ibid.*, pp. 534, 541.

linquishing its control over the island, Greece called upon the Assembly to consider the "Application, under the auspices of the United Nations, of the principle of equal rights and self-determination of peoples in the case of the population of the Island of Cyprus." In less obfuscatory terms, this meant union of Cyprus with Greece. Clearly no decision of the Assembly would be likely to sway either Greece or the United Kingdom from their respective positions, but satisfaction of Greek pride demanded that the complaint at least be given a hearing. After presentation of the views of the Greek delegation the committee adopted a New Zealand proposal, supported wholeheartedly by the United States in the interest of free-world solidarity, not to pass judgment on the matter. A face-saving amendment specifying that consideration would be suspended "for the time being" permitted the Greek delegation, which recognized the dangers in further pursuing the matter, to vote in favor of the draft and restore at least the gloss of unity. The plenary meeting ratified the committee decision.[63]

SUMMARY

Of all political questions, those arising from colonialism past and present have proved least amenable to United States influence. Often such questions have forced the United States to seek a compromise between conflicting values—to choose between the self-determination of peoples and the vested interests of good friends and allies. With exceptions, the United States has attempted to pursue a tortuous middle course, with the practical result of siding often against a majority. On only two occasions was a resolution passed over the American opposition vote, but many others failed only because of the two-thirds rule. On many questions, too, the United States voted for a compromise resolution with grave doubts as to its wisdom but even deeper reluctance to go on record against the general principle embodied in the resolution.

The treatment of Indians in South Africa was a perennial hair shirt for the American delegation. In the first session United States objections were overridden by a greater than two-thirds majority, and action was prevented in the second session only by the minority veto. A last-minute substitute measure supported by the United States failed to obtain even a simple majority. During subsequent sessions, the United States managed to vote with the majority, but this constituted no victory for American policies. United States representatives in the Assembly openly and repeatedly questioned the usefulness of continually belaboring South

---

[63] Resolution 814 (IX). The vote was 50-0-8. *Plenary Meetings*, 9th sess. (1954), p. 539. For committee discussion see *First Committee*, 9th sess. (1954), pp. 538-68. The vote in committee was 49-0-11. *Ibid.*, p. 567. Document A/2703 details the Greek complaint.

Africa, yet voted with the majority to prove their abhorrence of racial discrimination. Likewise, the United States heartily disapproved of Assembly action with respect to South African *apartheid* policies but chose to abstain rather than vote in the negative, in order not to give the appearance of condoning discrimination.

The questions of Tunisia and Morocco similarly provided difficult times for the American delegation. Conciliatory resolutions on both questions, which the United States could support with good conscience, were adopted by the seventh Assembly. But in the case of Morocco this resulted because the anti-colonial delegations, which commanded a majority but not a two-thirds majority, preferred a weak resolution to none at all. The following year the anti-colonial forces tried for the two-thirds majority but fell short by five votes. Happily for all concerned, a suitable compromise was arranged for the ninth session. The United States voted for compromise resolutions on both Tunisia and Morocco although it had originally evinced a preference for no resolution at all.

The United States was more determined and forceful in seeking a solution to the problem of Palestine. In the first special session of the Assembly the United States secured a fact-finding commission much to its liking, and, in collaboration with the Soviet Union, fought through the plan for partition of Palestine during the second session. From that point, however, the opposition became more formidable. In the spring of 1948 the American proposal for a temporary Palestinian trusteeship was buried in committee without coming to a vote, and an abortive American plan for a Jerusalem trusteeship failed to obtain a sufficiently large majority in plenary voting. The United States and Britain, working together, rallied in the third session to get Assembly approval for a Palestine conciliation commission, but many important features, including annexation of the non-Jewish portions of Palestine by Transjordan, were removed from the resolution. In the fourth session the United States could not muster even enough votes to prevent adoption by a two-thirds majority of a resolution to provide an international regime for Jerusalem. Subsequent policies initiated or supported by the United States, except those dealing with the refugee problem, were either drastically modified or rejected.

The United States had somewhat more success in promoting a settlement for the former Italian colonies but not before absorbing a resounding defeat with the collapse of the British-engineered compromise in the spring of 1948. Acquiescing in the apparent sentiment of the majority, the United States and Britain came to the fourth session prepared to advocate Libyan independence in the immediate future, without the previously contemplated ten-year period of tutelage. Assembly action on Libya and Somaliland coincided with the modified American views, but the United States was unable to secure quick action on Eritrea. The settlement subsequently decreed by the fifth session—federation with Ethiopia—represented a distinct compromise by the United States, which had expressed a preference for outright annexation by Ethiopia of all but the western province of Eritrea.

The record of the United States in dealing with legacies of colonialism in the Assembly and its political committees is thus one of compromise, retreat, and defeat, with only here and there a real victory for American leadership. Unquestionably, American influence is less evident and less effective in this area than with other types of political questions brought before the Assembly.

CHAPTER NINE

Organizational Questions

REPRESENTATION OF NON-GOVERNMENTAL ORGANIZATIONS

In contrast to the unanimity which characterized General Assembly action on most political questions in the first part of the first session,[1] a running battle was fought from the General Committee to the final plenary meeting over the representation of non-governmental organizations in the General Assembly and in ECOSOC. The issue was created by the requests of the World Federation of Trade Unions, the International Cooperative Alliance, the American Federation of Labor, and other similar bodies, to gain a voice in the councils of the United Nations. The Ukraine, supported by the Soviet Union and France, took up the cudgel in the General Committee for the left-wing WFTU, asking that it be given permanent consultative status in ECOSOC and the right to a hearing in the Assembly. The American representative opposed as an infringement of the Charter the admission of any organization to permanent participation of the kind suggested.[2] Without reaching any substantial agreement the General Committee passed the question on to the Assembly and its First Committee. The question of participation in the work of the Assembly was permitted to drop out of sight but sentiment in the First Committee favored recommending consultative status with ECOSOC for the WFTU. Consequently the American representative swallowed his objections to instructing another United Nations organ as to whom it should consult and worked instead to get equivalent consideration for the American Federation of Labor. The Assembly ultimately adopted a compromise resolution proposed by the United States. The WFTU, the International Cooperative Alliance, and the AF of L were mentioned by name, with precedence of order to the WFTU, and

---

[1] I.e., atomic energy, extradition of war criminals, and language rules. The question of language rules had been reviewed after the San Francisco Conference by the United Nations Preparatory Commission and was passed on to the first Assembly for final action. The First Committee made a number of recommendations for expansion of the interpreting service which were adopted unanimously by the Assembly. See Resolution 2 (I).

[2] *General Committee*, 1st sess., 1st pt. (1946), pp. 2-4, 8-10, 12, and document A/BUR/13. Article 71 of the Charter provides that "The Economic and Social Council may make suitable arrangements for consultation with non-governmental organizations which are concerned with matters within its competence."

other comparable non-governmental, national, and regional organizations were included as general categories.[3]

ADMISSION OF NEW MEMBERS

The fifty-one states which had proved their allegiance to the cause of peace by declaring war against the Axis became Charter members of the United Nations Organization. With a view to universality the United Nations Charter provided that other peace-loving states able and willing to fulfill Charter obligations might subsequently be admitted by action of the General Assembly upon recommendation of the Security Council.[4] Within the organization the desire to approximate universality more closely was strong, but disagreement among the permanent members of the Security Council concerning the qualifications of particular applicants barred the way to a growing list of prospective members. During the first year Afghanistan, Iceland, Siam, and Sweden successfully ran the gauntlet, but five others—Albania, Mongolia, Transjordan, Ireland, and Portugal—failed to win the Security Council recommendation. In the Security Council the United States was willing to compromise by recommending all five in a one-package deal. Australia, the Soviet Union, and the United Kingdom, however, insisted that each should be considered on its own merits. As a result the applications of Transjordan, Ireland, and Portugal were vetoed by the Soviet Union and the remaining two failed to win seven affirmative votes.[5] The Assembly accorded unanimous approval to the four states upon which the Security Council had agreed, but tempers flared over the five rejected applications. The Soviet representative contended that the most important factor in the determination of eligibility was the applicant's conduct during the second world war. The United States and most other delegations stood firmly on the expressed stipulations of the Charter. Australia, as spokesman for the small and middle powers, asserted the right of the Assembly to demand reconsideration by the Security Council of the rejected applications. This the United States was quite willing to admit, but in defense of the Security Council's prerogative it opposed another Australian proposal to establish, in terms which asserted the "primary and final responsibility" of the Assembly, a joint committee of the Assembly and Security Council for the formulation of precise admission rules. Both resolutions, however, were adopted by substantial majorities.[6]

---

[3] Resolution 4 (I). The plenary vote was 32-6 with 11 abstentions. *Plenary Meetings*, 1st sess., 1st pt. (1946), p. 534. For comments of American delegate see *First Committee*, 1st sess., 1st pt. (1946), pp. 16, 24.

[4] *United Nations Charter*, Article 4.

[5] Document A/108.

[6] Resolutions 35 and 36 (I). Voting was unanimous on the request for reconsideration of the rejected applications and 32-9-1 on the creation of the joint committee on

The joint committee met and formulated a number of rule changes which were subsequently adopted by the Security Council and the General Assembly.[7] But rejected applications continued to pile up in the files of the Security Council during 1947. To the five states previously rebuffed were added Austria, Bulgaria, Finland, Hungary, Italy, and Rumania, while Yemen and Pakistan succeeded in passing the barrier. Meanwhile the United States and the Soviet Union had reversed their positions with respect to admission: the Soviet Union was willing to entertain a package admission deal but the United States now insisted upon considering each application separately. Within the Assembly a number of delegations felt that universality should be the dominant consideration with respect to admission, but most shared officially the American conviction that the Soviet satellites were not qualified. The second session of the Assembly was presented with six separate recommendations that the Security Council favorably reconsider the vetoed applications of Austria, Finland, Ireland, Italy, Portugal, and Transjordan, respectively. The Soviet bloc tried to forestall action on these recommendations with a proposal that the Assembly adopt a single resolution requesting the permanent members of the Security Council to seek agreement through consultation on all of the pending applications. The Assembly accepted the communist suggestion for consultations but —over the opposition of the six communist states, Ethiopia, and India— adopted each of the six individual recommendations as well. On the initiative of the Belgian delegation the Assembly also voted to place the question of admission before the International Court of Justice. The court was asked to determine whether a member of the United Nations could make its consent to an application for admission dependent upon conditions not laid down in Article 4 of the Charter, such as the condition that other states be admitted together with the state in question.[8]

None of the vetoed applications was favorably reconsidered by the Security Council, but the International Court of Justice ruled that the enumeration of conditions for membership in Article 4 of the Charter

---

rules. *Plenary Meetings*, 1st sess., 2nd pt. (1946), pp. 993, 996. Only France, Norway, and the six communist states voted with the United States in opposition to the resolution. For pertinent discussion see *First Committee*, 1st sess., 2nd pt. (1946), esp. pp. 52-75, 80-81.

[7] The new rules specifically authorized the Assembly to request the Security Council to reconsider a rejected application and required it to submit to the Assembly a complete record of its dealings with membership applications whether it recommended admission or not. See document A/384 and Resolution 116 (II).

[8] Resolutions 113 A, B, C, D, E, F, G, and H (II). Voting on the request for an ICJ opinion was 40-8-2. The Soviet draft as amended was adopted 46-1-5. Voting on Ireland was 43-8-1; Portugal, 40-9-3; Transjordan, 44-8-0; Italy, 43-8-1; Finland, 44-8-0; Austria, 43-8-1. *Plenary Meetings*, 2nd sess. (1947), pp. 1078-80.

was exhaustive.[9] This gave the anti-communist states new grounds in the third Assembly to condemn the Soviet veto of membership applications. Otherwise discussion of the question proceeded much as before. The United States delegate, reiterating the need for each state to meet the requirements of Article 4, recommended that the Security Council be asked once more to reconsider the rejected applications of Transjordan, Ireland, Portugal, Italy, Finland, and Austria, this time in the light of the court's opinion. An Australian proposal that the Security Council act in accordance with the court opinion was subsequently approved, and seven vetoed non-communist applications, now including that of Ceylon, were recommended for reconsideration. The communist delegations received a small crumb of satisfaction in the adoption of a Swedish draft requesting the Security Council to review all applications, taking into account the particular circumstances of each case. This resolution was passed without opposition.[10]

With no essential change the question of admission came before the fourth session. The Assembly once more found the non-communist applicants, which now included the Republic of Korea and Nepal, eligible for admission, and rejected a Soviet proposal that all unapproved applications be re-examined together by the Security Council.[11] Two additional proposals also secured adoption. One was an Argentine request for the International Court of Justice to determine whether the Assembly could legally grant United Nations membership to a state without a Security Council recommendation. The other was an Iraqi appeal to the permanent members of the Security Council not to use the veto in questions of admission.[12] As was anticipated the International Court subsequently ruled that new members could not be admitted without a Security Council recommendation, and the Assembly in its fifth

---

[9] See document A/597.

[10] Resolutions 197 A, B, C, D, E, F, G, H, I (III). Plenary voting on the Australian proposal was 32-10-2, and on the Swedish draft, 33-0-10. Only the six communist states opposed the other resolutions. *Plenary Meetings*, 3rd sess., 1st pt. (1948), pp. 800-801. See U.S. comments, *ibid.*, p. 773, and *Ad Hoc Political Committee*, 3rd sess., 1st pt. (1948), pp. 77-78.

The State of Israel was admitted during the second part of the third session after recommendation from the Security Council. Because of Arab opposition the question was debated through ten committee sessions before a favorable decision was rendered. In the final plenary vote, 37-12-9, twelve Asian and African states were in the negative and nine other members, including the United Kingdom, abstained. *Plenary Meetings*, 3rd sess., 2nd pt. (1948-49), pp. 330-31. The United States voted with the communist bloc in approving the admission of Israel.

[11] Resolutions 296 A, B, C, D, E, F, G, H, I (IV). All were adopted with fifty or more affirmative votes. *Plenary Meetings*, 4th sess. (1949), p. 329. For rejected Soviet draft see document A/1079.

[12] Resolutions 296 J and K (IV). The vote was 42-9-6 and 34-10-9, respectively. *Plenary Meetings*, 4th sess. (1949), p. 329. The United States had on several previous occasions expressed its willingness to forego the veto in such cases.

session was content to adopt a single resolution asking the Security Council to keep membership applications under consideration in accordance with the resolutions adopted during the fourth session.[13]

A number of Latin-American delegations requested a place on the agenda of the sixth session for the question of admission in order to try a "new approach" to the problem. Costa Rica, El Salvador, Guatemala, Honduras, and Nicaragua jointly suggested that the International Court be asked to lay down criteria or rules for interpreting votes in the Security Council on questions of admission and, in particular, to determine whether the negative vote of one permanent member could nullify a recommendation receiving seven affirmative votes. This "new approach" proved so provocative that the sponsors later thought better of their proposal and offered a second draft to postpone discussion of the matter until the seventh session. The United States actively supported the postponement, and the Assembly concurred 36-5.[14]

Less quickly disposed of were two rival drafts submitted by Peru and the Soviet Union. The Peruvian proposal closely resembled previous resolutions in its hopes for universality, its unyielding stand upon Article 4 of the Charter, and its appeal for consultations among the five permanent members of the Security Council. One added feature, however, was an invitation to applicants to present proof of their qualifications for membership on the basis of the conditions laid down by the Charter. The Soviet draft called for Security Council re-examination of all previously rejected applications, excepting that of South Korea. The United States representative in the First Committee indicated readiness to support the Peruvian draft but strongly objected to the Soviet proposal because, in his view, it implied favorable endorsement of all pending applications. The omission of Korea was also deemed a fatal defect. The committee approved the Peruvian measure by a substantial majority and defied the American caveat by adopting the Soviet resolution as well, on a vote of 21-12 with 25 abstentions.[15] Plenary voting, however, was another story. The Peruvian draft was endorsed by a solid majority, but the

[13] Document A/1353 and Resolution 495 (V). Voting was 46-5-2. The question was disposed of without reference to a committee. *Plenary Meetings*, 5th sess. (1950), p. 586.

[14] Resolution 506 B (VI). The vote was 36-5-14. *Plenary Meetings*, 6th sess. (1951), p. 470. The original draft is document A/C.1/708.

[15] Vote on the Peruvian draft, document A/C.1/702 and Revs. 1, 2, and 3, was 36-9-12. For committee voting see *Plenary Meetings*, 6th sess. (1951), pp. 256-57. U.S. comments are found *ibid.*, p. 251. Document A/C.1/703 contains the Soviet draft. The New York *Times*, Jan. 26, 1952, p. 1, commented, "It was the first time a Soviet resolution strenuously opposed by the United States had been carried by the Political Committee and to that extent at least it was a diplomatic victory for the Soviet Union."

United States mustered an additional nine opposing votes to leave the Soviet proposal far short of the required two-thirds majority.[16]

The Security Council reported to the seventh session that the number of states rebuffed by the Soviet veto had been increased to fourteen by the addition of Libya, Japan, Vietnam, Laos, and Cambodia, and that an application from the communist-sponsored Democratic Republic of Vietnam had failed to obtain the necessary seven affirmative votes. In order to break the log-jam several Latin-American delegations were ready to declare admission a procedural question not subject to the veto or, alternatively, to regard as favorably recommended the nine non-communist states included in the Soviet package offer. In preference to such measures of questionable wisdom and dubious constitutionality the United States delegation supported a five-power Latin-American draft recommending the establishment of a special committee to explore the possibilities for agreement among the permanent members of the Security Council. Taking the more discreet course the Assembly settled on the five-power draft.[17] In addition the Assembly upheld past precedent by declaring that the states with freshly vetoed membership applications were qualified for admission to the United Nations.[18]

Hopes that the special committee might uncover new areas of agreement were disappointed. Its report to the eighth session was merely a record of deliberations without specific recommendations. Nevertheless the Peruvian delegation was ready to sponsor a new effort to reach agreement through a Good Offices Committee. Both the United States and the Soviet Union acquiesced in the creation of the committee, although openly skeptical of its success. With this dubious blessing the proposal was adopted unanimously.[19] The doubts, unfortunately, proved fully justified, and the Good Offices Committee was forced to report no progress to the ninth session. However, numerous smaller states were unwilling to disband the committee and the United States now affirmatively supported its continuation. In another show of unanimity the Assembly extended the committee's mandate for another year.[20]

[16] The Peruvian draft was embodied in Resolution 506 A (VI). Voting on the two measures was 43-8-7 and 22-21-16. *Plenary Meetings*, 6th sess. (1951), pp. 456, 469.

[17] Resolution 620 A (VII). The plenary vote was 48-5-6. *Plenary Meetings*, 7th sess. (1952), p. 479. Documents A/AC.61/L.31 and A/AC.61/L.30 contain the more extreme proposals. For comments of United States representative see *Ad Hoc Political Committee*, 7th sess. (1952), pp. 263-265.

[18] Resolutions 620 B, C, D, E, F, G (VII). Voting on the draft concerning Japan was 50-5-4; Vietnam, 40-5-12; Cambodia, 38-5-14; Laos, 36-5-14; Libya, 51-5-2; Jordan, 49-5-3. The United States voted in the affirmative in each instance. *Ibid.*, pp. 479-80.

[19] Resolution 718 (VIII). *Plenary Meetings*, 8th sess. (1953), p. 252. For comments of United States and Soviet delegates see *Ad Hoc Political Committee*, 8th sess. (1953), pp. 15-16, 51. Report of the special committee is found in document A/2400.

[20] Resolution 817 (IX). Although voting for the resolution as a whole the United

At this point unanimity on the question of admission ended. Scarcely was the Good Offices Committee endowed with authority to act for another year when a heated controversy developed concerning the desirability of recommending particular membership applications to the consideration of the Security Council. The committee entertained the usual Soviet proposal for en bloc admission of fourteen selected states, five communist and nine non-communist. In addition there was a French draft asking favorable reconsideration for Laos and Cambodia, a United States request of similar import with respect to Vietnam and South Korea, and a three-power Latin-American proposal which included all the other non-communist applicants. India, contending that further discussion of specific applications was inconsistent with the mandate given the Good Offices Committee, proposed that the committee resolve the question by sending all of the pending draft resolutions and a full record of committee discussion to the Security Council. This course of action found favor with many delegations, but the United States representative protested that the five communist applicants, which had never received a majority vote in the Security Council, should not be treated on a level with the non-communist applicants which had. Opinion was so evenly divided that the Indian resolution won committee approval by virtue of a single vote. With no possibility of securing adoption by the Assembly the Indian delegate chose to withdraw the motion before it came to a plenary vote rather than face the unpleasantness of a divided Assembly and certain defeat.[21]

CHINESE REPRESENTATION

The question of recognizing the Chinese Communist government as the representative of China in the Assembly was first raised at the beginning of the fifth session by the presentation of rival sets of credentials for the Chinese seat. India, among the first to accord official recognition to the Peiping government, urged immediate recognition of the communist credentials. But such action was not to be. Moved by the promptings of the American chief delegate to "vote now and vote it

---

States abstained in committee voting on one paragraph which seemed to imply that members of the Security Council would be in a better position to solve the problem of admissions at a periodic meeting under Article 28, paragraph 2, than at a regular meeting—an assumption which seemed unwarranted to the American delegation. *Ad Hoc Political Committee*, 8th sess. (1953), pp. 71, 116. For plenary voting see *Plenary Meetings*, 9th sess. (1954), p. 330. Document A/2720 contains report of the Good Offices Committee.

[21] *Plenary Meetings*, 9th sess. (1954), pp. 330-31. Committee vote on the draft, document A/AC.76/L.14, was 25-24-6. *Ad Hoc Political Committee*, 9th sess. (1954), pp. 124-25. U.S. comments are found *ibid.*, p. 122. Documents A/AC.76/L.7, A/AC.76/L.4, A/AC.76/L.13, and A/AC.76/L.9/Rev.1, are the proposals not acted upon by the committee.

down," the Assembly rejected the Indian proposal 16-33 with 10 abstentions.[22] Pending the report of a special committee established to consider the question of Chinese representation, the Nationalist government was granted full membership rights. The subsequent report of the committee made no recommendations whatever, and the Nationalist delegation continued to represent China in the General Assembly.[23]

Other organs of the United Nations had been beset with the same problem of conflicting claims to China's seat. The insistence with which the claims were pressed on both sides augured no quick and final settlement. Under these circumstances the Cuban delegation proposed that the fifth Assembly formulate a set of general criteria by which the organs of the United Nations might be able to judge more objectively between rival claimants to representation. At the suggestion of the United States the Cuban draft was sent to a subcommittee for detailed consideration. The subcommittee's recommendation, prepared under the vigilant eye of the United States representative, set forth specific criteria of eligibility under which the exclusion of the Peiping government could be readily justified. They included control of territory, consent of the governed, willingness and ability to carry out Charter obligations, and a consideration of the extent to which the governing authority was established by internal processes.[24] The whole Ad Hoc Political Committee was not as easily convinced as the subcommittee that the bases of future decision should be delimited so meticulously. The criteria of eligibility prized by the United States were wholly eliminated, and the remaining portions of the draft were rephrased into a loose directive to consider any question of representation in the light of the purposes and principles of the Charter and the circumstances of each case. Thus reduced to nothingness the resolution was adopted 36-6 with 9 abstentions.[25]

In subsequent sessions the question of Chinese representation continued to plague the Assembly but the adamantine stand of the United States blighted any hope of compromise in the absence of a general Far Eastern settlement. At the beginning of each successive session the Assembly decided not to consider proposals for the exclusion of the Nationalist government or to seat representatives of Peiping. Each time the proposal

---

[22] *Plenary Meetings*, 5th sess. (1950), pp. 6, 15.

[23] The vote on the creation of the committee was 38-6-11, and on Nationalist representation, 42-8-6. *Ibid.*, p. 16. For report of committee see document A/1923. The Assembly took note of the report in Resolution 501 (V), adopted November 5, 1951, by a vote of 36-5-2. *Plenary Meetings*, 5th sess. (1950), p. 749.

[24] The subcommittee vote was 8-4-2. See document A/AC.38/L.45, report of the subcommittee.

[25] Resolution 396 (V). The amended draft was approved by the committee 29-7-15. *Ad Hoc Political Committee*, 5th sess. (1950), pp. 388-89. For plenary voting see *Plenary Meetings*, 5th sess. (1950), p. 675.

carried by substantial majorities.[26] The attitude of the United States was clearly decisive in the voting. Many delegations whose governments recognized the Peiping regime abstained or supported the annual motion for postponement in order not to force a vote on an issue which found the Assembly so strongly and deeply divided.[27]

VOTING IN THE SECURITY COUNCIL

At San Francisco the smaller powers reluctantly accepted the Great Power veto in the Security Council in order to make agreement on a Charter possible. Their misgivings were proved portentous by succeeding events. By November, 1946, when the first Assembly met in resumed session, the Soviet Union had used the veto ten times to block decisions supported by a majority of votes in the Council and had forestalled action on numerous other occasions by threat of the veto. The dissatisfaction of smaller powers was evident in numerous draft proposals relating to the veto, ranging from suggestions for consultation among the five permanent members to the convening of a general conference for Charter revision.[28] The position of the United States was somewhat ambiguous. As one of the Great Powers which had insisted upon the unanimity principle at San Francisco, it still cherished the veto and recoiled from the thought of hasty Charter amendment. On the other hand the United States was willing voluntarily to restrict its own exercise of the veto, particularly with respect to the pacific settlement of disputes, and evinced interest in "clarification" of the voting formula through the development of "suitable practices and procedures."[29]

In the First Committee extremist proposals found little support. For practical consideration the field was quickly narrowed to two draft resolutions, one sponsored by the Chinese delegation and the other by Australia. The latter proposal contemplated easing the problem through consultation among the members of the Security Council and the adoption of standardized procedures for the application of the Charter

---

[26] See Resolutions 609 (VII), 800 (VIII), and 903 (IX). At the beginning of the sixth session the question of Chinese representation was discussed as a part of the General Committee's report to the Assembly and, although voted upon, was not made the subject of a resolution. The vote in the sixth session was 37-11-4; seventh session, 42-7-9; eighth session, 44-10-2; ninth session, 43-11-6. *Plenary Meetings*, 6th sess. (1951), pp. 99-104; 7th sess. (1952), p. 167-68; 8th sess. (1953), p. 10; 9th sess. (1954), pp. 11-12.

[27] See remarks of the British delegate in the ninth session, *Plenary Meetings*, 9th sess. (1954), p. 6. Others supported the United States proposals through conviction that Red China had not demonstrated the characteristics of a peace-loving nation. See, e.g., statement of Australian representative. *Ibid.*, pp. 6-7.

[28] E.g., documents A/C.1/34, A/C.1/42, A/C.1/49/Rev.1, A/C.1/52, and A/C.1/57.

[29] *First Committee*, 1st sess., 2nd pt. (1946), pp. 92-94, and *The U.S. and the U.N.*, report of President to Congress (1946), pp. 8-11.

voting formula. Its most controversial feature was an uncomplimentary allusion to past exercise of the veto right. Except for this paragraph the Australian draft corresponded closely to the expressed views of the American delegation. The Chinese draft was altogether less contentious. It urged that the Security Council use the voting right to facilitate prompt decisions but made no suggestions for consultations, the formulation of voting procedures, or other specific action. Of the two the Chinese proposal was preferred by the Soviet Union. In committee voting the Australian proposal received majority approval after the controversial paragraph had been eliminated.[30] Despite Soviet accusations that the United States and Britain were working covertly through Australia to wreck the unanimity principle, the Assembly adopted the committee recommendation unchanged.[31]

The United States delegation came to the second Assembly fully committed to liberalization of Security Council voting procedures. Other delegations, notably those of Argentina and Australia, went well beyond the United States in their demands for drastic limitation of the veto. However, the United States seized the initiative by proposing that the question be assigned to the newly created Interim Committee of the General Assembly for detailed study. This suggestion was accepted by the Assembly with the result that a substantive decision was deferred until the next session.[32]

The Interim Committee fulfilled its mandate by preparing for the third Assembly a detailed list of questions grouped in three categories: (1) procedural questions which under the Charter were not subject to the Great Power veto; (2) questions which ought to be decided by any seven affirmative votes, whether or not they were deemed procedural; and (3) questions presumably subject to the veto.[33] In the Ad Hoc Political Committee the United States, China, France, and the United Kingdom jointly sponsored a draft resolution requesting the members of the Security Council to consider seriously the suggestions of the Interim Committee and devise among themselves a code of conduct to govern the exercise of the veto. Neither the Soviet Union nor the extreme

[30] For committee voting see *ibid.*, pp. 290-92. Soviet and U.S. comments on the two drafts, documents A/C.1/121 and A/C.1/122, are found *First Committee*, 1st sess., 2nd pt. (1946), pp. 288-89.

[31] Resolution 40 (I). Plenary vote was 36-6-9. *Plenary Meetings*, 1st sess., 2nd pt. (1946), p. 1264. For Soviet comments see *ibid.*, pp. 1235-44, esp. pp. 1243-44.

[32] Resolution 117 (II). The plenary vote was 38-6-11. *Plenary Meetings*, 2nd sess. (1947), p. 1272. See comments of Warren R. Austin, New York *Times*, Sept. 17, 1947, p. 3, and address of Secretary of State George C. Marshall, *Plenary Meetings*, 2nd sess. (1947), pp. 24-25.

[33] Document A/578.

revisionists were pleased with the draft, but as a moderate step toward liberalization it easily won a substantial majority. Only the communist members voted in the opposition.[34]

THE INTERIM COMMITTEE

One method of mitigating the veto paralysis of the Security Council was to agree upon less restrictive voting practices and procedures. But real progress in this area was dependent upon agreement with the Soviet Union, an extremely unlikely possibility. An alternative was to compensate for the weakness of the Security Council by strengthening the Assembly. With this objective in view the United States urged upon the second Assembly the creation of an Interim Committee, with representation from all member states, authorized to function when the Assembly itself was not in session. If the Security Council were prevented by the unanimity rule from acting upon a threatening situation, the problem could be shifted to the Assembly or the Interim Committee, one of which would be in session at all times. The committee would, presumably, provide the further advantage of shortened Assembly sessions. Under the terms of the American proposal the committee would have broad authorization for investigation, discussion, and recommendation.[35]

The Soviet bloc termed the whole proposal illegal and refused to participate in the work of a subcommittee appointed to study the measure. Other delegations were sympathetic to the general principle but questioned the extremely broad scope of action proposed for the committee. Consequently the draft which emerged from the subcommittee more carefully delimited the competence of the Interim Committee than the original proposal. A number of the changes were accepted by the United States delegation without serious protest, but the stipulation that no item of business be discussed without the prior consent of a two-thirds majority went well beyond what the United States thought necessary or desirable. However, the United States accepted the amended draft in order to save the committee. The communist members denounced the proposal as an American scheme to circumvent the Security Council, and, when the resolution was approved by the First Committee, announced their intention not to participate in the work of the Interim Committee. Adoption, however, was assured.[36] At the following session of the Assembly the Interim Committee was continued in existence for

---

[34] Resolution 267 (III). The final vote was 43-6-2. *Plenary Meetings*, 3rd sess., 2nd pt. (1948-49), p. 129. Document A/578 contains the Interim Committee report.

[35] Document A/C.1/196.

[36] Resolution 111 (II). The vote was 41-6-6. *Plenary Meetings*, 2nd sess. (1947), p. 822. For attitude of communist delegations see *First Committee*, 2nd sess. (1947), pp. 178-79, 311-24, 333-36. Document A/C.1/240 is report of subcommittee activities.

a second year, and during the fourth session its mandate was renewed without a time limit.[37]

MACHINERY OF INTERNATIONAL COOPERATION

The Interim Committee was authorized under its original directive to study methods for promoting cooperation in the maintenance of international peace and security. In its report to the third Assembly the committee offered four specific recommendations relating to the pacific settlement of international disputes. They included continuation of the General Act for the Pacific Settlement of International Disputes with modification to substitute United Nations machinery for League machinery, appointment of a rapporteur or conciliator to assist in the settlement of disputes and threatening situations brought before the Assembly, appointment by the Security Council of a similar officer, and establishment of a General Assembly panel for enquiry and conciliation. All were subsequently endorsed by the Assembly except the recommendation for a General Assembly conciliator. At the suggestion of the United States this proposal was referred to the Interim Committee for consideration in connection with studies of Assembly procedure in the whole area of pacific settlement, which the committee was currently undertaking. Only the communist delegations opposed the majority.[38]

At the fifth session the Yugoslavian delegation proposed the establishment of a permanent commission of good offices to assist in the settlement of disputes and litigious questions on the agenda of the Security Council and the General Assembly. The United States representative in the First Committee objected to the creation of such a commission under the terms set forth in the Yugoslav draft on the ground that it would raise legal and political difficulties. He suggested that the proposal be referred to the Interim Committee in connection with its study of the machinery of peaceful settlement. This suggestion was adopted with a minimum of debate.[39]

GENERAL ASSEMBLY METHODS AND PROCEDURES

The excessive length of General Assembly sessions early became a source of concern to most delegations. One argument advanced in favor

[37] Resolutions 196 (III) and 295 (IV). The vote in the third session was 40-6-1, and in the fourth session, 45-5-4. *Plenary Meetings*, 3rd sess. (1948), p. 682, and 4th sess. (1949), p. 312.

[38] Resolution 268 (III). For plenary voting on the various propositions see *Plenary Meetings*, 3rd sess., 2nd pt. (1948-49), pp. 208-9. Document A/605 contains Interim Committee report. Note U.S. comments, *Ad Hoc Political Committee*, 3rd sess., 2nd pt. (1948-49), p. 5.

[39] Resolution 379 (V). Plenary voting was 45-5-3. *Plenary Meetings*, 5th sess. (1950), p. 429. For comments of U.S. representative see *First Committee*, 5th sess. (1950), p. 292. Yugoslav proposal is document A/1401.

of the Interim Committee was the need to relieve the overcrowded agenda of the Assembly. Despite the labors of the Interim Committee, however, the third session was more heavily burdened than its predecessors. In the hope of discovering some way to dispose of the work load more expeditiously, Denmark, Norway, and Sweden suggested the creation of an *ad hoc* committee for the revision of Assembly methods and procedures. All members of the Assembly were willing to let a special committee struggle with the problem, although the Soviet delegate objected to confining its terms of reference to technical matters when, as he believed, the increasing length of sessions was in fact due to loading the agenda with irrelevant items. For this reason the communist delegations abstained while all others voted in favor of the resolution. The United States approved but did not initiate the action.[40]

A UNITED NATIONS GUARD

Three years' experience in the operation of United Nations field missions, culminating in the assassination of Count Bernadotte, indicated a need to provide better protection for personnel and property of the missions. To meet this need the Secretary-General requested the third Assembly to establish an armed United Nations Guard of some eight hundred highly trained men, including personnel in transportation, communication, and other technical services. The Philippine delegation introduced a draft resolution to grant the Secretary-General's request forthwith; the Soviet Union opposed the whole plan as a usurpation of Security Council prerogative; and the United States called for careful study before taking a decision. The American view prevailed and the Philippine proposal was modified to provide for a special committee to study the problem. In this form it was adopted 47-6.[41] Because of contention evoked by his original proposal, the Secretary-General scaled down the request to a three-hundred-man field service, designed primarily to strengthen and systematize servicing functions already performed by the Secretariat, and a panel of field observers qualified to serve upon call of a competent United Nations organ. The special committee approved the new request with minor modifications and recommended it to the fourth session of the Assembly. Although some delegations questioned the workability of the proposed observers panel, the United

---

[40] Resolution 271 (III). The vote was 48-0-6. *First Committee*, 5th sess. (1950), p. 225. Soviet comments are found *Plenary Meetings*, 3rd sess., 2nd pt. (1948-49), p. 224.

[41] Resolution 270 (III). Cf. the original Philippine proposal, document A/AC.24/42, and Secretary-General's request, document A/656. The vote was 47-6-1. *Plenary Meetings*, 3rd sess., 2nd pt. (1948-49), p. 223. U.S. and Soviet views are presented *Ad Hoc Political Committee*, 3rd sess., 2nd pt. (1948-49), pp. 25-36.

States supported creation of both panel and field service. Both were ultimately approved by the Assembly.[42]

SUMMARY

Except for the admission of new members, an item which appeared on the agenda of every session, no resolution on an organizational question was approved as a whole in committee or plenary meeting without the United States affirmative vote. As with questions previously considered, however, most resolutions represented compromise, and in one or two instances the United States was defeated in paragraph voting or voting on amendments. This was notably true of the resolution on representation in organs of the United Nations. Where the United States attempted to exert influence, the result was usually a victory for the American position. Although abstentions were numerous and the opposition irrepressible, the United States each year beat down attempts to seat the Chinese Communist regime in the Assembly. After being on the defensive in early discussion of the veto, the United States shook free from its apprehensiveness of constricting the application of the unanimity rule and successfully took the initiative in discussions during the second and third sessions. The Interim Committee of the General Assembly was also a matter of American initiative and its creation a real triumph for American policy, even though compromise was necessary in delineating its competence and method of operation. Most of the remaining questions —those concerning language rules, the machinery of international cooperation, and Assembly methods and procedures—provided little occasion for exerting influence. The United States approved of the final Assembly action in each case. In debates on the representation of nongovernmental organizations and the creation of a United Nations Guard, later scaled down to a field service, the United States representative played an important but not dominant role.

Several defeats were absorbed, however, in voting upon the admission of new members. In the first session the American delegation joined forces with France, Norway, and the six communist members in vain opposition to a declaration by the Assembly of its precedence over the Security Council in matters of admission. This marked one of three occasions when a resolution on a political question was adopted over a United States negative vote. Once in the sixth session, and again in the ninth, the Assembly majority voted for the Security Council to reconsider rejected applications in terms which, to the United States dele-

---

[42] Resolutions 297 A and B (IV). Plenary voting was 46-5-3 for the field service and 38-6-11 for the panel of observers. *Plenary Meetings*, 4th sess. (1949), p. 334. For U.S. position see *Ad Hoc Political Committee*, 4th sess. (1949), pp. 98-99, 119. Documents A/AC.29/1 and A/959 contain recommendations of the special committee.

gation, seemed to place all applications on the same level. In neither case was the resolution adopted. The controversial draft did not even come to a plenary vote in the ninth session. But the United States objected strenuously to both drafts, and both were given majorities in defiance of American opposition. Throughout the course of nine sessions the United States actually attempted little constructive leadership on questions of admission. It fought resolutions it did not approve, and occasionally sponsored drafts recommending reconsideration of membership applications with which it was particularly concerned. But the initiative was usually left to others, and proposed drafts received American support with greatly varying degrees of enthusiasm. The United States position on admission, taken as a whole, does not even have the virtue of consistency, in view of the reversal on the issue of en bloc admission. The American record on questions of admission thus appears as mediocre and, with respect to the entire group of organizational questions, only spotty.

CHAPTER TEN

The Record: A Summary

In preceding chapters an effort has been made to indicate the extent to which policies advocated by the United States have been adopted by the General Assembly during its first nine sessions. Each political question has been briefly described as to its substance, the position taken by the United States, and the ultimate action of the Assembly. The record reveals, with few exceptions, that the General Assembly has adopted resolutions approved by the United States at least in principle whenever the United States has chosen to exert strong influence. Only three resolutions on political questions have been adopted despite the negative vote of the United States.[1] American influence has been particularly evident on questions of disarmament, atomic energy control,

TABLE 5. UNITED STATES VOTING RECORD FOR 86 ROLL-CALL VOTES ON POLITICAL QUESTIONS CLASSIFIED BY TYPES

	Number of votes	Times with majority	Times opposing majority	Absten-tions	Per cent of times with majority
Cooperation, propaganda, disputes	25	24	0	1	96
Disarmament and collective security	17	16	1	0	94
Organizational questions	14	11	3	0	79
Total non-colonial questions	56	51	4	1	91
Colonial questions	30	19	7	4	63
Total	86	70	11	5	81

[1] Two such defeats were absorbed during the first session, one resolution dealing with the admission of new members and the other with the treatment of Indians in the Union of South Africa. The third question on which the American negative vote was overridden by a two-thirds majority was the internationalization of Jerusalem, in the fourth session.

TABLE 6. MAJORITY AGREEMENT SCORES FOR 86 ROLL-CALL VOTES ON POLITICAL
QUESTIONS

Rank	State	Times Voting with Majority	Rank	State	Times Voting with Majority
1	Philippines	79	31	El Salvador	61
2	Bolivia	76	32	Lebanon	61
3	Liberia	75	33	Luxembourg	61
4	Uruguay	75	34	Thailand	61
5	Brazil	74	35	Colombia	60
6	Honduras	73	36	Egypt	60
7	Nicaragua	72	37	Turkey	60
8	Ecuador	71	38	Belgium	59
9	Mexico	71	39	France	58
10	Chile	70	40	Netherlands	58
11	China	70	41	Australia	56
12	United States	70	42	Guatemala	56
13	Argentina	69	43	Sweden	55
14	Cuba	69	44	United Kingdom	53
15	Ethiopia	69	45	Syria	51
16	Iraq	69	46	Pakistan	50
17	Panama	69	47	Saudi Arabia	50
18	Haiti	68	48	South Africa	50
19	Iceland	68	49	Afghanistan	44
20	Paraguay	67	50	Israel	44
21	Venezuela	67	51	Yemen	44
22	Iran	66	52	Burma	43
23	Norway	65	53	India	43
24	Dominican Republic	64	54	Yugoslavia	43
25	Peru	64	55	Indonesia	27
26	Costa Rica	63	56	Byelorussia	24
27	Greece	63	57	Czechoslovakia	24
28	New Zealand	63	58	Poland	24
29	Canada	61	59	Ukraine	24
30	Denmark	61	60	Soviet Union	24

and collective security. In propaganda battles, where its integrity and
motives have been questioned, the United States has never lost a major
vote. The same record holds for international disputes and threatening
situations on which a firm stand has been taken. The record is not as
good with respect to organizational questions, most notably the admission
of new members, and very indifferent for problems of dependent or
economically and politically submerged peoples. The fact must be under-
scored, however, that the United States has not taken the initiative in
most of the questions considered in this study as "legacies of colonialism."
American representatives have enunciated a position on such questions

but in most cases have not attempted to press hard for a particular decision. The very presence on the agenda of the Moroccan and Tunisian questions, for example, has been a source of great embarrassment to the American delegation. Because of conflicting values and loyalties the United States has not been in a position to lead out strongly in one direction or another. The delegation has tried rather to assume the role of a mediator between almost irreconcilable positions. Under these circumstances it is not surprising that the United States has frequently voted with the minority on colonial questions. This in no way detracts from the generalization that the United States almost invariably secures the required majority when influence is vigorously exerted. But it raises

TABLE 7. MAJORITY AGREEMENT SCORES FOR 56 ROLL-CALL VOTES ON POLITICAL QUESTIONS CLASSIFIED AS "NON-COLONIAL"

Rank	State	Times Voting with Majority	Rank	State	Times Voting with Majority
1	Philippines	53	31	France	45
2	Brazil	51	32	Norway	45
3	New Zealand	51	33	Argentina	44
4	Nicaragua	51	34	Costa Rica	44
5	United States	51	35	Denmark	44
6	Uruguay	51	36	Panama	44
7	Bolivia	50	37	El Salvador	43
8	Greece	50	38	Iceland	43
9	Honduras	50	39	Thailand	43
10	Turkey	50	40	Iran	42
11	Venezuela	50	41	South Africa	41
12	Cuba	49	42	Lebanon	38
13	Dominican Republic	49	43	Sweden	38
14	Liberia	49	44	Egypt	37
15	Australia	48	45	Guatemala	34
16	Belgium	48	46	Pakistan	28
17	Canada	48	47	Saudi Arabia	28
18	Chile	48	48	Syria	28
19	Ecuador	48	49	Israel	27
20	Haiti	48	50	Yemen	24
21	Luxembourg	48	51	Yugoslavia	22
22	Mexico	48	52	Afghanistan	21
23	China	47	53	Burma	21
24	Paraguay	47	54	India	19
25	United Kingdom	47	55	Indonesia	10
26	Ethiopia	46	56	Byelorussia	6
27	Iraq	46	57	Czechoslovakia	6
28	Netherlands	46	58	Poland	6
29	Peru	46	59	Ukraine	6
30	Colombia	45	60	Soviet Union	6

a presupposition that the effectiveness of American influence in the Assembly is limited by the nature of the issues.

Attention must also be drawn to the obvious fact that a record of voting frequently with the majority does not imply a series of clear victories for American policies. Some important draft resolutions initiated or strongly supported by the United States have in fact been adopted with little significant change. Such was the case, for instance, with the Uniting for Peace resolution of 1950. But on most questions the United States has been faced with the necessity of concession. The United States was strenuously opposed to the limitations upon the competence of the Interim Committee, on which many members insisted. Yet it accepted amendments to save the resolution as a whole. In December, 1946, the United States supported the resolution on the Spanish question with great misgivings, sacrificing its better judgment to the interests of greater unanimity. Such examples could be multiplied. If it is true that General Assembly resolutions on political questions, excluding colonial matters, usually embody the general principles of United States policy, it is equally true that most such resolutions differ in more or less significant detail from the proposals originally supported by the United States.

VOTING AGREEMENT WITH THE MAJORITY

Some aspects of the record can be precisely summarized and more easily comprehended in quantitative form. For this purpose eighty-six selected roll-call votes have been condensed into tabular form. Table 5 indicates how often the United States voted with the majority on the eighty-six roll-call votes classified by types; Tables 6 and 7 show majority agreement scores for all members, indicating the frequency with which each voted with the majority; Tables 8, 9, and 10 give scores of voting agreement with the United States. Given the initial assumption of American influence, the tables can provide a useful if rough index to the effectiveness of American influence. However, certain limitations of the statistical technique utilized must be carefully noted. The tables of agreement scores give no indication of the concessions which the United States may have made on particular questions in order to secure an effective majority on the final vote. Nor do they distinguish clearly between the resolutions with which the United States was vitally concerned as a leading protagonist and those in which a more passive role was assumed. The distinction is attempted in a general way through the separate tabulation of agreement scores for questions in categories designated, for convenience, as "colonial" and "non-colonial." This provides no more than a rough approximation, since the United States did not try to exercise vigorous leadership on all non-colonial political questions, and it took a very strong stand on a few in the colonial category.

Necessarily the results of the tabulations are conditioned by the representative character of the roll-call votes used in their construction. The criteria of selection were designed to provide data indicating the gross preference of Assembly members on as many political questions as possible, and, in lieu of any practicable system for weighting questions in terms of relative importance, to weight all questions equally by limiting the votes tabulated to one per question in all but a few instances. In the application of these criteria all roll-call votes on separate parts of resolutions were automatically eliminated from consideration. Although such

TABLE 8. SCORES OF AGREEMENT WITH THE UNITED STATES FOR 86 ROLL-CALL VOTES ON POLITICAL QUESTIONS

Rank	State	Times voting with U.S.	Rank	State	Times voting with U.S.
0	United States	86	30	United Kingdom	61
1	Nicaragua	77	31	Australia	60
2	Brazil	72	32	Mexico	60
3	China	71	33	El Salvador	58
4	Uruguay	71	34	Ethiopia	58
5	Honduras	70	35	France	57
6	Haiti	68	36	Thailand	57
7	New Zealand	68	37	Argentina	55
8	Panama	68	38	Iran	55
9	Bolivia	67	39	Sweden	55
10	Chile	67	40	Iraq	54
11	Cuba	67	41	South Africa	54
12	Netherlands	67	42	Guatemala	50
13	Canada	67	43	Lebanon	46
14	Dominican Republic	66	44	Egypt	45
15	Luxembourg	66	45	Pakistan	41
16	Paraguay	66	46	Israel	40
17	Philippines	66	47	Syria	37
18	Turkey	66	48	Saudi Arabia	34
19	Ecuador	65	49	Yugoslavia	34
20	Norway	65	50	Afghanistan	32
21	Peru	65	51	Burma	32
22	Belgium	64	52	India	31
23	Denmark	64	53	Yemen	31
24	Iceland	64	54	Indonesia	17
25	Liberia	64	55	Byelorussia	12
26	Venezuela	64	56	Czechoslovakia	12
27	Colombia	63	57	Poland	12
28	Costa Rica	62	58	Ukraine	12
29	Greece	62	59	Soviet Union	12

TABLE 9. SCORES OF AGREEMENT WITH THE UNITED STATES FOR 56 ROLL-CALL VOTES
ON POLITICAL QUESTIONS CLASSIFIED AS "NON-COLONIAL"

Rank	State	Times voting with U.S.	Rank	State	Times voting with U.S.
0	United States	56	30	Mexico	45
1	Nicaragua	53	31	El Salvador	44
2	Brazil	52	32	Ethiopia	44
3	Uruguay	52	33	Thailand	44
4	Chile	51	34	Norway	43
5	China	51	35	Denmark	42
6	Cuba	51	36	Iraq	42
7	Honduras	51	37	Iceland	41
8	Philippines	51	38	Iran	41
9	Bolivia	50	39	Argentina	40
10	Colombia	50	40	South Africa	40
11	Haiti	50	41	Sweden	36
12	Luxembourg	50	42	Lebanon	34
13	New Zealand	50	43	Egypt	33
14	Turkey	50	44	Guatemala	33
15	Venezuela	50	45	Pakistan	29
16	Belgium	49	46	Israel	24
17	Dominican Republic	49	47	Saudi Arabia	24
18	Greece	49	48	Syria	24
19	France	48	49	Yemen	20
20	Netherlands	48	50	Yugoslavia	20
21	Paraguay	48	51	Afghanistan	19
22	Australia	47	52	Burma	19
23	Canada	47	53	India	17
24	Ecuador	47	54	Indonesia	7
25	United Kingdom	47	55	Byelorussia	4
26	Liberia	46	56	Czechoslovakia	4
27	Panama	46	57	Poland	4
28	Peru	46	58	Ukraine	4
29	Costa Rica	45	59	Soviet Union	4

votes were undoubtedly significant in many questions, the vote on the
resolution as a whole was regarded as a better index of a member's attitude toward the resolution than its vote on any of the parts. Consistent
with the objective of limiting the tabulation to one vote per question,
a number of roll-call votes on whole propositions were omitted. In the
majority of questions involving roll-call votes on two or more different
whole propositions, one resolution was adopted by the Assembly and
one or more alternative resolutions rejected. Where this occurred only
the vote on the approved resolution was included in the tabulation.
Questions of the admission of new members, which sometimes eventuated
in the adoption by roll-call vote of as many as ten separate resolutions,

presented another problem. Here the practice was to select only one vote as representative of the whole group, since there was usually little variation in the voting between drafts. In four instances an exception was made to include two or three resolutions relating to one question but embodying separate action and adopted with significant differences in the voting alignment.[2] As a final consideration almost half of all political

TABLE 10. SCORES OF AGREEMENT WITH THE UNITED STATES FOR 56 ROLL-CALL VOTES ON POLITICAL QUESTIONS CLASSIFIED AS "NON-COLONIAL," EXPRESSED AS A PERCENTAGE OF TIMES VOTED

Rank	State	Per cent of agreement with U.S.	Rank	State	Per cent of agreement with U.S.
0	United States	100.0	30	Australia	83.9
1	Nicaragua	98.1	31	Canada	83.9
2	Haiti	96.1	32	United Kingdom	83.9
3	Paraguay	96.0	33	Mexico	81.8
4	Panama	95.8	34	South Africa	81.6
5	Cuba	94.4	35	Ethiopia	80.0
6	Honduras	94.4	36	Iraq	79.2
7	Costa Rica	93.8	37	Norway	76.8
8	Brazil	92.9	38	Denmark	75.0
9	Uruguay	92.9	39	Iran	73.2
10	Bolivia	92.6	40	Argentina	72.7
11	Luxembourg	92.6	41	Lebanon	72.3
12	Thailand	91.7	42	Guatemala	70.2
13	Chile	91.1	43	Sweden	67.9
14	China	91.1	44	Egypt	60.0
15	Philippines	91.1	45	Israel	57.1
16	Venezuela	90.9	46	Pakistan	55.8
17	Dominican Republic	90.7	47	Saudi Arabia	47.1
18	Peru	90.2	48	Syria	46.2
19	El Salvador	89.8	49	Yemen	41.7
20	Colombia	89.3	50	Burma	40.4
21	New Zealand	89.3	51	Afghanistan	35.2
22	Turkey	89.3	52	Yugoslavia	34.5
23	Greece	89.1	53	India	32.7
24	Liberia	88.5	54	Indonesia	21.9
25	Belgium	87.5	55	Byelorussia	7.4
26	Ecuador	87.0	56	Czechoslovakia	7.4
27	France	85.7	57	Poland	7.4
28	Netherlands	85.7	58	Ukraine	7.4
29	Iceland	85.4	59	Soviet Union	7.4

[2] There are other exceptions of a minor nature. In one case the vote used is a composite of plenary and committee voting on the same resolution. In another the roll-call on a rejected Soviet proposal is used in lieu of a vote on the approved resolution for which there was no roll-call. This deviation from the rule seemed warranted by the extremely close correspondence of the two votes.

questions are not represented in the tables, either because the voting was unanimous or because there was no final vote by roll-call on the resolutions concerned.

A word of caution must be enjoined with regard to interpretation of the tables. It should be emphasized that the tables of voting agreement scores do not constitute proof of American influence in the Assembly. Influence is not necessarily to be deduced from frequent concurrence with a majority. The tabulation of voting records for each of the sixty member nations shows that nine states voted with the majority more frequently than the United States. The Philippines, Bolivia, Liberia, and Uruguay—which ranked first through fourth, respectively—can scarcely be characterized as influential on that basis. The frequent concurrence with a majority becomes a significant index of influence only when coupled with attributes which neither the Philippines, Bolivia, Liberia, nor Uruguay possesses in marked degree: namely, the capacity to exert influence—in terms of a power base external to the Assembly—and a record of influence in the Assembly as evidenced by programs proposed and fought through to final adoption. The United States, on the other hand, pre-eminently fulfills these conditions. As a negative index of influence, the tables of majority agreement scores can stand on their own feet. Soviet Russia has proposed many more resolutions on political subjects than the United States, embodying far-reaching and significant programs. But by and large the Soviet proposals have not been adopted. In fact, the Soviet Union voted with the majority on only twenty-four of the eighty-six roll-call votes, fewer than any of the non-communist members. The Soviet Union has the external power base, it makes numerous proposals on significant matters, and it vigorously champions its own point of view. But in the absence of frequent concurrence with the majority the Soviet Union cannot be regarded as highly influential in the Assembly, except within its own tightly knit group. A table of majority agreement scores thus has significance for influence in the Assembly in a negative sense. A high majority agreement score cannot prove the existence of effective influence—a high score may in fact indicate judicious followership; but a low agreement score can effectively demonstrate its absence.

In this context the data presented in Tables 5 through 10 possess relevance for American influence in the Assembly as well as interest in their own right. Table 5 shows the United States voting record on the eighty-six roll-call votes classified by categories corresponding to the four subject-matter divisions adopted for Chapters Six through Nine of this study. Roll-call votes falling in the first three categories are further grouped into a fifth category of "non-colonial questions." Three of the succeeding five tables deal only with the fifty-six roll-call votes on non-colonial questions. This group of questions has been emphasized because, as indicated above, it includes on the whole those questions on which the United States has most actively exerted its influence.

On the scale of majority agreement scores for all eighty-six questions, in Table 6, the United States with seventy agreements ranks below nine other members—seven Latin-American states, the Philippines, and Liberia. Much farther down the list are the other three Great Powers— France, ranked thirty-ninth with fifty-eight agreements; the United Kingdom in forty-fourth place with fifty-three; and the Soviet Union at the bottom of the list with twenty-four. In the table of non-colonial questions, all of the Great Powers except the Soviet Union have relatively much higher scores. The United States is exceeded in the agreement column only by the Philippines. The United Kingdom ranks twenty-fifth with forty-seven agreements, France thirty-first with forty-five, and the Soviet Union with its satellites, once more at the end with a score of six. In general the Latin-American states and the small Western-oriented countries of Africa and Asia rank the highest on both scales. The explanation for this, certainly, is not hard to find: they voted with the United States on non-colonial questions and with the anti-colonial majority on colonial matters. Scattered over the broad center band of the continuum are the countries of Western Europe, the English-speaking members of the Commonwealth, and the more pro-Western countries of the Near East—Turkey, Iran, Iraq, and Lebanon. Near the end are Yugoslavia and the Asiatic neutralists with Burma, India, and Indonesia ranked the very lowest of the latter group. At the bottom of both tables stand the five communist members, whose extremely low agreement scores bear faithful witness to the many occasions on which they have stood in defiant opposition to a General Assembly majority.

VOTING AGREEMENT WITH THE UNITED STATES

Tables 8 and 9, showing voting agreement with the United States, like the two preceding tables give the total number of voting agreements recorded. In the calculation of agreement scores an absence, with the resulting failure to vote at all, has the same effect as a vote of disagreement or abstention. To equalize the factor of absence in Table 10, agreement scores are computed as a percentage of times voted rather than as a whole integer. Latin-American states dominate the higher ranks of all three tabulations, although this is especially noticeable in Table 6 where absence does not count as disagreement. In Table 6 the top ten, and sixteen of the first twenty, are Latin-American states. These sixteen states, on the average, voted with the United States 93.1 per cent of the time when non-colonial political questions were at issue. Even including the two renegades, Argentina and Guatemala, which rank well down in

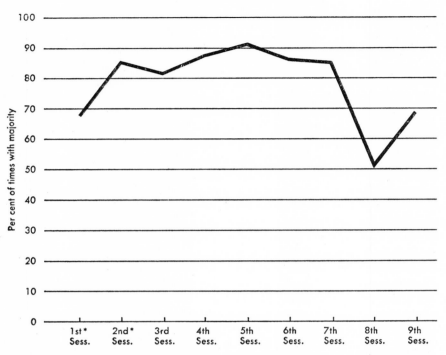

FIGURE 2. United States Voting Record for 86 Roll-Call Votes on Political Questions,
Tabulated by Session and Expressed as a Percentage

* Includes special session.

the second division of all three tables, the twenty republics to the south
on the average voted with the United States 90 per cent of the time on
this category of questions. Nationalist China on all three tables, and the
Philippines on the last two, rank within the first fifteen. Thailand is high,
taking twelfth place, on the table calculated by percentages. Of the
Commonwealth nations New Zealand consistently ranks the highest and
India, as might be surmised, the lowest. In Western Europe Luxembourg
appears as the most consistent supporter of the United States on non-
colonial questions and yields the honor to the Netherlands by a single
vote for the entire eighty-six issues. Sweden, of all Western European
states, unquestionably has voted least often with the United States.
Turkey votes more frequently with the United States than any other
country of the Near East, ranking as high as fourteen on Table 10 and
no lower than twenty-two on Table 8. Of the other Near Eastern States,
which, next to the communist members and the four South Asian
neutralists, vote least often with the United States, Iran and Iraq have
the highest scores. These data, when their limitations are borne in mind,
provide a useful index to states most amenable to United States influence.

VARIATION FROM SESSION TO SESSION

Thus far the influence of the United States in the Assembly has been treated almost as though it were an unvarying constant from session to session. The picture drawn has in fact been a composite view of American influence as it appears for the whole period 1946-1954. In terms of the voting record, American influence does not maintain constant strength throughout the first nine sessions. Table 11 and Figure 2 present data concerning the United States majority agreement record, session by session, for the eighty-six roll-call votes which have been used as a basis for other tabulations in this study. In Figure 2, where the agreement score is expressed as a percentage, the curve of agreement rises rapidly from 1946 to 1947, then, after a slight dip for 1948, curves gently upward to a peak in 1950 and descends gradually to 1952. The break from 1952 to 1953 is sharp, representing the fact that on three of the six roll-call votes tabulated for the eighth session the United States either abstained or voted against the majority. The curve rises slightly for the ninth session.

It is not to be contended that Table 11 and the graph in Figure 2 are a completely accurate representation of the trend of United States

TABLE 11. UNITED STATES VOTING RECORD FOR 86 ROLL-CALL VOTES ON POLITICAL QUESTIONS, TABULATED BY SESSION

Session	Votes per session	Defeats	Abstentions	Times with majority	Per cent of times with majority
1st and 1st spec.	6	2	0	4	67
2nd and 2nd spec.	7	1	0	6	86
3rd	11	1	1	9	82
4th	9	1	0	8	89
5th	14	1	0	13	93
6th	8	1	0	7	88
7th	15	1	1	13	87
8th	6	2	1	3	50
9th	10	1	2	7	70
Total	86	11	5	70	81

influence in the Assembly. The limitations of the voting sample and the inherent difficulties of expressing an essentially qualitative character in quantitative terms rule out all but tentative and rough-hewn inferences. However, the conclusions which may be tentatively drawn regarding the vicissitudes of American influence in the Assembly are in harmony with other evidence bearing on the subject. It will be recalled from the discussion of Chapter Three that the three basic ingredients of American influence in the Assembly were said to be national power, the dependence of other states upon American economic aid, and the need for non-communist unity in the face of Soviet imperialism. In 1946 the pattern of economic dependence and the threat of Soviet imperialism were not yet clearly established. By the opening of the second session, in the fall of 1947, the cold war had begun in earnest and sixteen states of Western Europe were in the process of planning programs for economic co-operation in anticipation of Marshall aid. The need for American aid as well as unity against the communist threat was brought home forcibly by aggression in Korea in 1950. This development coincides with the peak of the United States majority agreement curve in the fifth session.

More recently the decline of economic aid and the increasing economic independence of Western Europe and other parts of the world have been matched by growing communist emphasis upon the need for peaceful coexistence of nations. If the hypothesis regarding the determinants of American influence is correct, the rather sharp decline in American influence in 1953 and 1954, as measured by the majority agreement score, is the natural outcome of a shift in underlying power relationships.[3] As a further matter of interest, the majority agreement curve also coincides closely with the year-to-year observations of Thomas J. Hamilton, chief United Nations correspondent for the New York *Times*. His recorded evaluation of the fluctuations of American influence, or leadership, if put into statistical form, would describe a curve not far different from that in Figure 2. From an indifferent first session conspicuous for its lack of leadership, he reports marked increase in the effectiveness of American influence in 1947, reaching a peak in 1950 and decreasing noticeably in 1953 and 1954.[4]

---

[3] It will be recalled as well that the number of abstentions in the voting on questions involving direct opposition between the Soviet Union and the United States has tended to increase from year to year since 1950. This is particularly true of the Soviet propaganda proposals as noted in Chapter Six.

[4] In 1946 Mr. Hamilton wrote: "Great issues have been plentiful, but not great men to handle them." American leadership was reported to be "unquestionably" more effective in 1947 than previously. In 1950 he wrote: "Except for the countries of the Cominform bloc and the new nations of Asia, which are still reluctant to commit themselves to either side, we are the undisputed leader. . . . It was the Communist aggression in Korea and the prompt and decisive action of the United States in mobilizing the United Nations to put it down, that consolidated our influence. We entered the present General Assembly in a commanding position." And in October, 1953: "The decline in United States influence in the United Nations is in fact one of the most significant developments of recent months." See New York *Times*, Dec. 12, 1946, p. 6; Nov. 9, 1947, sec. IV, p. 5; Oct. 17, 1948, sec. IV, p. 5; Dec. 5, 1948, sec. IV, p. 4; Nov. 14, 1949, p. 4; Oct. 29, 1950, sec. IV, p. 4; Dec. 16, 1951, sec. IV, p. 4; Jan. 27, 1952, sec. IV, p. 5; Aug. 23, 1953, sec. IV, p. 3; Oct. 18, 1953, sec. IV, p. 5; Sept. 19, 1954, sec. IV, p. 3.

CHAPTER ELEVEN

Conclusions: The Task of Leadership

THE EXTENT OF INFLUENCE

In the introductory chapter to this study two problems were set. The first was to determine the extent of United States influence in the Assembly, the second the means by which American influence is exerted. As to the first problem—the extent of influence—the findings have been summarized in the preceding chapter. To state these findings succinctly, the United States has been a more successful advocate than any of the other Great Powers. Without exception political questions of vital concern to the United States have been decided in conformity with the major outlines of the American position. On other political questions the essence of the United States point of view has prevailed in most important aspects whenever the United States has attempted to exert a strong influence. American influence has been least evident and least effective with problems arising from efforts of colonial and erstwhile colonial peoples to obtain political self-determination and a status of equality. American influence has been most effective in matters relating to international peace and security. At the same time this effectiveness has varied from session to session, apparently reaching a peak in 1950 and declining markedly in 1953 and 1954.

THE METHODS OF INFLUENCE

In the exertion of influence the United States stands out from other members of the Assembly chiefly in the greater degree of success attending its efforts. The methods of influence are not unique to the United States or, in their essential nature, to international politics. Because of the influence that attaches to power, a simple pronouncement by the United States of its position on a given issue amounts to the exercise of influence. Influence is exerted through private negotiation and consultation with other delegations and their foreign offices. The strength of the pressure brought to bear upon Assembly delegations or through regular diplomatic channels increases with the insistence and the emphasis which American officials give to their arguments. The pressure, the strength of the effort to influence, flows from the insistence and the urgency with which the position is presented. Sometimes the fruit of successful importuning will be a *quid pro quo*, as pressure is met with counter-pressure. But the threat or bribe is avoided by the United States as the extreme of bad tactics.

Some delegations on some questions may be influenced on the basis of personal appeals as one friend to another. Much more frequently, however, the appeal must be based on self-interest. The successful exercise of influence, in the last analysis, lies in convincing other members that the adoption of a particular policy by the Assembly is in their self-interest. If the merits of the proposition are not sufficient, the reluctant delegation may be persuaded that it is more in its interest to maintain voting solidarity with the United States than to oppose the policy at issue. The task of leadership is to discover in each case an area of common interest which does not need to be broadened at great expenditure of moral and political capital. In principle, this fact is readily acknowledged by United States representatives to the Assembly and their co-workers in the State Department. In practice, expediency can lead to the exertion of pressure beyond the point of profitable returns.

Tests of Leadership

Because the United States is the most influential member of the United Nations, despite fluctuations from session to session, it has unrivaled opportunity for the exercise of leadership. Successful leadership, as has been observed, depends as much on the manner in which influence is exerted as on the capacity to exert it. Long-term successful leadership in a coalition of independent states must necessarily rest upon conversion, not coercion. This demands the espousal of programs which inspire the confidence of other states, programs which are conceived broadly enough to provide in themselves the necessary area of common interest. It demands also tact and consideration in their advocacy.

Failure to meet these demands puts an undue strain upon the staunch allies of the United States. Accepting the need for United States leadership, they are placed in a difficult dilemma when the United States insists upon a course of action which they regard unwise. Lester Pearson, as Canadian Minister for External Affairs, has pointed up the dilemma in terms which deserve quotation in some detail. Speaking to the Canadian Bar Association on March 31, 1951, he said:

We should gratefully recognize the special responsibility which the United States has accepted and the leadership it is giving in the struggle against Russian Communist imperialism. Such recognition carries with it the obligation to cooperate and to give support. But this support, if it is to have any value, does not mean an automatic response of 'Ready, aye ready' to everything that Washington proposes. It may mean constructive criticism of, and even opposition to, courses or proposals which we in Canada may think are unwise and concerning which it is our duty to express our views. I know that such criticism and opposition will be exploited by our Communist enemies for their own nefarious purposes. Because of this we should put forward our point of view, whenever we can, in private and try to persuade our friends as to its reasonableness. If we succeed, well and good. If we do not, we will have to decide whether to maintain our position in public or whether to abandon it because the acceptance of our viewpoint may not be so important as the maintenance of the united front.[1]

The problem at this time must have weighed heavily upon him, as he voiced almost identical sentiments in a speech ten days later to the Empire and Canadian Clubs of Toronto:

Our record in the United Nations is a worthy one. However, I do not think that we should be asked in the United Nations or elsewhere, to support automatically policies which are proposed by others if we have serious doubts about their wisdom. We must reserve the right, for instance, to criticize even the policy of our good friend, the United States, if we feel it necessary to do so. There are, however, two reservations to this. First, we must recognize and pay tribute to the leadership being given and the efforts being made by the United States in the conflict against Communist imperialism, and realize that if this leadership were not given we would have little chance of success in the common struggle. Secondly, we must never forget that our enemy gleefully welcomes every division in the free democratic ranks and that, therefore, there will be times when we should abandon our position if it is more important to maintain unity in the face of the common foe. This reconciliation of our right to differ and the necessity for unity, is going to be a tough problem for anyone charged with responsibility for foreign policy decisions in this, or indeed in any free country.[2]

Mr. Pearson doubtless had in mind the Korean conflict and the Far Eastern situation in general when these remarks were uttered. But the problem which he raised has a more general application.

Top-level American diplomats have not been unaware of the requirements of coalition diplomacy. They have, in fact, shown in numerous public utterances a statesmanlike grasp of the principles involved. John D. Hickerson, then Assistant Secretary of State for United Nations Affairs, in an address to the American Association for the United Nations, laid down three admirable tests of successful leadership. First, he said, the positions we take must be "sound and morally right" and "truly representative of American public opinion." Second, we must attain a "true partnership" with our allies through consultation with them and taking account of their views. Third, to gain the support of the non-Soviet members, "We must be able to persuade them of the essential correctness of our position. . . . To do this effectively, we must understand their doubts and answer them patiently and convincingly in terms of their own self-interests. We must welcome their constructive suggestions. We must seek to lead and not to dominate. This means that we

---

[1] Remarks reproduced in "Canada, the United Nations, and a Two-Power World," *External Affairs*, vol. 3 (May, 1951), pp. 154-57.

[2] *Ibid.*, pp. 157-60.

cannot always act as quickly or as decisively as we would sometimes like. But the end result will be worth the trouble." [3]

Former Secretary of State Dean Acheson, while in office, repeatedly expressed a kindred point of view. To quote him at length on one such occasion,

We should be forever grateful to the United Nations for furnishing a forum where the United States of America, to maintain its leadership, must enter and explain itself to the rest of the world, and do so under circumstances where the United States and its representatives listen to the representative of the smallest country in the world who has a point of view which he wishes to express, do so under circumstances where we make every effort to harmonize the views, adjust views, and may not force views down other people's throats. If we do that, then I believe the United States will lead into a new course in which the free nations will continue to be free nations, freely associated, freely, willingly, and eagerly accepting leadership which they believe considers their interests as deeply as it does its own. [4]

The Democratic administration did not have a monopoly of such sentiments. Henry Cabot Lodge, Jr., speaking to a House Subcommittee on International Organizations and Movements, recorded his conviction that our foreign policy should be aimed at "having people respect us and have confidence in us." He said, "We want a lot of people around the world who feel they are in business for themselves, and we don't want satellites. It should be the worst thing in the world for us to have satellites. We want people who are with us because they agree with us out of mutual respect." [5] John Foster Dulles, in his maiden address to the Assembly as Secretary of State, exhibited comparable statesmanship when he spoke of a willingness "to learn from others" and to accept defeat "philosophically." [6]

Although the principles of successful leadership in a world coalition of free nations are thus well known and accepted, the rub as always comes in applying them to the concrete situation. Such statements as those quoted above are made in all sincerity and are reflected in American attitudes in the Assembly. However, when in a particular situation the principles of successful long-term leadership are weighed against the desirability of an immediate policy goal, the principles are not always governing. To a degree this was the case with the condemnation of Chinese intervention in Korea. The United States did forbear pressing its condemnation resolution for more than six weeks while other alterna-

---

[3] Address in New York, Oct. 19, 1952, reproduced in *Department of State Bulletin*, vol. 27 (Oct. 27, 1952), pp. 644-49.

[4] Remarks to a group of magazine and book publishers, June 29, 1951, and reproduced in McGeorge Bundy (ed.), *The Pattern of Responsibility* (1952), p. 259.

[5] U.S. House, Subcommittee of Committee on Foreign Affairs, *Hearings on International Organizations and Movements*, 83rd Cong., 1st sess., p. 102.

[6] *Plenary Meetings*, 8th sess. (1953), p. 17.

tives were being tried. The delegation and the State Department perhaps felt that all the demands of consultation and concession had been met. So spoke Ernest A. Gross, at any rate, when he claimed that through acquiescing in the cease-fire offers the United States had created a majority for its resolution "solidly based upon the convictions of the peoples of the world" and would now command a unity of substance, whereas earlier the United States could have had "at best only the appearance of unity." [7] His estimate proved only partly true. The nations who voted for condemnation were clearly convinced that aggression had taken place, but many of them did not have an abiding faith that to say so at this time was the right thing to do. Weeks after the action the Canadian Minister for External Affairs reiterated his conviction that it had been unwise to force a vote on the resolution before a further and final effort at negotiation was made.[8] And on January 27, a few days before the final vote of condemnation, the British *Economist* wrote: "We must ask our American readers to take our word for it that great harm has been done to British confidence in America's ability to lead the free world." [9]

The refusal of the United States to accept Indian participation in the proposed political conference on Korea resulted in an even more clearly evident sacrifice of confidence and good will for the attainment of an immediate objective. Against the manifest will of the majority of members, including most of the Commonwealth and Western Europe, the United States doggedly persisted in its determination to defeat India's participation by the two-thirds rule if the motion came to a plenary vote. As it turned out India elected to withdraw. But the episode led one journalist to cite the classic statement of Pyhrrus, "Another such victory and we are undone." [10] The United States in both instances had real and compelling reasons to take the positions it did. And the results may or may not have justified the course of action. But both cases illustrate the difficulties inherent in the task of leadership.

In defense of United States policy, it is probably true that some delegations would be found to criticize no matter what course of action the United States might take. If the United States presses its viewpoint vigorously, some will talk of "pressure" and "cracking the whip." If the

[7] Address to United States Junior Chamber of Commerce, Roanoke, Virginia, Jan. 20, 1951, reproduced in *U.S. Mission Press Release*, no. 1119, Jan. 19, 1951.

[8] Address reproduced in *External Affairs*, vol. 3 (May, 1951), pp. 157-60.

[9] Cited in Soward, *op. cit.*, p. 129. Thomas J. Hamilton concluded that the "prestige of both the United States and the United Nations" had suffered despite the large majority voting for the resolution. New York *Times*, Feb. 4, 1951, sec. IV, p. 5.

[10] See "Going it Almost Alone," *New Republic*, vol. 129 (Aug. 31, 1953), p. 3; "To the Four Winds—Forward March!" *ibid.*, vol. 129 (Sept. 7, 1953), p. 3; "Politics on First Avenue," *New Statesman and Nation*, vol. 46 (Sept. 5, 1953), p. 247; report of Clement Attlee speech in New York *Times*, Sept. 20, 1953, pp. 1, 2; Hamilton, "Lesson of the India Debate," *Freedom and Union*, vol. 8 (Nov., 1953), p. 14.

initiative is left to others, the complaint may be that of failure to give the necessary leadership. Nor is the task of the State Department made easier by leaders in both political parties who do not hesitate to express their own ideas about the conduct of foreign affairs. Sometimes the State Department is forced to trim its policies and strategy in the Assembly to meet shifting political winds. Even when the Department, through the delegation, is pursuing the most statesmanlike course, an oratorical blast from some influential Senator may cause other delegations to question the real objectives of United States policy. To say that United States policies are sometimes influenced by domestic political considerations is not necessarily to criticize or to suggest that something can be done about it. But it calls attention to the fact that domestic political pressures at times place an additional strain upon American leadership in the United Nations.

The occasional deviation of American interests in the Assembly from those of other non-communist members, and even of close friends, can be avoided no more than the perennial complaints of the dissatisfied. The existence of partisan political pressures is another reality which can scarcely be ignored or removed. But some difficulties spring from the very fact that the United States insists on winning so often. Perhaps to Mr. Hickerson's three texts of leadership a fourth may be added. Let the moral position be sound; let our allies be consulted as in a true partnership; let our colleagues be persuaded of the essential correctness of our position when this is possible. But let leadership also be enhanced by learning to lose with grace. Costs are sometimes difficult to calculate in advance. Yet leadership is more solidly based if it can distinguish the occasions when strong exertion of influence will produce commensurate results from those in which political and moral capital may be expended out of proportion to the probable returns. This too is the task of leadership. And successful leadership then becomes measurable less in terms of voting records than in the respect and good will of nations.

Appendix A

Session	Representatives	Alternates
First	James F. Byrnes	Rep. Sol Bloom
(first part)	Edward R. Stettinius, Jr.	Rep. Charles A. Eaton
	Sen. Tom Connally	Frank Walker
	Sen. Arthur H. Vandenberg	John Foster Dulles
	Mrs. Franklin D. Roosevelt	John G. Townsend, Jr.
(second part)	Warren R. Austin	Rep. Charles A. Eaton
	Sen. Tom Connally	Rep. Helen Gahagan Douglas
	Sen. Arthur H. Vandenberg	John Foster Dulles
	Mrs. Franklin D. Roosevelt	Adlai Stevenson
	Rep. Sol Bloom	
First Special	Warren R. Austin	Herschel V. Johnson
Second	George C. Marshall	Charles Fahy
	Warren R. Austin	Willard L. Thorp
	Herschel V. Johnson	Francis B. Sayre
	Mrs. Franklin D. Roosevelt	Adlai Stevenson
	John Foster Dulles	Gen. John H. Hilldring
Second Special	Warren R. Austin	Dean Rusk
	Francis B. Sayre	John C. Ross
	Philip C. Jessup	
Third	George C. Marshall	Benjamin V. Cohen
(first part)	Warren R. Austin	Ray Atherton
	John Foster Dulles	Willard L. Thorp
	Mrs. Franklin D. Roosevelt	Ernest A. Gross
	Philip C. Jessup	Francis B. Sayre
(second part)	Warren R. Austin	Ray Atherton
	John Foster Dulles	Willard L. Thorp
	Mrs. Franklin D. Roosevelt	Dean Rusk
	Philip C. Jessup	Francis B. Sayre
	Benjamin V. Cohen	Erwin D. Canham
Fourth	Dean Acheson	Wilson Compton
	Warren R. Austin	Benjamin V. Cohen
	Philip C. Jessup	Charles Fahy
	Mrs. Franklin D. Roosevelt	John D. Hickerson
	Sen. John Sherman Cooper	Mrs. Ruth Bryan Rohde
Fifth	Dean Acheson	Benjamin V. Cohen
	Warren R. Austin	Sen. John Sherman Cooper
	Mrs. Franklin D. Roosevelt	Ernest A. Gross
	Sen. John J. Sparkman	Mrs. Edith Sampson
	Sen. Henry Cabot Lodge, Jr.	John C. Ross
	John Foster Dulles	

Session	*Representatives*	*Alternates*
Sixth	Dean Acheson	Sen. John Sherman Cooper
	Warren R. Austin	Ernest A. Gross
	Mrs. Franklin D. Roosevelt	Benjamin V. Cohen
	Rep. Michael J. Mansfield	Mrs. Anna Lord Strauss
	Rep. John M. Vorys	Channing H. Tobias
	Philip C. Jessup	
Seventh	Dean Acheson	Philip C. Jessup
	Warren R. Austin	Benjamin V. Cohen
	Mrs. Franklin D. Roosevelt	Charles A. Sprague
	Sen. Theodore F. Green	Mrs. Edith Sampson
	Sen. Alexander Wiley	Isador Lubin
	Ernest A. Gross	
	Henry Cabot Lodge, Jr.	
	James J. Wadsworth	
	John Foster Dulles	
Eighth	John Foster Dulles	Archibald J. Carey
	Henry Cabot Lodge, Jr.	James D. Zellerbach
	James F. Byrnes	Henry Ford II
	Rep. Frances P. Bolton	Charles W. Mayo
	Rep. James P. Richards	Mrs. Oswald B. Lord
Ninth	Henry Cabot Lodge, Jr.	James J. Wadsworth
	Sen. H. Alexander Smith	Mrs. Oswald B. Lord
	Sen. J. W. Fulbright	A. M. Ade Johnson
	C. D. Jackson	James P. Nash
	Charles H. Mahoney	Roger W. Straus

Appendix B

First Session

  Atomic energy control
  Language rules
* Representation of non-governmental organizations
  Extradition and punishment of war criminals
* Admission of new members
  Condemnation of persecution and discrimination
* Voting in the Security Council
  Troops of United Nations members stationed abroad
  Reduction of armaments
* Treatment of Indians in the Union of South Africa
  Declaration on the rights and duties of states
  Declaration on fundamental human rights and freedoms
* The Spanish question (acted upon in both parts of session)

First Special Session

* The Palestine question

Second Session

* The Greek question
  Condemnation of war propaganda and the inciters of a new war
  The independence of Korea
* Admission of new members
* The Spanish question
  Voting in the Security Council
* Treatment of Indians in the Union of South Africa
* The Palestine question
  The Interim Committee

Second Special Session

** The Palestine question

Third Session

* The Palestine question
  Appeal to the Great Powers to compose their differences
* The Greek question
  Reduction of armaments
* Atomic energy control
  Methods for the promotion of international cooperation
* The independence of Korea
  A United Nations Guard
* Admission of new members

* Indicates roll-call vote used in construction of Tables 1-3, 5-11.
** Indicates two roll-call votes used.

The Interim Committee
* Voting in the Security Council
* The former Italian colonies
* The Spanish question
* Treatment of Indians in the Union of South Africa
General Assembly methods and procedures
* Rights and freedoms in Bulgaria and Hungary
* The admission of Israel
The question of Indonesia

Fourth Session

* The Greek question
* The former Italian colonies
* Condemnation of preparations for a new war
** Threat to the independence and territorial integrity of China
The independence of Korea
* Rights and freedoms in Eastern Europe
* The Interim Committee
A United Nations field service
Admission of new members
* Atomic energy control
Reduction of armaments
* Palestine: the status of Jerusalem
Palestine: refugees
The question of Indonesia

Fifth Session

* The independence of Korea
* United action for peace
* Threat of a new war
Duties of states in the event of war
Establishment of a good offices commission
The Greek question
** Threat to the independence and territorial integrity of China
United States aggression
United States violation of Chinese air space
*** Chinese intervention in Korea
Rights and freedoms in Eastern Europe
* The former Italian colonies: Libya
The former Italian colonies: Eritrea
The former Italian colonies: boundary adjustments
* Treatment of Indians in the Union of South Africa
Representation in the United Nations
* The Spanish question
* Palestine: Jerusalem
Palestine: refugees
A Twenty-Year Program for Peace
Admission of new members
* Atomic energy control
* Representation of China

Sixth Session

* Regulation of armaments and atomic energy control

---

* Indicates roll-call vote used in construction of Tables 1-3, 5-11.
** Indicates two roll-call votes used.
*** Indicates three roll-call votes used.

* Methods to strengthen peace and security
* United States aggression
  Threat of a new war
* Admission of new members
* Threat to the independence and territorial integrity of China
* The independence of Korea
  Greece: border violations and guerrilla warfare
  Greece: repatriation of children
  Hostile activities of the Soviet bloc
* Treatment of Indians in the Union of South Africa
* German elections
  Palestine: conciliation
  Palestine: refugees
  The former Italian colonies: Libya
  A Twenty-Year Program for Peace
  Representation of China

Seventh Session

* Korea: prisoner-of-war repatriation
  Korea: reconstruction
* Korea: political conference
* The question of Tunisia
* The question of Morocco
* Austrian independence
  Greece: detention of Greek armed forces
  Greece: repatriation of children
  Methods to strengthen peace and security
  Regulation of armaments
* United States interference in the internal affairs of other states
* Investigation of bacteriological warfare charges
* Threat of a new war
  Aggression in Burma
  Palestine: refugees
* Palestine: conciliation
* Treatment of Indians in the Union of South Africa
* *Apartheid*
  The former Italian colonies: Eritrea
* Admission of new members
* Mass murder of prisoners of war
* Representation of China

Eighth Session

* The question of Morocco
* The question of Tunisia
  Investigation of bacteriological warfare charges
  Aggression in Burma
*Regulation of armaments
  Threat of a new war
  The independence of Korea
  Admission of new members
* Treatment of Indians in the Union of South Africa
* *Apartheid*
  Palestine: refugees
*Atrocities committed against United Nations prisoners of war
  Representation of China

* Indicates roll-call vote used in construction of Tables 1-3, 5-11.

Ninth Session

* Representation of China
* Detention of American airmen
* The independence of Korea
  Methods to strengthen peace and security
  Regulation of armaments
* The question of Tunisia
* The question of Morocco
* The question of West Irian
  The question of Cyprus
  Atomic energy for peaceful uses
  United States aggression
  Freedom of navigation in the China seas
  Palestine: refugees
* Admission of new members
* Treatment of Indians in the Union of South Africa
* *Apartheid*
  Aggression in Burma
* Prohibition of war propaganda

---

* Indicates roll-call vote used in construction of Tables 1-3, 5-11.

Appendix C

Any member state may request that an item be placed on the Assembly agenda simply by communicating the necessary information to the Secretary-General sixty days in advance of an Assembly session. The item is inscribed on a provisional agenda, together with matters proposed by other organs of the United Nations or awaiting consideration as a result of previous Assembly action, and circulated to all members of the organization. When the Assembly convenes the provisional agenda is sent to the General Committee, a small screening body whose chief function is to recommend which of the items submitted should be included on the final working agenda of the Assembly. The General Committee is composed of the president of the General Assembly, the seven vice-presidents, the chairmen of the six Main Committees, and the chairman of the Special Political Committee. By tacit agreement five of the vice-presidents are always representatives of the permanent members of the Security Council. Items affirmatively recommended by the General Committee are invariably accepted by the Assembly but a recommendation of disapproval is sometimes reversed.

After an item is approved by the Assembly for inclusion in the agenda it is usually referred to an appropriate committee. There are six Main Committees which remain in existence from year to year as part of the regular structure of the Assembly. These are (1) the Political and Security Committee; (2) the Economic and Financial Committee; (3) the Social, Humanitarian, and Cultural Committee; (4) the Trusteeship Committee; (5) the Administrative and Budgetary Committee; and (6) the Legal Committee. The Main Committees are frequently referred to by number rather than subject-matter designation, as, for instance, the Political and Security Committee is often called simply the First Committee. Until 1956 an Ad Hoc Political Committee was constituted anew each session. In 1956 it was renamed Special Political Committee and placed on a permanent basis. A few questions are acted upon in plenary meeting without reference to a committee.

Each committee is a little assembly in itself, where every member state has representation and debate is virtually unlimited. The committee submits to the Assembly in plenary meeting a report on every question considered, which may include a summary of major proposals and the text of a resolution decided upon. The committee report is usually adopted without significant modification. However, this is not always the case. On a closely contested issue the Assembly may even reject the committee recommendation. When such a reversal occurs it is due less often to the loss of a majority between committee and plenary meetings than to a lack of the two-thirds majority required for final adoption of "important" resolutions. Article 18 of the

---

[1] The best guide to Assembly procedure is *Rules of Procedure of the General Assembly*, published periodically by the Secretariat under the document symbol A/520.

United Nations Charter designates a number of "important" questions which must be decided by a two-thirds majority of those present and voting. These include elections of members to the Security Council, the Economic and Social Council, and the Trusteeship Council; questions of admission and expulsion; questions relating to the operation of the Trusteeship system; and budgetary questions. The determination of additional categories of questions to be decided by a two-thirds majority is made by a simple majority of members present and voting. A measure may thus receive approval by a simple majority of those voting in committee where the two-thirds rule is not operative, but fail to obtain the necessary additional votes in the plenary session. Committee recommendations on a number of political questions have in fact fallen short of the necessary two-thirds majority. This is one reason so few resolutions have been passed over the American negative vote. A General Assembly majority might often be mustered on certain types of issues despite United States opposition, but a two-thirds majority almost never, as the record will attest.

Bibliography

A. *United Nations Documents*

Disarmament Commission Documents. Three or four references are made to documents issued for the Disarmament Commission, designated by the symbol DC/.

Documents of the United Nations Conference on International Organization, San Francisco, 1945. 15 vols. These volumes contain records of debate in commissions and plenary meetings of the conference and other relevant documents. Only vol. 6 used in this study.

Official Records of the General Assembly. Official Assembly records constituted the principal source for the present inquiry. Records used numbered some sixty or seventy volumes and included the summary records of the *First Committee,* the *Ad Hoc Political Committee,* and the *General Committee* for the first nine sessions; verbatim records of *Plenary Meetings* for nine sessions; General Assembly *Resolutions* for nine sessions, published as supplements to the Official Records; *Annexes* to the Official Records, containing the most important documents issued during the Assembly session, and bound as separate volumes beginning with the fifth session; summary records of the *Ad Hoc Committee on the Palestinian Question,* second session; and summary records of the *Joint Committee of the First and Sixth Committee,* first session. Official Records are cited in the footnotes of this study only by the title of the committee or by *Plenary Meetings,* in addition to the session and the year. Official Records are published with a United Nations documents symbol according to the standard system of United Nations documentation. Thus the records of *Plenary Meetings* are numbered serially from the first meeting of the first session beginning A/PV/1; the *First Committee* records are in the series beginning A/C.1/SR.1, etc. Resolutions and other supplements to the Official Records have numbers in the general series of Assembly documents, designated by the symbol A/.

Other General Assembly Documents. In addition to the Official Records, heavy reliance has been placed upon other documents issued to the Assembly and its subsidiary bodies. The number of such documents cited in this study approaches four hundred. They include the text of draft resolutions and amendments thereto, committee reports to the plenary meetings, communications to the Assembly or its committees, and reports of special committees and commissions created by the Assembly, among other types of documents. Most of the documents cited can be found in the *Annexes* to the Official Records, published separately from 1950 and as appendixes to plenary and committee records prior to that time. Some, however, are available only in mimeographed form. A few documents identified in the footnotes only by symbol are published as supplements to the Official Records.

Security Council Documents. Several numbers of the *Official Records of the Security Council* were used. Like the records of the Assembly Main Committees these records contain only a summary of debate rather than a

verbatim record. A few references are also made to Security Council documents of the general series, designated by the symbol S/.
United Nations Charter.

B. *Other Public Documents*

Federal Register. Vols. 12 and 15.

Protocol of Proceedings of the Berlin Conference, July 17-Aug. 2, 1945 (Potsdam Declaration).

The United States and the United Nations. Annual report by the President to the Congress, pursuant to section 4 of the "United Nations Participation Act of 1945." After 1947 published under the title of *United States Participation in the United Nations.* The reports bear Department of State publication numbers 2735, 3024, 3437, 3765, 4178, 4583, 5034, and 5459, respectively. They contain summaries of major actions taken by the various agencies of the United Nations, with emphasis on the positions and activities of the United States.

U.S. House of Representatives. Subcommittee on International Organizations and Movements of the Committee on Foreign Affairs. *Hearings on International Organizations and Movements.* Mar. 27, May 20, June 23, July 8 and 29, 1953. 83rd Cong., 1st sess.

United States Relations with China, 1944-1949. Department of State Publication 3573, Far Eastern Series 30. 1949.

U.S. Senate. Committee on Armed Services and Committee on Foreign Relations. *Hearings to Conduct an Inquiry into the Military Situation in the Far East and the Facts Surrounding the Relief of General of the Army Douglas MacArthur from His Assignments in That Area.* 5 pts. May 3-Aug. 17, 1951. 82nd Cong., 1st sess. Only pt. 3 used in this study.

U.S. Senate. Committee on Foreign Relations. *Hearing: The Testimony of Ambassador Henry Cabot Lodge, Jr., the United States Representative to the United Nations and Representative in the Security Council.* July 23, 1953. 83rd Cong., 1st sess.

U.S. Senate. Subcommittee of Committee on Foreign Relations. *Hearings on Proposals to Amend the United Nations Charter.* 7 pts. Jan. 18 and Mar. 3, Feb. 12, Apr. 10, May 15, June 7, June 19, and July 10, 1954. 83rd Cong., 2nd sess. Only pt. 1 used in this study.

U.S. Senate. Subcommittee of Committee on Foreign Relations. *Hearings on Resolutions Relative to Revision of the United Nations Charter, Atlantic Union, World Federation, etc.* Feb. 2-20, 1950. 81st Cong., 2nd sess.

U.S. Senate. Subcommittee on the United Nations Charter of the Committee on Foreign Relations. *Review of the United Nations Charter: A Collection of Documents.* Senate Document No. 87. 83rd Cong., 2nd sess.

U.S. Statutes at Large. Vols. 59, 63, and 65.

C. *Books*

Bundy, McGeorge (ed.). *The Pattern of Responsibility.* Edited from the record of Secretary of State Dean Acheson. Boston: Houghton Mifflin Company, 1952.

Chase, Eugene P. *The United Nations in Action.* New York: McGraw-Hill Book Company, 1950.

Eagleton, Clyde. *The United Nations and the United States.* Arnold Foundation Studies. Vol. 2, New Series. Dallas: Southern Methodist University, 1951.

—— and Richard N. Swift (eds.). *Annual Review of United Nations Affairs, 1949-1953*. New York: New York University Press, 1950-54. One volume has been prepared annually since 1949 from proceedings of New York University summer Institute of United Nations Affairs.

Evatt, Herbert V. *The United Nations*. Revised from Oliver Wendell Holmes Lectures, delivered Oct. 17, 23, 24, 1947. Cambridge: Harvard University Press, 1948.

Fosdick, Dorothy. *Common Sense and World Affairs*. New York: Harcourt, Brace and Company, 1955.

García-Granados, Jorge. *The Birth of Israel*. New York: Alfred A. Knopf, 1949.

Goodrich, Leland M., and Edvard Hambro. *Charter of the United Nations: Commentary and Documents*. 2nd and rev. ed. Boston: World Peace Foundation, 1949.

Haviland, H. Field, Jr. *The Political Role of the General Assembly*. Carnegie Endowment for International Peace. United Nations Studies No. 7. New York: 1951.

Horowitz, David. *State in the Making*. Translated by Julian Meltzer. New York: Alfred A. Knopf, 1953.

Houston, John A. *Latin America in the United Nations*. Carnegie Endowment for International Peace. United Nations Studies No. 8. New York: 1956.

Hurewitz, Jacob Coleman. *The Struggle for Palestine*. New York: W. W. Norton & Company, Inc., 1950.

Leonard, L. Larry. *International Organization*. New York: McGraw-Hill Book Company, 1951.

Lie, Trygve. *In the Cause of Peace*. New York: The Macmillan Company, 1954.

Lilienthal, Alfred M. *What Price Israel?* Chicago: Henry Regnery Company, 1953.

Mikesell, Raymond F. *United States Economic Policy and International Relations*. New York: McGraw-Hill Book Company, 1952.

Millis, Walter (ed.). *The Forrestal Diaries*. New York: The Viking Press, 1951.

The United Nations Secretariat. Carnegie Endowment for International Peace. United Nations Studies No. 4. New York: 1950.

Schwebel, Stephen M. *The Secretary-General of the United Nations: His Political Powers and Practice*. Cambridge: Harvard University Press, 1952.

Weizmann, Chaim. *Trial and Error: The Autobiography of Chaim Weizmann*. 2 vols. Philadelphia: The Jewish Publication Society of America, 1949. Only vol. 2 used in present study.

Welles, Sumner. *We Need Not Fail*. Boston: Houghton Mifflin Company, 1948.

D. *Articles*

Acheson, Dean. "The Responsibility for Decision in Foreign Policy," *Yale Review*, vol. 44 (Sept., 1954), pp. 1-12.

"Assembly: Maneuverings Behind the Scenes," *Newsweek*, vol. 28 (Nov. 18, 1946), p. 48.

Ball, M. Margaret. "Bloc Voting in the General Assembly," *International Organization*, vol. 5 (Feb., 1951), pp. 3-31.

Barrett, George. "Our Global Embassy on Park Avenue," *New York Times Magazine*, Nov. 27, 1949, pp. 14-15.

Blickenstaff, David. "The General Assembly," *Annual Review of United Nations Affairs, 1952,* edited by Clyde Eagleton and Richard N. Swift (New York: New York University Press, 1953), pp. 23-39.

Bloomfield, Lincoln Palmer. "How the U.S. Government Is Organized to Participate in the U.N. System," *Department of State Bulletin,* vol. 35 (Sept. 17, 1956), pp. 442-44.

————. "The Department of State and the United Nations," *Department of State Bulletin,* vol. 23 (Nov. 20, 1950), pp. 804-11.

Bolles, Blair. "Will UN Members Follow U.S. on China Policy?" *Foreign Policy Bulletin,* vol. 30 (Jan. 26, 1951), pp. 2-3.

Brown, Benjamin H., and Joseph E. Johnson. "The U.S. and the UN," *Foreign Policy Association Headline Series,* no. 107 (Sept.-Oct., 1954).

Carter, Gwendolen M. "The Commonwealth in the United Nations," *International Organization,* vol. 4 (May, 1950), pp. 247-60.

Cheever, Daniel S. "The Role of the United Nations in the Conduct of United States Foreign Policy," *World Politics,* vol. 2 (Apr., 1950), pp. 390-404.

Cohen, Benjamin V. "The Impact of the United Nations on United States Foreign Policy," *International Organization,* vol. 5 (May, 1951), pp. 274-81.

Cordier, Andrew W. "The General Assembly," *Annual Review of United Nations Affairs, 1953,* edited by Clyde Eagleton and Richard N. Swift (New York: New York University Press, 1954), pp. 61-74.

Crossman, R. H. S. "Politics at Lake Success," *New Statesman and Nation,* vol. 34 (Oct. 25, 1947), p. 324.

Dennett, Raymond. "Politics in the Security Council," *International Organization,* vol. 3 (Aug., 1949), pp. 421-33.

Emerson, Rupert, and Inis L. Claude, Jr. "The Soviet Union and the United Nations: An Essay in Interpretation," *International Organization,* vol. 6 (Feb., 1952), pp. 1-26.

Fay, Sidney B. "Arabs, Zionists, and Oil," *Current History,* vol. 14 (May, 1948), pp. 270-76.

García-Granados, Jorge. "Behind the Palestine Reversal," *Colliers,* May 22, 1948, pp. 26, 76-77.

"Going It Almost Alone," *New Republic,* vol. 129 (Aug. 31, 1953), p. 3.

Goodrich, Leland M. "American National Interests and the Responsibilities of United Nations Membership," *International Organization,* vol. 6 (Aug., 1952), pp. 369-80.

————. "Expanding Role of the General Assembly," *International Conciliation,* no. 471 (May, 1951).

Gross, Ernest A. "The New United Nations," *Foreign Policy Association Headline Series,* no. 125 (Sept.-Oct., 1957).

————. "United States Policy in the United Nations," *Annual Review of United Nations Affairs, 1952,* edited by Clyde Eagleton and Richard N. Swift (New York: New York University Press, 1953), pp. 193-204.

————. "Why the U.S. Needs the UN," *Foreign Policy Bulletin,* vol. 34 (Sept. 15, 1954), p. 2.

Hamilton, Thomas J. "Lesson of the India Debate," *Freedom and Union,* vol. 8 (Nov., 1953), p. 14.

————. "Partition of Palestine," *Foreign Policy Reports,* vol. 23 (Feb. 15, 1948), pp. 286-95.

————. "Washington and the United Nations," *Nation,* vol. 165 (Sept. 6, 1947), pp. 219-21.

Haviland, H. Field, Jr. "The United Nations: Effects on American Government," *Current History*, vol. 22 (Jan., 1952), pp. 13-18.

Holmes, Olive. "U.S. Hedges on Action Against Franco," *Foreign Policy Bulletin*, vol. 26 (Dec. 13, 1946), pp. 2-3.

Houston, John A. "The United Nations and Spain," *Journal of Politics*, vol. 14 (Nov., 1952), pp. 683-709.

Howard, Harry N. "The Arab-Asian States in the United Nations," *The Middle East Journal*, vol. 7 (Summer, 1953), pp. 279-92.

——. "The General Assembly and the Problem of Greece," *Department of State Bulletin*, supplement, vol. 17 (Dec. 7, 1947), pp. 1097-1149.

Hyde, James N. "United States Policy in the United Nations," *Annual Review of United Nations Affairs, 1951*, edited by Clyde Eagleton and Richard N. Swift (New York: New York University Press, 1952), pp. 254-67.

——. "United States Participation in the United Nations," *International Organization*, vol. 10 (Feb., 1956), pp. 22-34.

Jordan, William M. "Handling of Disputes and Special Political Problems in 1950-1951," *Annual Review of United Nations Affairs, 1951*, edited by Clyde Eagleton and Richard N. Swift (New York: New York University Press, 1952), pp. 73-87.

Kennan, George F. "Foreign Aid in the Framework of National Policy," *Proceedings of the Academy of Political Science*, vol. 23 (Jan., 1950), pp. 448-56.

Kirchwey, Freda. "Apprehensive Allies," *Nation*, vol. 172 (Jan. 27, 1951), pp. 72-73.

——. "United Nations Victory," *Nation*, vol. 165 (Dec. 6, 1947), pp. 610-11.

Leonard, L. Larry. "The United Nations and Palestine," *International Conciliation*, no. 454 (Oct., 1949).

McClellan, Grant S. "Britain's Stand Forces U.S. to Reach Decision on Palestine," *Foreign Policy Bulletin*, vol. 26 (Oct. 3, 1947), pp. 2-3.

McKay, Vernon. "Success of Partition Hinges on Arab-Jewish Cooperation," *Foreign Policy Bulletin*, vol. 27 (Dec. 5, 1947), pp. 1-3.

Morgenthau, Hans J. "The New United Nations and the Revision of the Charter," *Review of Politics*, vol. 16 (Jan., 1954), pp. 3-21.

Padelford, Norman J. "The United Nations and Korea: A Political Resume," *International Organization*, vol. 5 (Nov., 1951), pp. 685-708.

Pearson, Lester B. "Basis of Canadian Far Eastern Policy," excerpts from statement in Canadian House of Commons, Feb. 2, 1951, as reproduced in *External Affairs*, vol. 3 (Feb., 1951), pp. 38-46.

——. "Canada, the United Nations, and a Two-Power World," text of addresses to the Canadian Bar Association, Mar. 31, 1951, and to the Empire and Canadian Clubs of Toronto, Apr. 10, 1951, as reproduced in *External Affairs*, vol. 3 (May, 1951), pp. 154-60.

——. "Mr. Pearson's Harvard University Speech," text of address to Harvard Univerity Alumni Association, June 11, 1953, as reproduced in *External Affairs*, vol. 5 (July, 1953), pp. 230-33.

"Politics on First Avenue," *New Statesman and Nation*, vol. 46 (Sept. 5, 1953), p. 247.

Potter, Pitman B. "The Palestine Problem Before the United Nations," *American Journal of International Law*, vol. 42 (Oct., 1948), pp. 859-61.

Richardson, Channing B. "The United States Mission to the United Nations," *International Organization*, vol. 7 (Feb., 1953), pp. 22-34.

Riggs, Fred W. "UN Record Mirrors Fundamental Split on China," *Foreign Policy Bulletin*, vol. 30 (Feb. 2, 1951), pp. 2-3.

Rivlin, Benjamin. "The Italian Colonies and the General Assembly," *International Organization*, vol. 3 (Aug., 1949), pp. 459-70.

Roosevelt, Kermit. "The Partition of Palestine: A Lesson in Pressure Politics," *The Middle East Journal*, vol. 2 (Jan., 1948), pp. 1-16.

Sanders, William. "Assignment to the United Nations," *Foreign Service Journal*, vol. 30 (Nov., 1953), pp. 24-27.

Schwebel, Stephen M. "Secretary-General and Secretariat," Commission to Study the Organization of Peace, *Charter Review Conference*, Ninth Report and Papers Presented to the Commission (New York: Aug., 1955), pp. 198-211.

Shultz, Lillie. "Democracy's Betrayal of Spain," *Nation*, vol. 171 (Nov. 18, 1950), pp. 455-57.

————. "The Palestine Fight—An Inside Story," *Nation*, vol. 165 (Dec. 20, 1947), pp. 675-78.

Soward, F. H. "The Korean Crisis and the Commonwealth," *Pacific Affairs*, vol. 24 (June, 1951), pp. 115-30.

Stone, Isaac A. "American Support of Free Elections in Europe," *Department of State Bulletin*, vol. 17 (Aug. 17 and 31, 1947), pp. 311-23, 407-13.

"To the Four Winds—Forward March!" *New Republic*, vol. 129 (Sept. 7, 1953), p. 3.

Wadsworth, James. "United States Policy in the United Nations," *Annual Review of United Nations Affairs, 1953*, edited by Clyde Eagleton and Richard N. Swift (New York: New York University Press, 1954), pp. 173-85.

E. *Other Materials*

Chicago *Tribune*, June 20 and June 30, 1955.

Department of State Bulletin, various issues, 1946-54.

New York *Times*, numerous issues, 1946-54.

United States Mission Press Releases, several numbers. Issued in mimeographed form, frequently but irregularly, by the United States Mission to the United Nations.

F. *Personal Interviews*

Interview with Ambassador José Vicente Trujillo, Permanent Representative of Ecuador to the United Nations, March 8, 1955.

Interview with Andrew W. Cordier, Executive Assistant to the Secretary-General of the United Nations, March 8, 1955.

Interviews with officials of the permanent missions to the United Nations of Canada, Norway, Peru, Saudi Arabia, the Soviet Union, and Yugoslavia, March 7-10, 1955.

Interviews with officials, present and former, of the United States Mission to the United Nations and the United States Department of State, March 1-10, 1955.

Index

Abdullah, King of Jordan: annexes Palestine territory, 133

Acheson, Dean: UN reaction to speech of, 34n; on Korean cease-fire appeals, 75n, 76; on Spanish question, 96n; proposes security program, 121; on U.S. leadership, 178

Ad Hoc Committee on the Palestinian Question: deliberations of, 47-50, 53-59

Ad Hoc Political Committee: discusses political questions, 5, 6

Admission to UN: Lie urges universality, 85n; Assembly action on, 149-54; U.S. influence on, 164

Advisers: to U.S. Mission, 12; to U.S. delegation, 16-17, 18, 18n; use of pressure by, 35-37, 62

Afghanistan: in Afro-Asian bloc, 22n; and Palestine ʻpartition, 51n, 59; seeks Korean settlement, 70n; and Austrian peace treaty, 104n; and Tunisia and Morocco, 142n; admitted to UN, 149

Afro-Asian states: discretion of Assembly delegations, 20; as voting bloc, 21, 22, 26, 171; in underdeveloped states bloc, 24n; and Tunisia, 43, 141-44; seek Korean settlement, 70-80 passim; oppose Chinese condemnation, 78; and germ warfare charges, 92; and Indians in South Africa, 125, 126, 127, 128; oppose apartheid policies, 128-29; and Morocco, 141-44; oppose Israel admission, 151n

Aggression: formula for determining, 122-23

Airmen, question of U.S.: and Secretary-General, 29n; Assembly action on, 105-6; and U.S. leadership, 107

Air space: violation of alleged, 90, 91

Albania: in Soviet bloc, 21n; admission to UN, 21n, 149; aids Greek rebels, 96, 97

Allied High Commission for Germany: proposes German elections, 103

American Federation of Labor: seeks UN representation, 148

Apartheid: Assembly action on, 128-29; U.S. attitude toward, 146

Arab-Asian states. See Afro-Asian states

Arab Higher Committee, 47, 48, 49

Arab League: as voting block, 21, 22, 26, 27; and Palestine partition, 47

Arabs: as Assembly bloc, 21, 22, 26, 27; pressure used by, 43, 67-68; oppose Palestine partition, 45-67 passim, 129-33 passim; and disarmament, 112; oppose U.K. Palestine policies, 129; and Palestine conciliation, 135; and UNRWA, 136; and Palestine refugees, 136-37; and Italian colonies, 137, 139, 140

Argentina: opposes bans on Spain, 95n; on UN membership, 151; on veto, 157; voting record of, 171-72

"Arm twisters," 35. See also Advisers

Armed forces: proposed census of, 86-87; use by UN proposed, 122n. See Disarmament

Armistice, Korean, 118, 119

Atlantic Charter: Assembly reaffirms, 85

Atomic energy: peaceful use of, 29n, 30n, 114-15; control of, 85n, 88, 89, 108-15; U.S. influence on issue, 123, 163

Atomic Energy Commission, 34n, 108-12 passim, 123

Atomic weapons: and Korean conflict, 68, 69n; prohibition and control, 87, 88, 89, 108-13 passim

Atrocities in Korea, 92